L-R

JIM LOCKHART
keyboards, flute, whistles, uilleann pipes, vocals

EAMON CARR
drums, bodhrán, percussion

BARRY DEVLIN
bass guitar, vocals

CHARLES O'CONNOR
violin, mandolin, concertina, guitar, vocals

JOHNNY FEAN
lead guitar, acoustic guitar, banjo, mandolin, vocals

First published 2013 by
The O'Brien Press Ltd,
12 Terenure Road East, Rathgar,
Dublin 6, Ireland.
Tel: +353 1 4923333; Fax: +353 1 4922777
E-mail: books@obrien.ie.
Website: www.obrien.ie

ISBN: 978-1-84717-586-1

1 2 3 4 5 6 7 8
13 14 15 16 17

Printed and bound in Poland by Białostockie Zakłady Graficzne S.A.
The paper in this book is produced using pulp from managed forests

COVER PHOTOGRAPHY
Front & hard cover: Ian Finlay.
Back: Miscellaneous / lyrics © Horslips
Author photo: Ian Tomey
Horslips logo: Billy Moore © Horslips

See Bibliography & Acknowledgements
for photography & memorabilia credits.

HORSLIPS

TALL TALES
THE OFFICIAL BIOGRAPHY

Mark Cunningham

THE O'BRIEN PRESS
DUBLIN

Longfield House, Cashel, 1972.

Dedicated to

the men

of the marsh

Tíolacaim an

leabhar seo d'fhir

an réisc

Horslips
(Eamon Carr, Barry Devlin, Jim Lockhart,
Johnny Fean and Charles O'Connor)
have co-operated fully with Mark Cunningham
in the creation of this official biography of Horslips,
and recommend it to their friends and fans
throughout the world.

Contents

The Man Who Built America photo shoot, 1978.

A FANBOY ODYSSEY

First impressions count, and they are often the most memorable. The first time I consciously heard Horslips, the experience was so profound that it was the catalyst for my eventual career in music. I blame Peter Hobbs, then a fellow resident of Corringham, Essex. One evening in November 1976, he placed an unusual album, called *Dancehall Sweethearts*, on his turntable. In the adjacent room, two pairs of ears pricked up. Pete's brother, Dean and I heard the sound of a fiddle playing over a gurgling Moog bass line. What in Cú Chulainn's name was this?

Since moving with my family to Corringham from east London during the legendary heatwave of '76, I had focused on developing my first real band with Dean, along with our friends Mark 'Odgie' Aldridge and Peter Simes. Upon hearing *Dancehall Sweethearts*, we instinctively knew that our initial lack of direction was cured. Along with further inspiration from Jethro Tull, Steeleye Span and Alan Stivell, Horslips would have a marked effect on the folk-infused brand of rock music that we would still be playing decades later. They gave us the road map.

Hot on the heels of this discovery, Horslips released what many have judged to be their magnum opus, *The Book Of Invasions: A Celtic Symphony*. I worshipped The Beatles for their spirit of experimentation, their sense of harmony, their occasional use of unusual instruments and their uncanny ability to rarely repeat themselves. I could hear all of these attributes in Horslips' music and more, particularly on this new album.

Barry Devlin, Jim Lockhart, Eamon Carr, Charles O'Connor and Johnny Fean had it all: a brickhouse rhythm section, bluesy guitar licks and multi-instrumental dexterity. Their combination of ancient melodies, slick harmonies, strident riffs and tales of Old Ireland sounded exotic to these teenage ears. And so, over the winter months of 1976–77, while our school mates were turning on to The Clash, The Damned and the Pistols, we were immersing ourselves in Celtic mythology and learning how to be real musicians. Four less fashionable kids were hard to find at Gable Hall School.

My first Horslips gig – at the Rainbow Theatre in London's Finsbury Park in November 1977 – finally sealed my fate as a fan. Touring that autumn in support of the *Aliens* album, they encored with Jethro Tull's 'Locomotive Breath'. Two weeks later, when we played our début gig in front of a bemused audience at our school's Christmas festival, we paid tribute by including 'King Of The Fairies' and 'Drive The Cold Winter Away', and took a leaf out of the Lipsos' book by ending with the same Tull number.

I have often pondered on why I was so drawn to the mystical themes etched out by Horslips when I was so distanced by geography. Perhaps my father's stories of his times in Cork and Kerry as a young man helped me identify with the tapestries Horslips were weaving.

With relatively few articles in the music press and very occasional airplay, Horslips appeared to receive scant exposure in Britain outside of touring. In the pre-Internet world, they remained something of an enigma and it was only natural to deduce that we had discovered something rare and very personal to us. In reality, the music of Horslips touched a much wider audience than a bunch of spotty would-bes from the Thames Estuary.

For a generation in their homeland, Horslips provided a life-changing escape from a dreary, post-World War II existence. During an era of devastating social and political crises, they pioneered a new live rock circuit, playing ballrooms normally accustomed to cabaret – ballrooms that have since been turned into furniture warehouses or simply erased from view. They helped to revolutionise Ireland's live musical landscape forever, and countless artists have benefitted ever since.

Unlike most other bands, Horslips, because of their embracing of traditional music and their political neutrality, encouraged a sense of unity amongst their fans at live gigs in the North. Those gigs offered a rare chance to put aside differences and simply enjoy the craic.

If Celtic Rock can be defined as the creative marriage of traditional Celtic folk tunes and original, contemporary rock'n'roll, then this is a genre that Horslips unquestionably pioneered. And yet, while their influence on later bands such as Runrig, Counting Crows, The Corrs, The Waterboys and U2 is indisputable, they never enjoyed similar commercial success internationally. As such, they could be regarded as being among the most profoundly important under-achievers in rock history.

Horslips' journey – of highs, lows, artistic integrity, commercial successes and failures, missed opportunities and ultimate disagreements over musical direction – is a journey shared by so many artists. Only hindsight can suggest how things might have been approached differently for the greater good. But what the band achieved in the 10 years of their original lifespan continues to delight and inspire people all over the world.

Many years after Horslips' decade of invention came to a halt, I started a career as a writer, and became acquainted with members of the band and also struck up regular contact with former road crew members, Robbie McGrath, Steve Iredale and Peter Clarke. In 1995, it was a thrill to interview the band individually for a serialised Horslips history in Ireland's leading music magazine, *Hot Press*. Although self-effacing, the band members remained unanimously proud of the legacy they had left behind. With their individual careers blooming, it was made clear that Horslips belonged only to the past. But then came a few flickers of life. And a miracle...

In 2004, the opening of the Horslips exhibition, organised by Jim Nelis, Paul Callaghan and Stephen Ferris, provoked a surprise, low-key live reunion of all five members. This experience provided the spark for a flurry of activity that included *Roll Back* (an 'unplugged' reworking of past glories) and the documentary DVD, *The Return Of The Dancehall Sweethearts*.

And they kept coming back. In the wake of numerous TV and radio appearances, the unthinkable happened when Horslips – with drummer Ray Fean deputising for Eamon Carr – went out on a brief Irish tour in winter 2009, rounding it off with a show at Dublin's O2, where both they and the crowd were on fire. For many, it was the greatest concert of their lives.

Those winter gigs were repeated in 2010, and since then Horslips have appeared live on a semi-regular basis, notching up memorable performances with orchestras, and playing 'special guest' spots at events and festivals in Glasgow, London, Galway, Cork, Cropredy and Switzerland. In Belfast, *Arthur's Day* saw Eamon reclaim his place behind the kit, proving that the spirit is as alive as it ever was.

It is a relief for me that, thanks to the enthusiasm of The O'Brien Press, this book has finally seen the light of day, because its gestation period is almost as long as Horslips' original career. During this long wait, I've been lucky to forge relationships with many fans, from Ireland, England, Scotland, Wales, North America and

L–R: Jim Lockhart, Johnny Fean, Mark Cunningham, Charles O'Connor, Eamon Carr and Barry Devlin in 2012.

Europe, some of whom have become firm friends. They form a diehard brigade beyond compare.

This book is based on the hours upon hours of interviews I have conducted with the band (collectively and individually) and their associates, and these were always eventful. One glaring omission, however, is original guitarist Declan Sinnott. A person well-known for maintaining a negative opinion of the band he left, he declined more than one request to be interviewed. His own explanation for leaving Horslips is provided by way of a brief *Hot Press* feature extract from 2000.

Each band member has been tremendously hospitable and accommodating. When I spent a few days with Charles and his partner Numi at their Whitby home, I was given access to a treasure trove of photographs and rare artwork. During an evening at Jim's house, he casually presented a box whose contents amounted to a Holy Grail of paraphernalia, including original handwritten lyrics, recording session notes, promoter contracts and internal memos. Touring colleague Steve Iredale also

donated several of the rare items that he salvaged from the Horslips office when it closed in 1981.

In many ways, what you are reading is the result of teamwork, and I often feel that my role has been more of a curator than a writer. Many people have been helpful in sharing their memorabilia and nuggets of information, and I cannot thank them enough.

Rather than approach this as an intellectual review, this is mostly 'Horslips In Their Own Words' with relatively little narrative interference. For aesthetic reasons, I have avoided listing each and every concert, TV and radio appearance (this detail will become available online), and concentrated on the most important events within the chronology and the stories behind them.

This only leaves me to thank Horslips themselves for indulging my project. It has often been said that you should never meet your heroes, for you may be disappointed. The person who came up with that theory has never met Barry, Jim, Eamon, Charles and Johnny.

Mark Cunningham

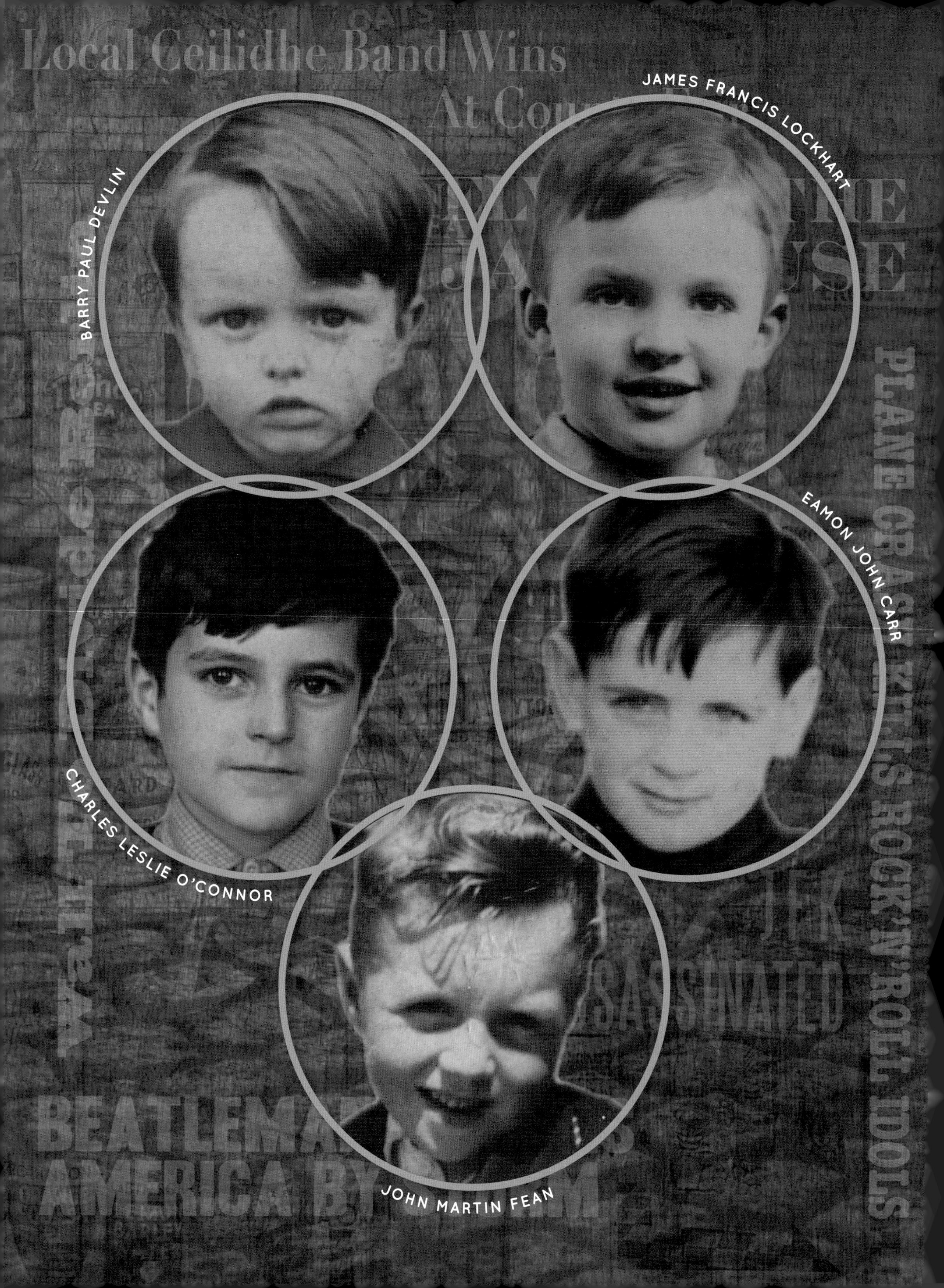

Local Ceilidhe Band Wins
At Cou...

BARRY PAUL DEVLIN

JAMES FRANCIS LOCKHART

EAMON JOHN CARR

CHARLES LESLIE O'CONNOR

JOHN MARTIN FEAN

CHAPTER 1

GROWING UP

BARRY PAUL DEVLIN
NOVEMBER 27 1946
NEWRY, COUNTY DOWN, N. IRELAND

My family home is in Ardboe, County Tyrone, which is where I grew up. My father, Tommy, had this great idea that whenever my mother Eileen [née O'Hare] came to her confinement, he sent her off to visit her sister in Newry, which, like most of my family, is how I came to be born in the town's Daisy Hill Hospital. It's still there.

As a writer, I have problems with my very rural childhood – it was embarrassingly idyllic. You're supposed to have angst in you if you're going to be a writer.

I was the only boy of seven children. My sisters Anne, Marie, Polly, Valerie, Clare and Helen and I grew up on a farm on the shores of Lough Neagh. My mother was a teacher at the first public elementary school in the area, and my father was a publican, fish merchant and general merchant. We had a couple of cottages on the farm, which accommodated two families who worked for us, the Croziers and the Coyles, so there were probably 21 kids roaming around.

Polly wrote a book about it in 1983, called *All Of Us There* [right], which she dedicated to me. It paints a very accurate picture of the family bonds, the rural

environment and the shenanigans that went on as we grew up in the 'fifties.

We lived in a house that had lots and lots of books, beside a big Celtic cross that was kind of a metaphor. Ireland was pretty much dominated by the cross, and life revolved around a cycle of religion, so it played a big part in my childhood.

Our mother was a very careful parent who made sure we went to bed early, by 7.30pm, even in the summer. From our bedrooms, we'd hear the Crozier and Coyle kids playing outside, and we'd listen to the fun they were all having. Then, one summer, we were allowed to stay up until 9.30 for the first time. I went out to our front gates to find a couple with a portable radio. They'd tuned into Radio Luxembourg, and someone like Johnny Tillotson was playing. I didn't know anything like this existed. There was this extraordinary noise ... and life after 7.30pm.

It was the first time I'd connected music with this yearning and this new world you could see ahead of you. My horizons multiplied; the world suddenly had an extra

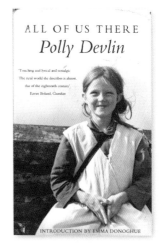

ALL OF US THERE
Polly Devlin

'Touching and lyrical and nostalgic.
The rural world she describes is almost
that of the eighteenth century'.
Eavan Boland, *Guardian*

INTRODUCTION BY EMMA DONOGHUE

dimension and nothing was ever the same again.

Somewhere inside me, I knew that music was important and that I wanted to be part of it. Not that I had access to a guitar. We had a piano on which my sisters would play pieces like 'Für Elise', but that was hard and nothing like this rock'n'roll that excited me on the radio. So I played lead hurley stick along to Cliff Richard, Billy Fury, Tommy Steele and whatever was cool in 1959.

A year earlier, when I was nine, I won a talent contest, singing Elvis' 'Teddy Bear'. It was at one of Clarrie Hayden's touring variety shows, or 'fit-ups' as they were known, in a big tent that came to the Battery Field near to us in Ardboe. They'd do a play like 'Frankenstein' every night and also have dancing girls and a sax player, and then there'd be a talent contest. I vied for first place with a girl called Philomena Cassidy, but being small and cute, I got the prize.

I never saw a live gig, but on a Saturday night you could hear the distant sounds of a showband being carried across the shores of the Lough. It resonated with me and yet it seemed so untouchable. We had a local dancehall, but it was largely for ceilidhe bands – our parish priest hated the thought of pop music, so the chances of hearing anything vaguely modern were zero.

Later on, music began to be a very personal thing for me. I was often ill at boarding school, because I didn't like it, and being in the infirmary was a way out, especially if there wasn't really anything much wrong with you. You'd just go in there and listen to the bells all day.

One day in November '62, when I was in the third year, I heard 'Love Me Do' in the infirmary on a transistor radio lent to me by a friend called Tom McGurk. I told my schoolmates about this great new band called The Beedles. No one knew what the hell I was talking about, least of all myself.

By March '63, however, when 'Please Please Me' was out, everyone was starting to become Beatle mad. I had the kudos, because I'd been espousing their cause for a good few months.

Discovering The Beatles was my real awakening. They were, and have remained, the reason I wanted to be in a band. Of course, I moved on and got into other kinds of music, but I still believe they wrote the book and will continue to be the standard to which every band aspires. There's something about the noise they made together that was absolutely remarkable and irreplaceable. You could argue that it was all about the time and the place, but even my children recognise them as being special.

Something quite profound happened the following year. I had a 'St Paul on the road to Damascus' conversion. I'd been brought up as a Catholic, and as a 17-year-old boy I decided that if any of it was true, then that was the most important thing in life, and that's what I should attend to.

So in September 1964, after I did my senior certificate and left school, I joined a missionary order called the Maynooth Mission To China – which, strangely, wasn't in Maynooth and didn't go to China at the time; it was in Navan and went to Peru, Japan and the Philippines. It was more interested in building than theology, and they were a great bunch of guys who are still out there doing the good work, even though the Missionary no longer exists in the way it used to.

I stayed there for four-and-a-half years, and for the first half I wasn't allowed to listen to rock and pop music. Every so often I'd be out in the grounds of the monastery and hear a car passing with the radio on,

playing the latest Rolling Stones record or whatever. I particularly remember the distant strains of the riff from 'The Last Time', which teased and rankled with me, I'll admit. It was very frustrating.

A part of me knew that I was being robbed of my teenage life, at what history would later determine as the most exciting time in pop music. This was the very birth of pop culture, if you like, and I missed it so unutterably much. But then, for some reason, the ban was lifted. In 1967, I was allowed to hear rock music, so I got to listen to *Sgt. Pepper's Lonely Hearts Club Band*, Jimi Hendrix and the soundtrack of the Summer of Love. The world outside had turned colour, but I was still immersed in a very black-and-white existence.

Polly bought me a nylon six-string guitar for my 21st birthday in 1967, and I was allowed to play it in the seminary for brief periods in the evening – songs like 'Mr Tambourine Man' that I'd picked up from those passing car radios.

Opposite page:
'Little Barry' with his sisters Anne, Polly, Marie and Valerie; his father, Tommy Devlin.

This page:
The young Devlins and Croziers with Ardboe neighbours in the early 1950s.

Despite everything, I really did enjoy my time in the seminary. I felt I had a chance to do something good and interesting, and I really was the swotty student. I spent nearly all that time searching, looking for 'the answer' and wondering where He was. But He didn't want to show Himself. So I eventually left in 1969, because I no longer believed in God, and I've felt the same ever since.

Being an ex-seminarian in my generation isn't as unusual as it might seem. I was the last of a generation of Irish men who viewed the clergy as being a reasonably sensible vocation. Gabriel Byrne and John Hume went through the same experience as I did, and came out the other side wanting to do something other than be a priest.

During my last two years in the seminary, I had attended University College, Dublin and completed my BA in English, and I started getting more serious about playing the guitar. Neil Jordan, who played guitar and was in the year behind me, came over to my flat in Harrington Street with Brendan Corry, another guitarist. They made me green with envy because they were so good.

I wasn't learning the instrument with any ambition to be in a band. It was all 'Michael, Row The Boat Ashore' and really bad Peter, Paul & Mary numbers, but when I came out of the seminary, I played for a while in a folk trio called The O'Carroll, named after our singer, Phil O'Carroll. We did about three gigs and, even though we were pretty dire despite rehearsing a lot, I loved the experience of making music together.

What The O'Carroll did inspire, however, was the thought of being in a real band. At the end of 1969, Polly – who lived the most exciting life imaginable as the features editor for *Vogue* – invited me over to Italy, to the beautiful converted farmhouse she had in Castellina, Tuscany.

Chrissie Shrimpton and other very famous English models were all there, and I was in my element, racing around the Italian roads in a white Mini Moke like I was in an episode of 'The Prisoner'. I thought everybody did this.

I remember saying to Polly, 'I want to be in a band and I'm sure you can help me.' I'll never forget her words. She said, 'The way you get to be famous is by wanting it.' I thought it was such a cliché and I was so cross with her, because it felt like she was fobbing me off. I realised later that she was right, of course.

The thing was, no one was going to let me be in their band, so I'd have to start my own.

I met Jim at UCD whilst playing with The O'Carroll. Jim was a really gifted actor and we toured together with the Irish Dramatic Society [Cumann Drámaíochta]. After I left the seminary, I went back to UCD as a layman to do my MA in English at UCD, but did all my research at Queen's University in Belfast, where the best resources for the subject existed.

I was there in August '69, when The Troubles erupted in Derry. It was horrendous. Then the British Army came in, and from that moment we would live our lives in the fearful knowledge that anything could happen, anywhere, at any time.

"No one was going to let me be in their band, so I'd have to start my own ..."

The boy Lockhart with his parents in Phoenix Park, Dublin.

JAMES FRANCIS LOCKHART
FEBRUARY 3 1948
DUBLIN, IRELAND

My mother, Molly [née Lennon], was from Strokestown, County Roscommon. My father John hailed from Belfast, where his grandparents, James and Susannah, had a spirit grocer's in California Street. Mum and Dad met in Dublin and we lived in Terenure until I was about 10 years old, when we moved to James's Street, above my Dad's butcher shop, right next to the Guinness brewery.

I was an only child and, as I had no siblings to play with and I wasn't especially sporty, I tended to read a lot. When I was small, Billy Neville was effectively my minder while my mother worked in the shop. Billy was a friend and neighbour of my aunt Peggy, who had a sweet shop in New Street, just up from St Patrick's Cathedral. He was known locally as 'Billy The Sailor', because he'd been in the British Navy in WWI and fought at the Battle of Jutland under Admiral Beatty, as he never tired of telling. Billy was like my substitute grandfather, because my actual grandparents in Belfast died before I was born. I used to polish his medals on Remembrance Day.

One of the regular customers in the butcher's was a Mrs Cluskey, whose sons Con and Dec had a group called the Harmonichords, soon to be The Bachelors,

Left: Lockhart's great-grandparents at their shop in Belfast, circa 1900; butcher John Lockhart; young Jim enjoying a day on the farm.

Ireland's first UK chart-toppers. My Dad was keen for me to play piano, and so I inherited the Cluskeys' music teacher, Noel Curtin. Noel was connected with the Royal Irish Academy Of Music, and he started coming to teach me the regular classical pieces that youngsters are subjected to. From the age of 10 on, I got stuck into it in a big way, and really liked the challenges he set me.

When we moved I went to James's Street Christian Brothers School, which also had amongst its pupils Terry Woods (later of Sweeney's Men and The Pogues), Tom Dunne of Something Happens and Newstalk, and Michael Colgan of the Gate Theatre. When I was 16 or 17, a folk group was formed for a school concert – Dylan and Clancy Brothers type of stuff. Our teacher thought we should have a tin whistle in the band and the finger was pointed at me. So I went and bought one, and learned how to play the thing.

That was interesting, because learning the piano was a daunting prospect. You had to learn to read music and it was all very formal and structured. A lot of people who learn that way have great difficulty improvising, and in some cases they find it impossible to jam.

So it was great when I started on tin whistle, because I found myself playing traditional tunes but 'bending' them in my own way, completely by ear. Then I began to play jazz tunes, like 'Take Five' and 'Blue Rondo À La Turk'. That gave me an open door into jamming and not being tied to a score. It also gave me the confidence to quit my lessons and start playing piano more freely.

I had been reading everything about jazz and blues that I could lay my hands on. So I had a very good handle on the theory and historical background, and despite not having a record collection, I knew about all of the key musicians and how they fitted into the development of the genres.

I was also swotting up on traditional music. I would frequent the folk clubs in Mount Street and stand at

Jim Lockhart: from schoolboy to 18-year-old hiker.

the back, scribbling down the words of Scottish folk songs, and also spend time in the library, reading the big coffee-table-sized books of old song collections by Breandán Breathnach, Colm Ó Lochlainn, PW Joyce and Donal O'Sullivan.

Going away to Irish College in the summer was a rite of passage for many Irish teenagers, and from age 10 to 16, I went to Brú na Mí, in a former army camp in County Meath. From then I attended Ring College [Coláiste na Rinne] in County Waterford.

As well as the swimming and sports, one of the things you'd do there was sing a lot in the Irish language. I learned a lot of Irish songs that I would never

have discovered otherwise, as well as poetry and Celtic mythology.

There had been a fair amount of emphasis on all things traditionally Irish at the Christian Brothers School, but there was much more focus on these things at Irish College, and I seemed naturally drawn to everything laid before me.

I was becoming more and more exposed to the elements that were at the heart of Irish culture, and listened to Ciarán Mac Mathúna's programmes on Radio Éireann, whose folk collections deeply fascinated me. So when The Chieftains and Seán Ó Riada arrived on my radar, I was primed.

19

Just like everyone else, I was listening to Radio Luxembourg and the pirate stations, so I was equally exposed to rock and pop music in my teens. By the late sixties I started getting into 'Kid Jensen's Dimensions', his late night 'progressive' show on 208. Bruce Springsteen once talked about being in his mother's car when he first heard 'Like A Rolling Stone', and we all had those jaw-dropping moments. There are so many rock and pop songs that awakened me – far too many to mention – but in terms of my contribution to Horslips, I'd say that the music of Seán Ó Riada was at least as influential, because it showed there were more ways than one of engaging with the tradition.

You couldn't go anywhere in the summer of 1964 without hearing 'The House Of The Rising Sun' by The Animals. I first heard it when I was sitting in my cousin's Ford Consul and it came bursting out of his car radio. Eric Burdon's vocals sounded like they were going to tear a hole in the little speakers, they were so raucous and powerful, and Alan Price's bluesy solo on the Vox Continental had me staring at the dashboard in complete awe.

I knew I recognised the song. Dylan had done a version of this old folk song a couple of years earlier, although I wasn't very aware of that. It had first been recorded in the early 1930s and countless other people had covered it, from Woody Guthrie to Nina Simone. I guess it was just in the air. The Animals' version has an enigmatic sound about it that sums up a period for me, and every time I hear it, I'm right back there.

In 1966, I left school and went on to study for a BA in Economics and Politics at University College Dublin, and went on to get my Master's Degree in Economics. Then, just as UCD was moving out of its campus at Earlsfort Terrace beside St Stephen's Green, I worked out of a new office on my Ph.D in Environmental Economics, which was a bit far-sighted in 1969. I started to look at how certain industrial processes were affecting the environment, and I was collating information that could be used as a coherent, theoretical tool for people who wanted to campaign for change on a rational basis rather than emotive. We haven't actually progressed much further.

Before Horslips, I'd played tin whistle in a few random groups of musicians during college, including Paul Boxberger. We played together as Freddie Slack & The Cow-Cow Boogie Whistle Ensemble at various parties and hotel gigs. There was another band I played in with Maurice Sweeney, Mick Friel and Jodie Barrett, and there was one memorable concert that we did in the Great Hall at UCD.

We would play jazzy-blues numbers by Mose Allison and Dave Brubeck, boogie-woogie and English and Irish folk songs. It was quite a mishmash, and I suppose it gave me a good grounding for fusion.

I'd do anything I could to distract me from studying at UCD, and ended up getting involved with the Irish Dramatic Society, the Cumann Drámaíochta. I got on very well with Seán Ó Briain, the director and creative driving force of the group. He was a couple of years older than the rest of us and was doing an extended Master's degree.

Unlike DramSoc [the English-speaking drama group], which would do its productions in college, the Cumann Drámaíochta appeared at Irish language drama festivals around the country. We'd pile into a single-decker bus with some recycled scenery and costumes, and trundle off to do a full-length play and a few shorts.

"The music of Seán Ó Riada showed there were more ways than one of engaging with the tradition ..."

Right: The university graduate with mother Molly.

Below: Frances Swift, Lockhart's future wife.

It was backstage in Athlone during the production of one of Sean's one-act, one-man plays that he wrote for me that I met Barry, who, along with Don O'Donnell, had been roped in to be a stage manager. Barry first became aware of my existence when he saw Mick Friel and me at a piano working out the chords to some Beatles song, and he joined in. It was our shared passion for Beatles songs that got us together as mates.

Barry was doing his Master's while I was approaching my final exams. I'd never particularly noticed him around college – the clerical students didn't form part of our social scene. There were lots of them, they wore black, they studied diligently and they didn't spend half the day in the pub. But as we got to know each other through the drama group, we discovered a lot of shared enthusiasms and increasingly hung around together.

I was also working on *Campus*, the college paper, as production manager, and got to spend a lot of time with the printers. It was letterpress, very old-school, with compositors making the pages up laboriously by hand on the 'stone', even doing the headlines letter by letter. That was a real privilege, to be in on the tail end of a living tradition that went right back to Gutenberg.

It was around this time that I met Frances Swift, who was also studying at UCD, but tended to frequent Trinity College more. As it happened we didn't become a proper item for a couple of years. We were married in 1979.

The band that later became Horslips was just starting to get going a little while into my research. Paddy Lynch, who was the Professor of Economics, took me aside one day and said, 'Mr Lockhart, we see you more often on the television these days than we do along the corridors of our department.' He was right – I didn't know it, but I was about to run away with the circus.

Early days for Charles O'Connor, a.k.a. 'Little Les', long before facial hair took up residence.

**CHARLES LESLIE O'CONNOR
SEPTEMBER 7 1948
MIDDLESBROUGH, ENGLAND**

Like a large proportion of the Middlesbrough population, I come from a Catholic family. My father, Charles Leslie O'Connor, served during the war in the 1st Division of the SAS and was badly injured in Tobruk. He may have felt that he wasn't going to live very long, which is possibly why I was given his name, Charles Leslie, Jr., and was taunted with 'Little Les' all through my childhood.

Dad married my mother, Gwendoline Iris [née Pearson], during the 'thirties and before I came along, they produced a lovely daughter called Maureen, who we very sadly lost in 2011. Like me, my big sister hated her name. She was born as Gwendoline, after my Mum, and changed it to Maureen as soon as she could. We grew up in Grove Hill, a satellite housing development in Middlesbrough, built in the 1950s to bring people away from the town centre and into the green belt of Teesside.

My love of music obviously came from my parents, who favoured Noël Coward, Ivor Novello, Al Bowlly and anyone with a good voice. My father was a professional singer, who performed with Harry Lester's Hayseeds, the comedy hillbilly outfit, while my mother continued to be a very competent pianist all her life. We had a piano at home, so I became naturally attracted to music – it was simply part of family life.

I was always interested in art and modelmaking, from as early as infant school. At age five or six, I made cardboard cars and cranes, and impressed teachers with what I suppose was quite a mature talent for my years. Mr Bresslaw was the first person who set me on my future path as a designer. He would take me out of my music class – which I hated – to teach me how to mix flour and water with poster colour, and make a paste out of it that would resemble oil paint. He was very kind to me, and realised that I had some imagination for this kind of thing. He would encourage me to create pictures that got displayed on the corridor walls.

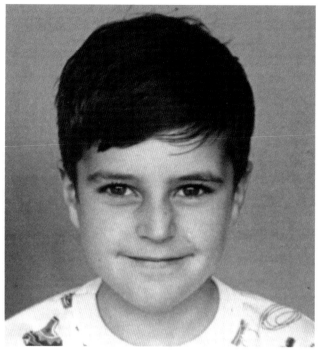

Schoolboy O'Connor in the 1950s.

Maureen got me my first guitar in 1958. She stole it from her boyfriend, and I began to learn some basic tunes, like Lonnie Donegan's 'The Grand Coulee Dam'. As a kid, I would go to the nearby flea market and buy old fiddles and banjos, then go home and try to make some noise out of them. I also bought a dreadful second-hand bowl-back mandolin and picked out tunes.

I had a vague interest in Irish music, possibly because of a distant family connection and the large Catholic population in Middlesbrough, and I liked to find tunes that weren't too difficult to play The social clubs seemed to have quite a focus on Irish music, and I'd be dragged into the singsong.

My mother sent me to piano lessons when I was 11. My music teacher, Mrs Hutchinson, wore fingerless gloves and gave me a sweet if I was good. I forfeited the mint humbug many times by not playing the Chopin she wanted me to play. Instead, I'd play a rock'n'roll number and she freaked! Formal lessons often had a way of putting you off this music.

I heard rock'n'roll for the first time at Rea's Ice Cream & Coffee House on Linthorpe Road in Middlesbrough, owned by Camillo and Gaetano Rea, the Italian father and uncle of rock star Chris Rea and his brother Nik, who became a touring stage manager. Camillo controlled the wholesale of many ice-cream items in Middlesbrough. His coffee house was the place where the local kids would hang out, other than the cinema if you could afford it, and I spent a lot of time there.

It was a very elaborate and impressive café, and the default place to meet girls. Chris started cleaning tables there before his teens. They had the big, noisy Gaggia machines that produced exotic, foamy coffee, and there was a log-walled room at the back and a goldfish pond.

"Formal lessons often had a way of putting you off this music ..."

If you paid the extra penny for your coffee, they let you throw things at the fish and listen to the juke box in the corner.

Just up the road from Rea's was Fearnley's record shop. The strains of all the latest sounds would pour out of Fearnley's. 'If You Need Me' by the Stones [from the *Five By Five* EP] always reminds me of those times, along with the early Dusty Springfield records like 'Island Of Dreams'. I had a thing for Dusty; in fact, I think I fell in love with her without realising it. The little short skirt and the Ronettes-like beehive hairdo she wore were so cool. There was no one like her.

From 11 to 15, I went to Brackenhoe Technical School on the Prissick School Base in Marton Road, where the pupils were trained to be useful to the coal, metal and steel industries in the northeast of England, whether they liked it or not. Metalwork was fun, and I was showing signs of becoming a draughtsman. The pencil craft skills I developed taught me a lot about drawing and, although I didn't recognise it at first, I was showing all the signs of being a worthy art student, which wasn't what the teachers at Brackenhoe would have had in mind for me. But my sister was telling me how cool art college would be and it was gradually feeding my imagination.

It suddenly dawned on me when I was in my last year at Brackenhoe that in order to get into art college, I needed to get a GCE in Art. So I explained to one of the teachers that this was what I wanted to do, and if I had to drop a subject – which was Draughtsmanship – to make way for me to cram Art, that's what I'd do. And so, after just a month-and-a-half of seriously intensive and dreadful work, I not only passed my O Level but got a Grade A to boot.

At 16, I arrived at Middlesbrough College of Art [later Teesside College of Art], dressed in a green, skin-tight Blackwatch suit with a slightly baggy arse in the trousers, a very tailored waist, a shirt with a tiny wing collar and knitted tie, hair backcombed in Mod style

and smoking a tab. Our principal, Sidney Spedding, shouted at me: 'Hey, O'Connor, put that cigarette out!' I didn't like college at all in the beginning, but it was hip. Eventually I got in with a few friends and began to find my feet.

All of the British bands were starting to happen. I was very lucky to have been just the right age when The Who, The Animals and The Pretty Things were breaking through in '64 and '65, and they would come to play at the two clubs in Middlesbrough – the Purple Onion, owned by the McCoy family, and The Scene, which was run by my uncle from a basement underneath four council houses. I'd started college without much of a grant, but I made it stretch and certain gigs had to be seen.

The Northern Mod phenomenon had started long before it was recognised, and there was a definite style you had to follow. For me it would be check shirts, gardeners' jackets, square-toed slip-ons and tweed trousers, and there were boutiques everywhere that catered for these fashions. Although I aspired to being a Mod with my appearance, I didn't go the whole way and get a scooter. I suppose I was 'Mod lite'.

Clothes were always important to me and still are. My Dad taught me good dress sense and the importance of smart shoes, and my sister was also quite influential, as she made her own clothes and was a good 'barometer' for coolness. We weren't a well-off family, but we made an effort and it showed.

When The Pretty Things played at The Scene, supported by the great John Lee Hooker, I was completely mesmerised. I watched through the gaps of fighting fists and bodies while Phil May screamed out 'Do you really love me, Rosalyn? Yeah, I gotta know!' This was my first real introduction to live gigs, and although I was naturally more driven towards traditional music, I think 'cool' overcame that for a while and Mod influences pushed me more in the direction of bands like the Small Faces.

Teenager O'Connor strikes a chord.

In my late teens, I spent a lot of time dreaming of getting away from Teesside and seeing the bright lights of London. That was where everything was happening – all the pop groups, the artists, the movers and shakers, the fashion gurus and the girls. Middlesbrough was great and so were the people, but I'd seen enough for a while. I needed excitement ... and, boy, what a time to be looking for it.

The Animals' 'We've Gotta Get Out Of This Place' literally described my situation. The moment I heard that first verse – *'In this dirty old part of the city / Where the sun refused to shine / People tell me there ain't no use in trying'* – all these feelings my girlfriend and I had been harbouring suddenly felt valid. It was probably the first record that really spoke to me. I didn't go to London for some time, but I did get out of 'that place' eventually.

I began playing mandolin in the Art College Ceilidhe Band. I saw myself as a bit of a musician, but it was more of a pikey vision than a career move. There was one very funny episode when the college's gay and lesbian society had put up a poster for a ceilidhe, and someone scrawled across it, 'There's nowt as folk as queers'!

A better mandolin came my way when I could afford one, and I also started to play with the Stockton Blue & Golds Morris team, whose fiddle player, Jack Keane, had a lovely, simple English style. He had an incredible knowledge of traditional tunes, and was probably the biggest influence on the musician I became.

I did the Society of Industrial Artists course at college, but didn't become a Fellow because the membership fee was too expensive. Instead of taking a Fine Art course like my daughter Aphra, I studied Graphics, which involved typography, printmaking and photography. It set me up as a graphic designer and I amassed a very impressive portfolio with which to get a good job.

Music was still a hobby. I regarded art as the foundation of my career – the idea of graphic design for packaging was something that really motivated me. When I finally got my SIA qualification in 1970, I was offered a job at the college by my course lecturer, Hans Linder, but I fancied the idea of getting away.

I applied for as many jobs as I could, including one with Philips in Holland, one with a furniture design company in the North of England, and another with a Dublin advertising agency called Arks. Philips wrote to offer an interview, but before that could be arranged, Eamonn O'Flaherty, the creative director at Arks, had seen my work and contacted me to ask if he could meet me while he was staying at the Piccadilly Hotel in Manchester.

Eamonn looked like Clement Freud, while I was like a miniature, hairy Georgie Best, and we laughed at each other when we met. He'd already made up his mind that I could do the job, but just wanted to check me out and ask when I could get over to Dublin and start on £12 10/- a week.

The Silver Star Band in 1944 with Eamon's grandfather Johnnie Carr (far right) and uncle Paddy on drums.

EAMON JOHN CARR
NOVEMBER 12 1948
KELLS, COUNTY MEATH, IRELAND

Joe Carr was my Dad; my mother was Mary, and her maiden name was Ginnity. I was their eldest child, followed by my sister Irene and brothers Declan, Nodlaig [Noel] and Jude, who surfaced with the Irish punk fanzine *Heat*. My Mum died in 1957, and my Dad got married again to a lady called Joan Brodigan. I have two sisters from that relationship, called Anita and Sinéad.

Kells was a small town, 40 miles from Dublin, with a population of a few thousand, but, like much of County Meath, is very rich in Celtic artefacts, like the Market Cross of Kells. Newgrange and Tara are both in County Meath, and the sacred River Boyne runs through the county.

I was just a child when my paternal grandfather, Johnny Carr, played accordion with his Silver Star Cei-

lidhe Band. They were active in the 1940s and 1950s, and were top-notch and won various prizes at festivals. Two of my uncles – his sons Paddy Carr and Michael Carr – played with him at various times, as did my Dad.

At a very early age, I was presented with an accordion, but I couldn't master it at all. There was actually a drum kit in my grandfather's house as well, a sort of twenties-style kit – a big bass drum with a fantastic painting on it and a wood block and a snare. That held much more allure for me, and it obviously would have been the initial spark.

When I was five or six, I saw the Silver Star Ceilidhe Band in action at an afternoon tea dance. There was a real old-school ballroom in Virginia, County Cavan, about 12 miles from Kells, called Lough Ramor Farmers' Ballroom. One of my earliest clear memories was being taken to this adult gig. At some point in the proceedings, I was brought up and seated on the drum kit. I remember a sea of smiling faces as I was lifted in.

This style of music gave me my introduction. My

Dad got his own 'old time' band together, called the Round Tower Ceilidhe Band, which got shortened to the Round Tower. They were more of a dance band, with piano and a saxophone.

I grew up as a child with my Mum in the house and her girlfriends, who were good fun. In the evenings, my Dad would be off with the band, and he and the musicians would come back after gigs. It was exciting and fun.

We were the third family in the town to have a TV, and all my mates came back to the house to watch kids' programmes – sports and things like 'Boy Meets Girls' and 'Six-Five Special' with its house band Don Lang and the Frantic Five. Suddenly you were exposed to all this rock'n'roll stuff. You weren't just hearing it on Radio Luxembourg – you were actually seeing these guys: Billy Fury, Adam Faith, Joe Brown. I used to think Joe was God, and Adam Faith had an amazing persona. I didn't look at the drummers. With Adam, you felt that he was human, whereas Billy Fury was sort of raw and superhuman. Elvis was so exotic that he just didn't register with me.

My mother was a huge Buddy Holly fan, and his songs are the only ones I can remember her singing. She had four brothers, one of whom was Noel Ginnity, an Irish comedian who, in the '60s, was part of the Irish ballad boom. He was a member of the Ramblers Three, with Johnny McEvoy and Mick Bonner. They toured with The Dubliners, part of that gang. Luke Kelly was best man at his wedding. Oddly enough, it was Noel who introduced me to what I would have considered hardcore traditional music at that point. I was hearing the Chieftains and Seán Ó Riada's music through Noel.

I spent a lot of time in hospital as a kid. I was in the sanitarium for six months and in another hospital for three months. I had severe bronchiectasis; it was a near-death business back in 1956. Even then, you had hospital radio, so you're hearing everything that's going on, like Lonnie Donegan and other skiffle bands. I tapped along to those sort of things, so I thought that once I got out

From top: Eamon Carr, schoolboy and dog lover; a school play cast photo with Carr (back row, left) and future band colleague John Olohan (front row, far right); Toneage live in 1966.

27

of hospital and back to school, I might try to muscle into the school flageolet band at the CBS in Kells, and get the little uniform. I wanted to be a drummer.

A guy who had played the bass drum in the school band took me under his wing and showed me what you had to do: keep the beat! So I did that, and graduated to the snare and kettle drum. But I still had to sit through all the music classes with the 30 flageolet players. I knew the tunes, and some of them even wound up in the Horslips repertoire: 'King Of The Fairies' is the classic example. I was already kickin' ass on that tune in 1958 with the CBS band!

Between the ages of about 13 and 17, I went to St Finian's College, an all-boys boarding school in the Diocese of Meath. In hindsight, apart from playing Gaelic football every day, which helped toughen me up, its big advantage was a good grounding in both Latin and Greek.

Radios and TV sets were banned there, but a friend lent me his crystal set. Late one night, while I was in my room, on came Howlin' Wolf's 'Smokestack Lightning' – probably the weirdest-sounding music I'd ever heard. The effect was doubled by the foggy landscape I was seeing outside my dorm window, like an eerie movie scene playing out in front of me. Hubert Sumlin's guitar playing on this was absolutely seminal, and it continues to influence musicians today.

'Love Me Do' was the catalyst for so many musical careers, and I was certainly one of its victims, just as Barry and Jim were. It was late one night on Radio Luxembourg that I heard this echoey harmonica and thought it sounded amazing. I used to get the *NME*, and there was a little ad in the back for this single by a band called the Beatles. When 'Please Please Me' came out, everything clicked. It was astonishing ... and accessible. And they were from Liverpool, with Irish-sounding

names. You felt you could do this, as they all seemed so personable and funny, sharp and witty, like normal people. Like us.

The phenomenon of the showbands that developed in the late 1950s fulfilled a function, in that they were a gigantic jukebox. They played all sorts – not just the charts, but waltz music, foxtrots and whatever else was in demand. I don't think the rock'n'roll thing really kicked off in Ireland until the Beat Boom. Suddenly, you had beat clubs opening up in the major cities and young people started forming beat or R&B groups.

Some of the clubs just had DJs playing the latest hits, but in a few clubs, bands started to form. An important group was the Greenbeats. The name sounds naff, but the main guy was John Keogh, a great piano player who became a television producer with RTÉ.

We finally got it together around 1965–66 and called ourselves Toneage. The bass player was Gene Mulvaney, who crops up later in the Horslips story. We were practising, hanging out and playing in John Olohan's front room. Then we decided to do a gig. We said, 'But how are we going to amplify the piano?' So we rang John Keogh.

John's aunt lived in Blackrock on the same road as Keogh, and they knew each other. So we rang his house. This guy's on TV – I can't believe we're ringing him. John was really personable and helpful. He advised us to get an old skull microphone, lift the lid, dangle it down into the piano, close the lid, turn up the amp and hit the piano keys. So that's what we did.

We played a pile of gigs around County Meath, and it was a lot of fun. We would get paid, and a gang of people our own age would follow us. It felt like being in a beat group.

The general feeling was that groups were hip and showbands were not. Although it wasn't creatively challenging,

"The general feeling was that groups were hip and showbands were not ..."

Carr and John Olohan on O'Connell Bridge, circa 1964; Toneage (Olohan, Gene Mulvaney, Carr & Joe Rourke).

a lot of the showband musicians were brilliant players and good singers, but they would learn the charts note by note, and just go and do it. As it happens, a lot of the beat groups were doing exactly the same thing. They weren't writing their own material, just doing R&B covers and covers of English or Scottish beat groups.

Toneage's set list was filled with numbers by Chuck Berry, John Lee Hooker, Jimmy Reed, Bo Diddley, The Shirelles and The Animals. You'd turn their singles over and find out what was on the B-sides, do those songs and people thought it was cool. It was a hipper scene.

As things began to develop, bands began to write their own material, and a few of them began to get records released. In Cork you had Rory Gallagher and Taste, while Belfast obviously had Van Morrison and Them, who occasionally played in Dublin. There were a lot of other very good, interesting bands. Those who did get signed had one single or album out and then disappeared. These were bands such as Ditch Cassidy and the News, Granny's Intentions and The People, who featured Henry McCullough and later changed their name to Eire Apparent. We once supported The People. Our guitar amp started giving trouble and the guy who hopped up from the front of the stage to fix it was Dave

Robinson, who was a sort of a roadie, man-about-club type in Dublin, years before he set up Stiff Records.

I didn't see too many bands from America and England. If they didn't play the old Adelphi Cinema or the Caroline Club in Dún Laoghaire, where I saw The Animals, they tended to be brought on to the showband circuit. If you wanted to catch The Tremeloes, you'd have to endure an hour-and-a-half showband set before they came on for their 30 minutes. It began to change at the end of the 1960s, when promoters put bands on in the National Boxing Stadium in Dublin. Led Zeppelin, The Nice, Jethro Tull and Fleetwood Mac were the kind of acts coming in, but not necessarily selling 2,000 seats.

Toneage actually did some really big gigs, especially in Navan. More memorable ones were at the CYMS Hall and the Rugby Club, as well as Vincent's Hall in Kells and The Scene club in Dublin, which was a big deal for us. We were just into staging events for the sheer hell of it, so we roped in a couple of Dublin bands that we knew and said, 'Let's put on a package tour. A big beat festival.' A few thousand people turned up and, at the time, we weren't prepared for it. And neither was the so-called box office. Everything was crazy, like 'Hey, this is rock'n'roll!'

We managed to do some recording with Colum Fitzsimons, a local businessman and DJ from Kells who was a bit of a sound geek and had built his own studio at home. The tracks we did weren't bad, but the tapes sadly went missing.

Toneage continued for a while, with Pat Dunne replacing the outgoing guitarist Joe Rourke, but things were becoming fractured. The other guys had fallen under the spell of more acoustic-based music like Simon & Garfunkel and The Mamas & The Papas, and I was being seriously distracted with my new alt-scene discoveries.

I took to going to Liver-pool on the old cattle boat. It went from the North Wall and the cattle were downstairs, with the passengers upstairs. We were sailing on real old rust buckets and some of us who were on deck, we thought we were fuckin' Jack Kerouac! I mostly went on my own, just checking it out, to see what was happening, and had actually made my first visits around 1965. The first port of call was the old Cavern Club, as it was.

To bridge the gap between the quarterly Capella magazine, we are issuing monthly broadsheets. This is Chapter 1 of the series.

Peter Fallon, Eamon Carr,
Editors.

People were really friendly. Women that you would meet would be intrigued that you were Irish and had come over. Then they'd discover that you had nowhere to stay and you had hardly any money anyway. They were really cool and always found you some food and places to bunk down for the night. They were brilliant.

When I started going back regularly around 1967, I met some people like Roger McGough and Adrian Henri, who were reading poetry in pubs. This was a serious eye-opener. I would get to crash at 64 Canning Street, and I recall sidling up to McGough and asking if he'd mind having a look at stuff I'd written. He was really positive. 'Yeah, you've got to keep doing this, why don't you read a bit in public?' he advised. Roger later attended at least one Horslips gig which he enjoyed.

There was something in the air – all these guys were scribbling bits and pieces of notes and poems, people wanted to be painters. So we'd get together on Saturdays in a hotel in Navan and just start reading poetry and arguing about philosophy and music.

Out of that, we organised a couple of poetry readings in Navan under the heading 'The Meath Poetry Group', and we published a couple of little magazines. BP Fallon, who I knew, told me that his brother Peter was writing poetry and asked if I'd take him to the readings. Suddenly it was a scene!

Peter was a lot more serious about it, and we agreed to move it all to Dublin. We began a poetry workshop in Parnell Square once a fortnight, and loads of people would turn up and sit around. A very nervous Philip Lynott dropped in to read occasionally.

I'd already published wee things with the poetry group, so I said, 'I think we should try and publish a magazine.' So we edited a thing called *Capella*. We took poems from a lot of people who turned up and we tried to sift out what would work and what wouldn't. We also issued a broadsheet called *The Book Of Invasions* [above] – pre-dating the Horslips album by about seven years. We put that out to bridge gaps between issues of *Capella*.

We had everybody in it – even stuff by Marc Bolan. Jim Fitzpatrick did all the artwork and, of course, Jim went on to do some great work for Thin Lizzy's album sleeves.

I told Peter that I knew a fair-haired guitarist called David Costello. David was trying things out with our poetry and then we added a second guitarist, Paul

Tara Telephone in early 1970.
L-R: Peter Fallon, Lucienne Purcell,
Bernie Barrett, Andrew Robinson,
Declan Sinnott and Eamon Carr.

Kennan. I'd get the bongos out and it all evolved from there. We needed a name for the poetry readings, and that became Tara Telephone. We started appearing on TV and radio, and although I didn't have a long-term vision for any of this, we worked quite hard at it over a couple of years.

An active involvement in blues music started for me towards the end of the sixties and during Tara Telephone's embryonic period, I also began playing with another band, Empire State Express.

I'd become a member of the Dublin Blues Appreciation Society, which had been established in 1969 by Larry Roddy, with regular sessions at Slattery's in Capel Street. It was a great thing to be a part of if you wanted to hear music that wasn't on the radio. People would play records by Blind Willie Johnson and then deliver lectures about them.

An English guy called Pat Martin came to play Big Bill Broonzy songs and he was joined by Shay Fogerty on harmonica the following week. Another musician who impressed everyone was Brian Fry, who'd been playing on the jazz circuit. He brought with him Red Peters, a legend of the Dublin blues scene, who had a magnificent blues voice that made the room shake. Over the next few weeks, they started to play as one unit and, after mentioning that I had a washboard, I was invited into the fold.

Very soon, this thing suddenly gained legs. It became Red's vehicle, and he gave us the name Empire State Express. It was like a jug band. We did some interesting gigs, including playing support to Champion Jack Dupree and performing at the one-day *North South*

Blues Festival in Dublin's Mansion House alongside Blueshouse, a fantastic outfit with Ed Deane on guitar and Dermot Stokes [brother of *Hot Press* founder Niall] on piano, who ended up being the house band at the Appreciation Society's sessions. Gary Moore sat in with them occasionally, and it was such a thrilling vibe.

I played with the Empire State Express on the side for about nine months whilst progressing Tara Telephone, which extended its line-up and began doing even more live appearances as the 'seventies got underway.

The wee Johnny Fean.

JOHN MARTIN FEAN
NOVEMBER 17 1951
DUBLIN, IRELAND

Although I would never class myself as a Dubliner, I was, in fact, born in Dublin due to unforeseen circumstances. My mother, Maureen [neé Murray], had some complications with her pregnancy and it was decided that the Rotunda Hospital in Dublin would be better equipped for her labour than the local hospital in Limerick, where our family was based. So she went off to stay with her aunts in Dublin a month before I was born, and returned a few weeks afterwards to our small bedsit flat in Upper Mallow Street, close to the People's Park in Limerick.

My Dad, Jim, grew up on a farm near Bruree, County Limerick, as part of a large family, while my mother came from Claremorris. Her Dad, Dan, came from Scottish ancestry in Donegal and worked for the Great Southern Railway as an engine driver. After being stationed for a number of years in Claremorris, he and the family moved to Limerick.

My parents met in Limerick – at the time, my mother was a waitress at the Savoy restaurant in Limerick City. Dad was working at Shannon Airport as an oil tanker driver for Esso, helping with the refuelling of aeroplanes.

I was the first of six children. Donal followed when I was about three, around the time we moved to a ground-floor flat in nearby Henry Street, and the family gradually expanded with the arrival of Seamus, or 'Shearie' as he's known, then Gail, Ray and, finally, Corna in 1966.

The Fean family in 1966. L–R: Gail, Johnny, Donal, baby Corna, Maureen, Jim, Ray and Shearie.

Our flat in Henry Street was just 100 yards along from the flour mill owned by Ivan and Mildred Harris, whose nine children included Richard Harris, later to become a famous actor and the voice of 'MacArthur Park'.

Being the oldest, I was usually the ringleader when we played games together, and always the protective one if there were ever any skirmishes. I seemed to be attracted to mischief and danger, and my fascination with cars nearly got me into a lot of trouble.

There was a local insurance salesman doing his house-to-house collecting round one evening, and he parked his car on a hill on the corner that led down to the docks, but left his car door open. I must have seen this as an invitation, because as soon as I saw him go into a house, I jumped into the driver's seat and released the handbrake. The car very gradually moved downhill in the direction of the River Shannon. As it gathered speed, Richard Harris was walking up the hill towards me, but because I was so small, what he saw was a moving car without a driver. He sprinted into action. He quickly jumped into the car, jammed on the handbrake and saved me from disaster. Richard frogmarched me up to my front door and told my mother what had just happened. I think there may have been a few tears shed that evening.

Ireland was way behind the rest of Europe when it came to television. Telefís Éireann didn't start broadcasting until December 1961, so the only entertainment we had at home was the radio, which was often pretty dull, or the Pye radiogram, which had a rich, bassy sound. There was always a big pile of 78s in our house, because Dad was a huge jazz fan.

Dad particularly loved Louis Armstrong, Nat 'King' Cole and Dean Martin. He had quite an advantage over other music lovers in the neighbourhood, because he got to know a lot of the American pilots, and often asked them to bring over the latest jazz 78s from the States that you couldn't get anywhere in Ireland.

When Dad was at work, Mum used to play those records and sing along with them while I was in my pram, so they formed the soundtrack to my very early life. Later on, my Dad bought me the first record I ever owned – 'Mary's Boy Child' by Harry Belafonte.

We moved to Garryowen in Limerick City in 1957. We were only there a few months before I heard 'Heartbreak Hotel' for the first time. Elvis Presley made such an impact on our household with that song, and I would hear my Dad humming it around the house for weeks afterwards. It's difficult to express to young people today just how exciting that was, because it came out of nowhere, as if there had been nothing until that moment.

But it was when 'Jailhouse Rock' started to get airplay towards the end of 1957 that my ears really opened up, because I immediately focused in on Scotty Moore's guitar playing. It was the greatest sound I'd ever heard, and that was when my lifelong interest in the instrument really began. Hearing Little Richard's 'Lucille' for the first time was similarly devastating.

From that point on, I'd tune in to Luxembourg in the evenings, and whenever a new record came over the airwaves, I homed in on the guitars and kind of dissected the sounds in my head. It was only going to be a matter of time before I took up the guitar and, sure enough, my Dad came home one day in 1958 with a wonderful present under his arm.

Dad knew a guitar player from Limerick in the 'fifties, and had loaned him some money, because times were hard back in those days and the guy was a bit down on his luck. A few months passed, however, and my Dad hadn't seen him or had the money repaid. One day, while Dad was working at his job in Shannon Airport, he was surprised to see this guy returning from Spain with a nylon-string Spanish guitar that he'd acquired. He and my Dad met and chatted for a while, and during their conversation Dad suggested that if he wanted to write off the debt, he could do so by giving him this guitar instead. I now had my first guitar, and that was the beginning of everything.

In 1961, we moved to Shannon. A lot of American families were also living there and working at the airport, or the associated support companies on the new Shannon Free Zone industrial estate. It was pretty exciting to suddenly find myself in the company of people from America, Europe and Australia who had come over to start a new life.

For some unexplained reason, my first guitar was left behind when we moved to Shannon and I didn't play for about a year. But, for Christmas in 1962, my Mum paid about £3 10/- for a crude steel-string guitar. This time I really got stuck into it. One of the first tunes I learned to play quite well was 'Diamonds' by Jet Harris and Tony Meehan. I was completely self-taught, and the thing is that a bad guitar makes you work harder, and I guess that if it had been a better instrument I might not have developed in the same way.

For a while, it seemed as if the music I loved, the wilder rock'n'roll, had gone into limbo. Cliff Richard was having a stab at being the British Elvis, but he wasn't too convincing. But The Shadows were influential.

The sound and tone that Hank Marvin achieved on 'Apache' and 'Wonderful Land' was absolutely unique. His Fender Stratocaster looked like something that had fallen off an alien spacecraft.

"I now had my first guitar, and that was the beginning of everything ..."

Christmas 1962 coincided with the first time I heard The Beatles' 'Love Me Do', which was the start of an entirely new period. In the spring of '63, I progressed to an electric guitar, an Egmond Lucky 7. It was rare to find anybody who owned an electric guitar. But because the Egmond was a jazz model with an f-hole, I could play it acoustically.

While I was attending the Christian Brothers School in Sexton Street, Limerick City, I met two Canadian lads who were into music. Their father was a boss at a local factory. One of them was a drummer and the other played guitar and owned a five-watt Vox Domino combo. It was the first amplifier I ever played through. We would go to the local community hall in Shannon on Sunday afternoons and make a bit of a racket, playing all of George Harrison's wonderful licks from the latest Beatles songs.

The very first time I played to an audience was in 1963, at a Christmas concert at the same community hall. It was a local gathering, and anyone who sang or played was invited to get up on the stage and do a number. My Dad played a Larry Adler instrumental on his chromatic harmonica and I backed him on my acoustic guitar. Dad was a big Larry Adler fan and actually played very well, having taught himself as a boy.

Over the next year, another couple of guys from school joined in to form a little nameless band. We would practice on the stage in the hall as a way of amusing ourselves at weekends. Just as we were becoming

half decent, the Canadians had to move back home, and I borrowed £5 from my Dad to buy their Vox amplifier. My folks were very supportive of my guitar playing. There was always a lot of encouragement, because everyone loved music.

My next band was called The Shady Blues, and the lads all came from Limerick. Our repertoire included things like 'The House Of The Rising Sun', 'You Really Got Me' and a number by The Downliners Sect called 'Baby What's Wrong'.

In summer '64, I got a job working on one of the building sites around Shannon, with the aim of earning as much as I could so that I could buy a solid-bodied electric guitar. I spent 36 guineas – a fortune at the time – on a red, three pick-up Futurama III, a Czechoslovakian instrument that looked a little like a Strat to the uninitiated. The Futurama III was also George Harrison's first electric guitar, the one that he took to Hamburg in 1960, and his was just like the one I had.

The new British R&B groups began to champion the blues and, in fact, it was the blues that probably influenced my guitar playing more than any other style. 'Around And Around', 'For Your Love' and 'Over Under Sideways Down' were just a few of the songs that I painstakingly learned to play. It was in early '65 that I started to listen to blues music. I'd bought a compilation album called *Rhythm And Blues All-Stars*, which featured all the big Chicago and Delta blues artists, and for a while I listened to nothing else. I felt like

I was getting an education, because I was discovering what originally inspired bands like the Stones and The Animals.

As my Dad learned himself years earlier, one of the big bonuses of living where I did was that all the new American singles and albums would be brought into Shannon, so I heard the Phil Spector and Motown records way before they became big outside of the States. This was when the 'sixties really started, and the world was a very colourful place.

In 1966, after spending two years at the Technical School in Ennis, I started at St Patrick's Comprehensive School in Shannon, the very first comprehensive school to be opened in Ireland. Suddenly I was sharing classes with girls. That was quite an experience for a teenage boy!

I was becoming quite interested in classical music, and I bought a nylon-string classical guitar so that I could learn the fingerpicking style to complement what I was doing on electric. Classical music was always in the background, but it was hearing things like George Martin's Elizabethan-style electric piano solo on The Beatles' 'In My Life' that made me take more notice.

A friend of mine played classical guitar and could read music. He played a couple of Bach pieces – 'Bourrée' and 'Prelude In D Minor' – and showed me how to play in this style, although I never read music and always picked things up by ear. I saw how Bach's use of bass notes were a major part of his composition, and it opened the door to a lot of things for me.

While I was getting to grips with classical guitar, around 1965–66, I taught myself to play two Irish instrumental: 'The Foggy Dew' and 'The Rocky Road To Dublin'. I played them as guitar instrumentals, as I had no interest in their lyrics. I now realise that I was sowing the early seeds that led to me inventing Celtic Rock guitar.

At the same time as I was learning classical guitar, I chanced upon the American guitarist Charlie Byrd's music, and this got me into the Bossa Nova/Latin style. I bought a couple of his albums and studied the different rhythms that he used. The great discovery for me came when I risked some money on an album by Django Reinhardt and Stéphane Grappelli's Quintet of the Hot Club of France. John Renbourn and Wes Montgomery also informed my playing.

When I returned to school after the summer holiday in 1966, *Revolver* had just come out. One of the American kids had bought a copy of the LP and played it down at the community hall. I was fixed to the spot. You could tell that rock music was becoming an art form. The 'Beano' album by John Mayall's Bluesbreakers

THE SWEET STREET

ENQUIRIES :—
JIMTON PROMOTIONS
" MARYVILLE,"
DUBLIN ROAD, LIMERICK.

"YOUNG AT HEART"
DANCE
Shrove Tuesday, February 27
FRANCISCAN HALL
Music by
SWEET STREET SECT
8 to 11.55

Opposite page: Fean performing in 1967. Above: The Sweet Street; Fean jamming with the band's Eugene Wallace.

with Eric Clapton was also new, and it was essential listening for any guitar player. Eric's was the first Les Paul I ever noticed, and it really turned my head. That Les Paul sound was pretty crucial in me deciding on the kind of tone I was looking to achieve myself.

I left the Comprehensive in 1967, after doing my Intermediate Certificate, and took up a job as an apprentice, by which time I'd joined my first serious band, The Sweet Street – a Limerick-based outfit that was very much 'of the time', with the paisley shirts and new, post-Mod psychedelic fashions that defined the period.

Eugene Wallace was a fantastic singer; we had Noel Franklin on bass and Eamon Walsh on drums, and Joe O'Donnell [later of East Of Eden], who lent me his Hofner Verithin guitar, was probably the first electric violinist that anyone had seen. He was classically trained and played through a 100-watt amp and two 4 x 12" cabinets, and got an incredible sound.

The Sweet Street hardly ever played outside of Limerick, except for a few gigs in Cork and Dublin, but word got around. One of the gigs I'll never forget was when we supported John Mayall's Bluesbreakers at the 006

Club in Cork, when Mick Taylor was their lead guitarist. It was probably the first time I had ever drooled over a guitar. Mick was playing a sunburst Les Paul, and as soon as he played the first notes I just stood there, wide-eyed and rooted to the spot at the front of the stage. I was in heaven. Mick borrowed Joe's stack because it was already set up on stage when they arrived – we forgave him for blowing one of Joe's speakers that night!

Two years after we formed, The Sweet Street came to an end in 1969 without ever making any recordings, which was a real pity. Meanwhile, I joined a group called Silver Spoon, another R&B outfit that featured Mick Fraser, the original lead singer with The Sweet Street, and a great keyboard player called Teddy McCoy. The group name later changed to Jimmi Skinner, but it didn't last too long after that.

This was a period during which I was trying to find something that fitted well with what I wanted to do as a guitarist. After Silver Spoon/Jimmi Skinner, I briefly reunited with Eugene Wallace in The Play Ground, but he very soon went off to join Macbeth with Pat Quigley and Joe Staunton, and that was the end of that.

Jeremiah Henry in 1971: Jack Costelloe, Guido DiVito & Johnny Fean. Below: Johnny with Maggie in 1972.

For about two-and-a-half years, while I was busy playing gigs in the evenings, by day I had been working as an apprentice plumber for a company that serviced the new factories on Shannon Industrial Estate. I became pretty handy and if it hadn't been for the music,

I think I would have made a career of it. But I didn't get to finish the apprenticeship because, in 1970, a new band I had formed was developing so well that I left the job and took the plunge to go full-time as a musician.

I teamed up with Guido DiVito [drums and vocals] and [bassist/vocalist] Jack Costelloe of Granny's Intentions to form Jeremiah Henry, and we gigged all over Ireland, travelling in a big, old motor with a trailer for all the equipment. It was similar to the Buffalo Springfield/country-rock vibe that was becoming fashionable.

We rented a huge mansion in Parteen, County Clare, for a year, where we lived, rehearsed and hung out with other musos, like Skid Row and Lizzy, who were just starting out. Whenever Phil, Brian and Eric Bell were playing in the area, they'd always come by and stay over. We became good friends.

I think the idea of us all in this big house was probably inspired by Traffic and their famous 'getting it together in the country' period – we'd be gigging in the evening and rehearsing or writing during the day. I was starting to write my own songs then, two of which were called 'Got It In My Head' and 'Leavin' Today'.

Throughout 1971, Jeremiah Henry started to

make a name for being a great live band in Ireland. Through that exposure I started to gain a reputation as a guitarist. We were a three-piece and, as with all the classic rock trios from that time, the guitar was the main thing. It was through the influence of Hendrix and Cream that I learned how to become a frontman, guitarist and singer, and how to lead a trio.

I met Maggie [Margaret Clarke] at an outdoor picnic at a place called Carraig Rock in County Limerick, over the Easter holiday in 1971. It was love at first sight when our eyes met, and we've been in love with each other ever since that day. Maggie is the greatest woman and soulmate I have ever known. She has stayed with me through thick and thin, and we were finally married on May 30 1992 in Limerick City.

When Jeremiah Henry eventually split up, at the end of July 1972, I moved back home to Shannon for a time, and played tenor banjo and a bit of mandolin at seisiúns in County Clare. I began playing quite regularly with Ted Furey, a great fiddle player, the father of the Furey Brothers and a wonderful teacher and mentor. You couldn't ignore the musicianship of some of those traditional players. I suppose that as I became more mature as a guitarist, I began to appreciate what these guys could do, and got interested in the tenor banjo as a second instrument.

There was a thriving folk scene down in Limerick, and it was there that I met Mick and Diane Hogan, a husband and wife duo. They asked me if I would go down with them to Curtin's pub [The Roadside Tavern] in Lisdoonvarna one afternoon in the summer. The place was filled with these incredible concertina, fiddle and banjo players, and that gave me the encouragement to start picking up as many tunes as I could and learn them on the banjo.

I returned from Lisdoonvarna that September to find that someone had been looking for me. Charles O'Connor came all the way over to Shannon to ask if I'd join Horslips.

A brand new chapter in my life was about to unfold.

Eamon Carr in the Dublin mountains, cast as a poet for a Parker pens advertisement — one of several assignments as a male model during his time at Arks Advertising.

CHAPTER 2

WHEN STARS COLLIDE

 Adding two new members to the line-up, Tara Telephone progress further at the start of the new decade ...

Carr: We got to a point with Tara Telephone where we'd pushed our two guitarists as far as we felt we could go in the existing format. We came across a woman called Lucienne Purcell who had a divine voice, and Peter Fallon found two more experienced guitarists in Wexford, Bernie Barrett and Declan Sinnott, who agreed to come to Dublin. When viola da gamba player Andrew Robinson joined we were complete. We were now like an Irish version of Pentangle.

There were indications that John Peel might do an album with us for his Dandelion label. He'd already produced the first Liverpool Scene album, and their guitarist Mike Hart's début solo album. There was a connection, and we were inviting English and Scottish poets to read at the *Dublin Arts Festival* and so on.

Just as this was developing, I started working at Arks advertising agency. Arks was at 16–18 Harcourt Street in Dublin, and probably the hottest Irish ad agency at the time. I'd already gained a bit of experience in advertising at an agency called Arrow, and went to Arks as a media campaign planner. The head of copy, Frank Sheerin, was

a good mentor. He'd taken note of what I'd done as a writer with Tara Telephone, and asked if I'd become a copywriter. My life was about to take a serious detour.

Charles O'Connor was a visualiser/designer on another floor, and Barry Devlin had just arrived as one of six copywriters spread across three groups, so we got to know each other well.

O'Connor: Arks found me digs in Harold's Cross with Mr & Mrs Kelly, a friendly couple that were used to accommodating the new starters. The agency was based in the most beautiful Georgian building. On any given day, I'd be working for Harp, Carrolls cigarettes and Guinness, whose account was a particularly big deal.

Carr: The week I joined the copywriting department I was diagnosed with hepatitis, so I was out for three months. It was a miserable, desperate fuckin' business. When I came back to Arks, Charles and Barry came to see Tara Telephone do their thing. Charles was a musician, and musicians were always interested in what we were doing.

O'Connor: Like most of the stuff I was experiencing in Dublin, it was a new awakening. If you recited poetry in Middlesbrough, people would club you to death! There was never any talk of me joining Tara Telephone as far as I was aware, although it was known that I played a bit.

What they were doing was interesting, but I didn't think it was my bag. The great thing about that scene was that Eamon was one of the prime instigators behind encouraging Phil Lynott to start playing music seriously, and that's not something that is widely appreciated.

Devlin: I was in a pub with my then girlfriend some-time in early 1970, and we saw Edison Lighthouse, who had just had a No.1 single ['Love Grows (Where My Rosemary Goes)']. That was the moment when I knew a music career was what I eventually wanted. So when thinking about a job, I figured that if I could find some-thing through which I would meet like-minded souls, I might end up in a band.

Advertising and publicity seemed like a suitable avenue, because the people that worked in it were crea-tive and cool, and the younger ones had the clothes and the artistic vibe that I could feed off. Pretty girls always seemed to be around, but I was so shy and innocent, as would befit a lad who hadn't long escaped from a monastery.

That April, a travel editor friend of mine, Dennis Smith, took me with him on an assignment to Bergen in Norway, giving the excuse that I was his photog-rapher. We met a beautiful blonde lady, a model called Vibeke Steineger. We got on so well that she gave me her number and suggested that I call her sometime.

Dennis and I went off to another town the next day, and I noticed Vibeke's name in a local paper, so I asked someone if it was a common name over there. The guy said, 'You mean Miss Norway?' I was astonished. So when we returned to Bergen to continue Dennis' work, I called her and we went out for dinner. It only went as far as a kiss, but as first romantic encounters go, Miss Norway was an impressive start.

My Masters degree probably helped me win my job with Arks – a real melting pot of artistic creativity that inspired on-the-hoof thinking. Eamon, Charles and I weren't big pals outside of the office, but we started to knock about together after a while, and music was inevitably the topic of conversation. All I knew about was white trash pop, while Eamon seemed to be a universal authority.

Carr: There was a really exciting thing going on in Dublin around 1970, because Dr Strangely Strange, Sweeney's Men and Brush Shiels' Skid Row had come through; the young Philip Lynott's star was beginning to shine, and Gary Moore was hanging around.

We always had musical guests at the Tara Telephone poetry workshops, and one night Jim played 'Blue Rondo À La Turk' and a traditional air on tin whistle. I just knew Jim from hanging around, because Dublin was a lot smaller then. Everybody tended to congregate. And on this night, 'everybody' also included Charles, playing a pile of strange instruments.

O'Connor: As I began to settle in at Arks, I decided to see if there were any opportunities to play some music. I also met Liam Weldon, and we started a folk club at Slattery's in Capel Street called The Stalling Sark. Anyone could form a club like this if you attracted enough beer drinkers. We briefly formed a group called The Wild Geese with Tommy Peoples and Johnny Flood. I was playing concertina, a bit of mandolin and bad fiddle, and Liam was singing a lot of old Irish songs.

Liam was like my Irish dad for a while. He took me up to Ballyfermot, where I hung out with the Fureys and met their dad, Ted. It was a few months before I started to bond and socialise with Barry and Eamon.

Devlin: Like Eamon, I worked on Arks' Harp and

"Advertising and publicity seemed like a suitable avenue – the people that worked in it were creative and cool ..."

POETRY IN IN PARNELL SQUARE

Eamonn Carr (left) and Peter Fallon of the Tara Telephone.

By JIM LOCKHART

HEADS BOWED and faces intent, over 60 young people sit around on benches, chairs or on the floor. Their ages range from 17 to 21. From the walls pictures of the 1916 leaders peer down; the room has an intimate atmosphere reminiscent of a time gone by. An attractive, dark-haired girl finishes reading three of her poems and the others clap appreciatively.

This is the scene that greets the visitor to the Poetry Workshop in 51 Parnell Square. Most of the city's younger poets have gravitated there since its inception last January to read their own work and to hear what others were writing. Recently the workshop held the last of its fortnightly sessions until September.

"We're breaking up for a while beause a lot of the people who come are going away for the summer, and also to prevent anyone in particular from having too strong an influence on the younger writers," says quiet-spoken Peter Fallon.

Peter and fellow-poet Eamonn Carr, with guitarist David Costello, make up the Tara Telephone, a regular attraction at poetry-and-music sessions in Dublin.

The group came together last November. "At the time," says Peter, "there was nowhere in town where readings were open to anyone who wanted to take part." So they rented the room in Parnell Square and from then on news of the Workshop spread gradually.

"In the beginning we thought it would just be a small group of a dozen or so reading to others, but it developed as it went along."

In fact once they got off the ground the sessions occasionally drew attendances of 100 or more, many of them drawn from the city's secondary and technical schools with a sprinkling of university students.

One of the stickiest problems to confront the aspiring young poet is the danger of becoming narrowly ingrown in his style and subject-matter. This is effectively overcome by the regular cross-fertilisation of ideas that occurs in the workshop. In addition, gatherings like this put poetry into a context that is more relevant and alive than that of the schoolroom or textbook — poetry, it has been said, only finds its true meaning when it is spoken.

The sessions also have a musical leavening. To date guests have included Danny Doyle, John Ledingham, Brendan Shiels and Paul Kennan. Rent for the room is made up by passing the hat around.

MAGAZINE

Some weeks ago the group published the first issue of "Capella," containing a cross-section of the best of the poetry that has emerged in the Workshop. Before long, all 700 copies were sold, no mean achievement for a poetry magazine costing 3s. 6d. Encouraged by this early success, Peter and Eamon are already planning the second issue.

A more ambitious plan concerns the future of the Workshop. An expanding Arts Laboratory is envisaged, with bigger premises catering for experimental films, plays and concerts as well as poetry readings. However, such a project is still very much up in the air.

Meanwhile, nobody stops writing just because the meetings are over for the moment. As one girl put it: "We're really going to be flooded out with stuff in September." And if the sensitivity and eagerness of these young people is anything to go by, she was probably right.

Lockhart: "While I was at UCD, I wrote a few pieces for the *Irish Independent* including this one in early 1970. I'd been to some of the Tara Telephone workshops and offered to write about what was going on there."

Guinness accounts, and I was the very proud recipient of the Greenhorn Award within my first year. It was exciting to go to London and work with John Carter of Ivy League and The Flower Pot Men fame, and also one half of the Carter–Lewis songwriting team. Together, we re-wrote The Love Affair's 'Bringing On Back The Good Times' as 'Bringing On Back The Goodness' for Guinness, and we did an all-night shoot with a crowd of models, which was a lot of fun. What really put Eamon, Charles and I – and Jim – together was a Harp commercial that I didn't write.

Carr: We had all appeared in different ads. Charles was actually a fashionable male model. In one ad, I was cast as a poet who only used Parker pens, and was photographed up in the Dublin mountains with Spud Murphy's dad's bike, dressed in my normal everyday clothes, which fitted the part perfectly.

One day I was in my little cubicle at Arks, slaving over copy for a marmalade ad, when I heard some excitement down the corridor. It was Charles, Barry and another guy, who was a visualiser. I heard Charles saying, 'Well, you've got the guitar,' and Barry's saying, 'Yeah.' So I asked them what was happening. The boys said, 'They're looking for a band ... a commercial for Harp lager.'

They said, 'We're trying to put a band together, because they can't find a band.' Charles said, 'And Barry plays the guitar, so we're going to go down and say we're in a band.' They didn't have a drummer, so I quickly said that I'd played drums before I played the bongos, and I suddenly had the gig.

The director, Gerry Poulson, had auditioned a lot of rock bands, but everybody looked too bedraggled. We were earning a salary, so we weren't decrepit, but we were suitably hairy. Poulson said, 'Okay, you look like a band, but there are only three of you.'

We had to find a keyboard player. Barry said, 'I know Jim Lockhart.' I said, 'Oh yeah, Jim. The guy who plays the whistle? Where is he?'

Devlin: Arks was just up from St Stephen's Green and I had a strong feeling that if I popped over there, I'd find Jim. Sure enough, he came around the corner and I asked if he was free. He was keen.

Lockhart: Devlin said, 'You'll be great ... you can play the organ, can't you?' But I didn't. He said, 'Ah, but tell 'em you can. It's only miming.'

Carr: Jim came back, all dressed up. We didn't have to play; we just had to mime to a non-specific backing track. We were the 'band on a stage', playing to a

Above: Devlin, O'Connor & Lockhart in 1970. These are the earliest-known photographs of any Horslips members together.

trendy audience, which included future U2 manager Paul McGuinness as an extra. It was like something out of 'Blow-Up', with us wearing dandy cravats like The Kinks, circa 'Waterloo Sunset'.

Devlin: Poulson was a very animated director, shouting at us through his megaphone to look a bit more like a groovy rock band. We were called The Gentle People, or at least that's what it said on the bass drum. Unfortunately, the footage appears to have vanished. There were free drinks and lots of girls, and we thought, if this is what being in a pop band was like, maybe we should look into it!

Carr: After the ad shoot, we went to a café on Suffolk Street. We'd had an enjoyable day, and we looked like a band, so I suggested maybe we should try to get together and see if we could knock out a couple of tunes. It was arranged that we'd go to Jim's house in James' Street. Jim had a piano there, Charles brought some instruments, Barry brought a guitar, and I came with bongos and a bodhrán. It was just lads hanging out. Someone would play something by The High Level Ranters or the Everly Brothers. It wasn't like a band, but we were doing that for a while and having a laugh.

Devlin: We'd sometimes use the resources at Arks to make things interesting, and we'd certainly keep the dream alive by recording demos for presentations at the agency. One of our clients was a clothes chain called Penny's, and we'd record jingles for them.

O'Connor: Quite soon, Sue Calvert, my childhood sweetheart, came over to Dublin to live with me. We went to parties, where we'd sing some English songs together. It was at one of these gatherings that I saw Martin Byrnes, a fiddle player who remains a hero of mine. He played the polka 'After The Battle Of Aughrim' brilliantly – I'd never heard playing like that before. Surrounding myself with great players like Martin made me want to improve my own playing. Something in me was changing. I just needed a catalyst, and it gradually dawned on me that Barry, Eamon and Jim might just be that catalyst. It got to the point where the four of us decided it would be a fine idea to play a gig. And that was how Horslips began to evolve.

We wanted to do something, but we weren't sure what it was, and there was a lot of fumbling around and toffee chewing. All of us were fairly shite, and yet we recognised there was a Celtic connection and a rock connection that brought us together. We daydreamed about wild parties and screwing gorgeous models in much the same way as you did at art school, but there was something about being a musician that we thought might make all of this possible.

August: Kieron 'Spud' Murphy (born August 24 1946), an Arks staff photographer, is persuaded to join the still-unnamed outfit.

Murphy: I started working as a photographer in April 1968, soon after I graduated from University College Dublin, where I did it as a hobby. I worked for Tony Higgins, the top fashion and advertising photographer in Dublin, for about two years, and one of my clients was Arks. Eamonn O'Flaherty took me out to a very posh restaurant one night in 1970 and got me absolutely leathered, and then asked if I'd work for him.

Barry, Eamon, Charlie and I found each other quite quickly. We were kindred spirits, particularly Barry and I. I had got into pop and rock music in the early to middle 'sixties, but I'd given it up as a bit of a bad job by around 1969, and turned my attention to jazz.

They had already done the Harp commercial when I started jamming with them on guitar. It was suggested that if four guys from an advertising agency can't hype a band, they should be lined up against a wall and shot! That was the genesis of the band that we created, even though we realised that, with the exception of Charlie and Jim, the traditionally-inspired members, we were quite limited as musicians.

Devlin: It was my idea to recruit Spud as lead guitarist. He was a very tasteful player who looked like Roy Kinnear, and we nicknamed him 'Stormy Trousers' because of his big, wide, flared pants. For the first couple of months we would meet, occasionally hire equipment and get together to play Beatles and Cream songs, and discuss how we were going to be the biggest band in the world. The thing is, if all your energy goes into learning songs properly, you're fucked, and you should just be a bar band. But if you concentrate on what it'll be like when you do get it together, you're on the right track, and we certainly had that.

Murphy: We began to attempt writing some original songs. Barry was very keen and he brought some numbers of his own to the gatherings over at Jimmy's flat. I contributed a little instrumental that I'd written myself, and I thought we should model our sound on The Band, who I loved.

O'Connor: Jamming at Jimmy's was great fun, because his dad would offer me a glass of poitín. 'Come on, you Brit bugger, try some of this,' he'd say, even though it was 11 o'clock on a Saturday morning. 'Just get it down your neck,' he would insist.

The Lockharts were lovely people and so hospitable. Jimmy's mum cooked us an enormous fried breakfast. All of our jamming sessions were fuelled on fat and poitín, and I have no idea how we got anything done. This became a ritual that lasted for several years. Even when we became very well-known, we would pop over there for a fry-up before we played the National Stadium.

"If this is what being in a pop band was going to be like, maybe we should look into it ..."

The first promotional photographs of Horslips
with Kieron 'Spud' Murphy (centre).

Carr: The possibilities seemed endless. Working with a little bit of lyrical content and a concertina was rootsy. Jim had this jazzy traditional thing going on and Barry had a strong folk input, so we had this big common ground straight away.

Murphy: That we weren't very good didn't seem to be too much of an issue for the others. We decided to make this concept of a band more real by staging a photo session on Sandymount Beach – I got my Arks colleague Shay Lattimore to take shots that I set up for him.

They were the very first photographs of the band and, being the master of style that I wasn't, I made sure to wear my trilby hat as we leaned down into the camera's wide-angle lens.

October 12: Horslips are born. Whilst dining at the Kum Tong Chinese restaurant in Dublin, the fivesome finally decide on a name for the band.

Murphy: We thought the name 'Apocalypse' would be interesting, although none of us really liked it. There was a rehearsal one day at Jimmy's that didn't go well, and we got quite depressed about it, so as a consolation we took ourselves off for a Chinese, the only form of exotic cuisine in Dublin at the time.

We were joshing around with different uses of this word when someone said that maybe we should call ourselves The Four Horsemen Of The Apocalypse. I said, no, we played so badly that it should be The Four Poxmen Of The Horselypse. Everyone laughed loudly, pointed at me and said, 'Yes, that's it ... Horselypse!' It was just a joke spoonerism that I thought was shite. I couldn't believe they stuck with it!

Devlin: I've always claimed that monosodium glutamate poisoning must have taken hold of us, but good old Spud made history right there and then! The Four Poxmen wouldn't have been right, as Punk hadn't kicked off yet, so Horselypse it was, until we quickly modified it to Horselips, and finally Horslips, all within days.

October 16: The band attract their first press coverage when Pat Egan's Group Scene column in Ireland's top music magazine, *Spotlight*, describes Horslips as a 'new rock-orientated group'.

November 5: Their first gig – at CYMS Hall in Navan, County Meath – is cancelled when the local curate withdraws permission for the use of

the venue as the event is, he says, 'immoral and designed to seduce the girls of Navan'.

In the *Sunday Independent*, Jim Lockhart complains: 'Naturally, we were very disappointed … it meant heavy financial loss, as we had already spent about £40 in advertising.'

Carr: I had the idea of hiring the hall in Navan for our own event: a 'Funky Ceilidhe'. We'd run a couple of buses from Dublin for our mates and colleagues, and turn it into a magical mystery tour to Navan. Charles designed the poster. He took a graphic from a woman's magazine – a pair of bright red lips – with us 'trapped' inside them and a long, phallic cigarette dangling out with a red tip on the end. Charles was good with the double entendre.

We had to have good lighting, so to make the poster look even more interesting we added the words 'The Afro-Dizziac Light Show'. We knew an electronics buff who had found out how to build a strobe unit … or so he said.

With the hall hired, we plastered posters on walls everywhere. Unfortunately, O'Connor had put his number on the bottom of the poster, in case someone might like it and give him some work. But it backfired. Within a couple of days, Charles received a phone call from the top priest in Navan, who told him that he'd never seen anything quite so disgusting in his life.

So I rang to smooth the waters, but I didn't get the priest. I spoke to someone who told me that 'twenty good fathers and true had called up to the presbytery and demanded that this filth not be allowed to infect the town'. For some bands that might have been a seriously damning blow, but the ban was our saving grace really, because we hardly had much of a set, and our lighting guy's strobe didn't work either.

Coming from advertising, we were more savvy than most, and turned the situation to our advantage. We contacted the newspapers with a story involving God and his fight with the Devil's music. Within days, headlines such as 'Bingo Priest Bans Pop Group' were screaming from the news stands. Without ever playing a note in public, Horslips were all over the national press – an exercise in pure Situationism.

Late November: A chance meeting gives Horslips an opportunity with RTÉ.

Carr: I bumped into Áine O'Connor from RTÉ. She was about to start work with Joe O'Donnell on a new TV series called 'Fonn', and asked me if I knew of a band that would be interested in doing a theme tune and appearing on the show. I told Áine that I was finishing with Tara Telephone. I said, 'Have you heard of a band called Horslips? They've been all over the newspapers …' at which point I produced the latest copy of *Spotlight* magazine, with our picture in it and a write-up by Pat Egan. I told her we played funky ceilidhe music … sort of folk-rock. Naturally, she wanted to hear some material, so she asked if she could attend a rehearsal to get a feel for what we did.

Up to this point, we were really just an acoustic band, and we played a few tunes like 'Flower Amang Them All'. Joe O'Donnell said, 'Great, but I believe you're a rock band. Can I hear you play with the electric gear? You can play electric, right?' 'Oh yeah, we're good,' we said, 'but the gear's in the truck and it broke down on the way back home last night. It's in Kinnegad, 40 miles from here.'

This was a complete lie, but we had the best of intentions. We felt that we could write if only we had electric instruments or a drum kit, and it was clear that this TV gig rested on our ability to deliver what they wanted. We had to buy some new instruments.

Murphy: The demo we recorded for 'Fonn' was supposed to have included original material, but we just couldn't get it together, and I suggested we do a simple blues jam. I was playing a really cheap old Spanish gutstring guitar.

Devlin: We recorded a jam session with electric guitar,

the gig of writing the theme for 'Fonn' thanks to Spud's 'See See Rider', but by the time we got on the show, Spud had departed.

December: Murphy leaves the band and heads for London to develop what will become a lucrative, star-studded photography career with the newly-launched _Sounds_ magazine.

As well as his famous shoot during John Lennon's _Imagine_ sessions, Murphy also earns the title of Marc Bolan's 'court photographer'. Meanwhile, Declan Sinnott, Eamon Carr's sidekick in Tara Telephone, is brought in to replace Murphy on lead guitar.

Carr: Declan had also been thinking of dropping out of Tara Telephone, and I told him about this new band and our television opportunity. I could vouch for his musicianship, so I ran it past the others and suggested that he come along and check out what we were doing. He eventually became a vital component of Horslips' early music.

Devlin: We saw what fun you could have with traditional tunes, but we were much more like a West Coast act. There was a pretty cavalier attitude towards a rhythm section, and a strong advocacy of interesting and eccentric melodic lines and instrumentation. We purposely didn't try to emulate what Fairport Convention were doing, in the sense that they were English folkies playing rock instruments. We sensed that we wanted to do something quite different, which was to deconstruct tunes and use them as the basis for new material. What you look for is a tune that isn't busy, but has a cadence to it that you can lift for something like 'Trouble (With A Capital T)'.

bass, fiddle and bongos, I think, and as an after-thought Spud played a solo instrumental version of 'See See Rider', which was a very neat piece of picking. What we thought Áine had received was a tape of Spud's number at the start, followed by our jam as an addendum. The reality was the reverse.

Lockhart: Then she called us and complained that we must have sent her the wrong tape, because there was this terrible noise, and she had to keep fast-forwarding until a very lovely guitar number appeared. I said, 'Ah, I think we may have taped over something.' So we got

"We wanted to deconstruct tunes and use them as the basis for new material ..."

Horslips, with new members Declan Sinnott (far right) and Gene Mulvaney (third from left) on RTÉ's 'Fonn'.

January: Formerly of Carr's mid-'60s band Toneage, Gene Mulvaney joins as bass guitarist, and rehearsals in Jim Lockhart's front room become more frequent.

Carr: Joe O'Donnell asked us to be free to start recording the show, 'Fonn'. It was only at this point that he mentioned the word 'series'. He said, 'Yeah, it's six shows. Our idea is that you might open or close the show, or maybe do two or three numbers during the show.' We had to keep a straight face and say, 'Right, sure, no problem.' But really, we were in shock.

Our role was to be the house band. Joe was really pushing for us to play as an electric band, but we were keen to avoid that pressure. We asked, 'Would it be better if we start acoustically and then gradually build up ... ?' 'No,' he interrupted, 'we must go electric the first week. Be here Sunday next at 12 noon, we'll do some rehearsals, some camera shots, take a break for tea, and we'll come back and shoot the thing.' So that was that.

We sat around wondering how the fuck we were going to pull this off. But to get through the first week, all we had to do was get two or three tunes together, so it didn't seem too much of a stretch.

Then we realised that not only did Declan need to buy an electric guitar, I also needed a new set of drums. So I hurried down to the Drum Centre to see this guy, John, and tell him I was desperate but could only afford something cheap. He said, 'You're in luck, a

51

second-hand drum kit has just come in, and it's really good.' He opened a door to reveal a great-looking blue sparkle Premier job. He agreed to take a small amount up-front, followed by installments, and even threw in some cymbals.

When I quizzed him about where the kit came from, he told me that Brian Downey from Thin Lizzy had just brought it in because the band were going to England, and he needed a new kit. I realised I'd seen Brian playing these drums, and they sounded great. John said, 'Before that, the kit was owned by Noel Bridgeman of Skid Row.'

I took the kit down to the smelly basement of an art gallery [Galerie Langlois] that Jimmy had arranged for rehearsals, and we had a week to shape up. But first we needed a bass player. I immediately thought of Gene Mulvaney, who came down for a workout.

Lockhart: Bits and pieces of what we did in those six weeks eventually turned up on *Happy To Meet*. Things like 'The Clergy's Lamentation', 'Johnny's Wedding', 'The Musical Priest' and probably 'Flower Amang Them All' and 'Comb Your Hair And Curl It' all surfaced during those sessions. It astonishes me how much doing that series was responsible for shaping what Horslips became. That kind of pressure forces you to focus sharply.

Everyone was still working during the day and obvi-

ously this deadline was on our minds all the time. We'd speed over to the art gallery by 6pm and knock out an arrangement, move on to another one and come back and review and tighten up what we'd done that evening.

We worked towards compiling a list of songs that we might be able to perform at later gigs. It generally involved sitting around, playing some traditional jigs and reels, and seeing how we could work that music into something of a contemporary nature.

We weren't into pastiche; we didn't want to make up traditional-sounding tunes. Everything we did was the genuine article – tunes that had been passed down through the generations. It was very much an experimental period; we were just feeling our way.

Recording for 'Fonn' begins on January 24 and continues on January 31 and February 7, 14 and 21, leading up to RTÉ's broadcast of the first episode in the 9.30pm time slot vacated by The Dubliners' regular show. A nation catches its first sight of a curious band …

Carr: The nature of 'Fonn' was slightly complex. It was an Irish-language programme that worked out of a small budget at the national television station. I think they recycled sets from the Chekhov play 'Uncle Vanya', and they had a quirky mix of musical talent, including a pianist playing Percy French tunes or

The brief six-piece line-up with Gene Mulvaney (second from left)

Thomas Moore's Irish Melodies, a fiddler, and a tenor singing a couple of songs.

Devlin: We were playing a hybrid of traditional Irish airs and rock'n'roll that was received warmly but cautiously by the audience. No one had ever given Irish music this treatment.

Carr: It was exciting, because we had to come up with a couple of new tunes for each performance. It gave us something to work towards, and by the end of the series we had cracked a repertoire of sorts.

O'Connor: There wasn't much money involved, but the promise of appearing on television was staggering. We had made this abrupt move from the shallow end into the deep end. We didn't want to sing Irish songs, but take the melodies that were inherently Irish or Celtic and put them into a different form of music.

On one episode I corpsed – I went into this dry funk and couldn't remember for the life of me what I should be playing. And Jimmy managed to get on camera picking his nose, which was probably a first in Ireland. To my great surprise, the music didn't fall to bits. It was a great lesson to learn early on, that you need to have your shit together if you're going to play at this level. I think we took on more than we could chew, although, if anything, it set us up for what was to come.

Devlin: As well as giving the band national profile, 'Fonn' yielded another significant benefit for me. It was on the day of the first shoot that I met the lovely Caroline Erskine, a future broadcaster and journalist, who was then a Trinity student and the roommate of Declan's girlfriend, Pat Eastwood. Pat invited Caroline along and, as fate would have it, 11 years later we were married.

"By the end of the series we had cracked a repertoire of sorts ..."

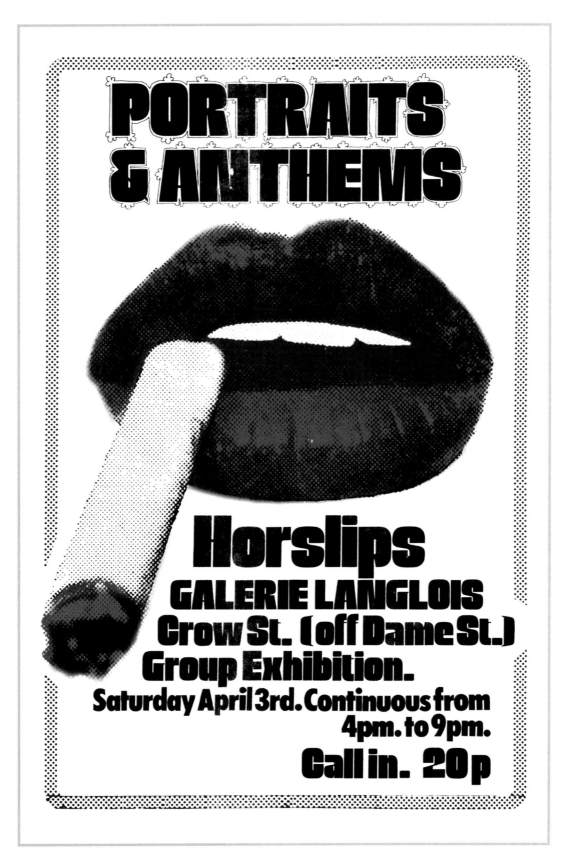

Portraits & Anthems: Horslips' first live public performance.

Further recording for 'Fonn' occurs on March 6 and 7, after which Mulvaney leaves the band and Devlin moves from rhythm guitar to bass.

Devlin: I could see that there wasn't going to be much of a future in this band for a Marmalade-style rhythm guitar player, so I decided it would be a really sensible move to learn the bass. Gene was getting increasingly fed up with commuting to Dublin for rehearsals and the TV shoots, especially as he was busy with his day job as a carpenter back in Kells, but to be brutally honest, we just didn't ask him back. We weren't wicked, just young, and it can make you feel guilty later in life.

Declan had been giving me some bass lessons. I knew so little that he was literally telling me what to play, note for note, on things like 'The Ace & Deuce Of Pipering'. I didn't have much time to get my act together before our first public gig, so I was putting in a lot of practice.

April 3: On the same date that Horslips are featured in the final 'Fonn' episode, the band's official public live début is staged at Galerie Langlois in Dublin's Crow Street. They play as part of a five-hour 'extravaganza', titled *Portraits & Anthems*. To satisfy public demand, the event is repeated on May 1.

O'Connor: By the end of the TV series, we'd started to attract a bit of a cult following and were starting to get gig offers. The thing was, it was going to be hard to get gigs on our own terms, because the music was too oddball, too experimental, and didn't have dance beats. We wanted to independently style our own shows.

Carr: Galerie Langlois was a fairly bohemian art gallery in the Temple Bar area, run by a friend of the band called Brendan Langlois Kennedy. He let us use the gallery as our rehearsal base, but we ended up owing rent and electricity money. We thought we could drum up some hype, perform in the actual gallery and earn some money to pay our way. That some of the people who came might also be interested in buying the paintings was a great incentive to the owner.

Lockhart: We hired a PA and did all the normal organisational stuff. It was very loose. Eamon read a few poems and Declan sang a couple of songs. We played our 12-song set three times. People could wander in, pay a few bob, and then wander out.

Carr: We turned it into an afternoon/early evening event. It worked for us, because it meant that we got the experience of performing live without a lot of the inherent trauma. I came up with the *Portraits & Anthems* title; it was like our version of 'Pictures At An Exhibition', echoing The Strawbs' album title *Just*

A Collection Of Antiques And Curios. And we charged a good value admission fee of 30 new pence.

Devlin: Our early live performances were incredibly ropey. We were a far cry from the dancehall band we later became. Any money that we did make from gigs was ploughed into buying amps and instruments.

O'Connor: There was a lot of 'unseen' promotion work going on all the time in the background, all very homemade. We would stand on vans in O'Connell Street and put up 6' x 4' posters that I'd designed at work when I wasn't asleep. It was dangerous – we'd be slipping off the vans with the wallpaper paste and the police were chasing us.

June 5: *Sligo Sounds '71 Whit Weekend Festival* (June 4–7), with Fairport Convention, Tír na nÓg (Sonny Condell and Leo O'Kelly), Bridget St John and The Chieftains. It will be Horslips' only live appearance with Fairport until August 2011, when they are special guests at *Fairport's Cropredy Convention.*

Lockhart: I was so impressed with Dave Swarbrick's vibe and coolness. His fiddle playing for Fairport was a knockout. It was the first time I'd seen them and I thought they were a fabulous band, and very worthy of all the acclaim they were getting.

Carr: We were way down the bill, but we went down very well, because unlike most of the other performers, we were kind of a rock band. Fairport were the business; they were so tight, while we were really loose.

Dave Pegg (Fairport Convention): We'd been hearing a lot about Horslips around that time. People in England who were into folk-rock knew about them, and were telling us that we should check them out. They were great. I got their first album, *Happy To Meet, Sorry To Part,* and it made a really good impression on me.

Simon Nicol (Fairport Convention): It was an absolutely beautiful evening and after the gig, everybody retreated to the appointed hotel to partake of a fair amount of alcohol until sunrise. Horslips were with us before and after our set at the festival, and I was like a sponge soaking it all up. It was a great time to be a young man and the company we kept was first class.

I suppose that Horslips were still at the point where they were trying to discover their strengths and work out their direction. I recognised that, because Fairport were in the same position about five years earlier and yet it still felt very fresh.

Horslips certainly had something going for them, even in 1971, and I think all of us appreciated what they were about.

Like them, we were taking the threads of old songs and tunes, although the end results tended to be quite different because we both came from different cultures. Just breathing the same air together was probably very inspirational to both camps.

A late addition to the *Sligo Sounds '71* bill are Jeremiah Henry, whose 19-year-old lead guitarist, Johnny Fean, earns a standing ovation.

Lockhart, Carr, Sinnott, O'Connor & Devlin: summer '71.

Fean: We did a lively set early in the programme. Philip Lynott had recommended us to the organisers, and we were added to the bill within a couple of days of the gig. I didn't get to see Horslips that day, although I heard great reports from countless people.

The summer includes appearances at RDS, Dublin, supporting Donovan (June 26); the *Clare Festival* (July 3), where Johnny Fean and Jeremiah Henry once again share the bill; RTÉ's 'Songs And Sounds Of Tomorrow', with Richard Harris and Tír na nÓg (July 16); the National Stadium, supporting Thin Lizzy (August 7); *Rock In The Hollow* in Blackrock Park (August 8); an indoor festival at Alice's Restaurant (August 21); and the *Blackrock Festival* on August 29.

Lockhart: The *Blackrock Festival* was on a concrete island in the middle of an artificial lake, and it was a lovely summer affair. The *Irish Times* gave us a great review and published a picture of me playing flute and wearing the low-necked top with three-quarter sleeves and a vest that I favoured for a year or two.

September 7: Coinciding with Charles O'Connor's 23rd birthday, disaster strikes while Horslips are recording a session at RTÉ Studios in O'Connell Hall, Dublin.

Horslips live on RTÉ's 'Discaset', June 26 1971.

O'Connor: We used RTÉ's studios that day to record some cover versions, including 'Southern Man' by Neil Young, that we'd enjoyed playing live. During the session, Sinnott nearly killed himself, because his guitar was incorrectly wired and he received a massive electric shock when he touched the microphone. He went flying and one of the acoustic screens fell on top of him, knocking him out.

Devlin: The engineer, Gerry Fitzgerald, freaked out, probably thinking that the corporation would be sued. The situation could have been a whole lot worse, but fortunately Declan's injuries were very temporary.

September 11: *Headland Festival* **at Dublin's RDS. Horslips appear alongside Arthur Brown's Kingdom Come, Alan Price and Georgie Fame, Donovan, Manfred Mann's Earth Band and Mellow Candle. Attracting several thousand fans, the event is promoted by Michael Deeny and Paul McGuinness.**

Carr: The audience brought their cushions and sat down, smoking dope or doing whatever floated their boat. There were funny lights and all the stuff you might have associated with the freak-outs at the Roundhouse. We started with 'The Clergy's Lamentation', and the weird thing was that it worked. Horslips actually were an Irish underground band when you think about it. Audiences were getting off on us.

Horslips are the most talked-about band of the event. They impress Michael Deeny, who immediately offers a management deal.

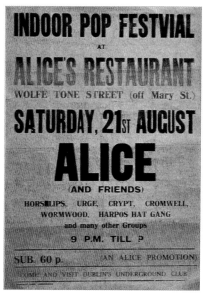

Deeny: I had known Paul McGuinness for some time, as a friend of my younger brother Donnell. They met at Clongowes Wood College and went on to Trinity College together. Paul suggested that he and I team up to promote music events in Dublin. Having a chartered accountant involved appealed to his sharp business sense even then.

I was a music fan; I'd seen bands like the Rolling Stones at the Ulster Hall in 1964, and The Pink Floyd at Middle Earth in 1967, when I lived in London. I had a very eclectic taste, for everything from early R&B to New Orleans jazz. So I had been pre-programmed for a life in the music business, and was very interested when Paul wanted to set up Headland Promotions with me.

It was my money that funded our concerts. Our first was headlined by Donovan at the RDS [Royal Dublin Society] – the biggest indoor

Signing with manager Michael Deeny in September 1971.

venue in Dublin for any major exhibition, and regularly used for horse shows. It had never been hired for rock'n'roll concerts and so I had to be very sensitive in my negotiations. It helped that I wore a pinstriped suit and tie, and came across as well educated, because I don't think they would have taken me seriously otherwise.

I was able to talk them into giving us the RDS, and the Donovan gig in June '71 was a success. In fact, Horslips were one of the support bands, but I'm ashamed to say I didn't pay much attention.

The success of that gig encouraged Paul and I to plan another one at the RDS that September, called the *Headland Festival*. The bill was to be topped by The Who, but they hadn't signed a contract by the time we announced it and they pulled out. Along with the other well-known bands, one of the Irish acts we booked to open was Horslips, who got a fantastic reaction.

It was impossible to be in Dublin and not be aware of Horslips, because they were creating such a buzz and were constantly in the press. When I finally saw them for the first time, at our festival, I was immediately impressed by their originality and spirited performance. There wasn't anything else like them in Ireland, or indeed the world.

I could also see that they were very intelligent, likeable, rational people. This wasn't rare amongst rock musicians but it also wasn't common, so they made an instant, positive impression on me. I instinctively knew that I must get involved with them.

O'Connor: We'd received a number of management offers – including one from Tony Wilson, a reporter with the Dublin *Evening Herald* – but we were holding out for someone interesting and special, possibly someone with a bit of that Peter Grant [Led Zeppelin manager] clout.

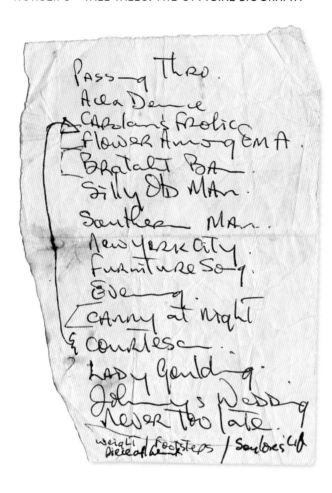

A set list from a gig in Bray on September 24.

Terry O'Neill had been looking after us informally for a few months, but it wasn't going to last, because he didn't approve of our musical direction.

Michael was different. Being as he was an accountant, we thought he was lowering his standards by surrounding himself with hairy rock musicians. He wore a cape and carried a swordstick ... nothing if not eccentric. He had the brass neck to tell me he could only give us the fee less £15, as he'd lost money on the gig. That he succeeded in getting us to accept this told me that we must have this guy on our side.

Late September: An active member of the Anti-Apartheid movement, Michael Deeny (born November 12 1944) officially becomes Horslips' manager. He opens serious discussions about the

band's future career strategies – one of which is to explore their potential as a recording outfit.

O'Connor: Michael was very influential in us making the transition into the ballrooms, which became a big focus. When we started playing them we noticed that people didn't know how to dance to folk-rock. The trick was to just fling yourself around and have a laugh!

Carr: It wasn't properly announced until the November. We agreed to work with Michael for something like six months, but it soon became obvious how crucial he would be for us, so it was soon cast in stone. Like Brian Epstein, he would say, 'Guys, you're going to have to get your act together, and you probably need to have a few good dancing tunes in the set.'

We'd be sitting around at Michael's late at night, and he'd suggest Rolling Stones numbers – which weren't too out of place, as we'd started out playing John Lee Hooker songs. We threw in 'Jumping Jack Flash', and a couple of beat numbers like 'I Saw Her Standing There'. We also did the CCS instrumental version of 'Whole Lotta Love', and 'Passing Through', a great Steamhammer number that we often played as a long, drawn-out piece that seemed to go on for hours. The set was mixed, but we drew from it to match the venues we played.

Devlin: We packed our set out with anything we could think of, including dire originals. I wrote a Tull rip-off called 'Looking Back', and another called 'Margarine' – a very bad song that we dropped from our set as soon as we could.

Deeny: Persuading the ballroom owners to take a chance and let us in to play gigs was an uphill struggle, and we had to do it on a town-by-town basis. The more successful gigs we had under our belt, the more evidence we could present that we could pack out a hall and be profitable for everyone. So the province previously 'owned' by uniformed showbands and cabaret singers was now being shared by hairy rockers and a largely grateful audience, who suddenly had their own rock stars. It changed everything.

Original lyrics for 'Motorway Madness'
from the October Trend Studios session.

. . . .

October 4-5: Trend Studios, Dublin.

Lockhart: Pretty much immediately after becoming our manager, Michael booked us into Trend Studios. One of the songs we'd written and were featuring in our live set – even in the later years – was the notably un-folky 'Motorway Madness'. Michael liked it and thought we should record it. Barry sang and Declan Sinnott rocked out on lead guitar. It's probably a telling sign that it would remain unreleased until it was included as one of the rarities on *Tracks From The Vaults*.

Devlin: On our first visit to Trend, the engineer, John D'Ardis, played us a recording he'd done of The Freshmen doing Neil Diamond's 'Soolaimon', and I was incredibly impressed by how slick the production was. It was a bit intimidating to think that we'd be up against those guys, because we sounded so raw.

Carr: At those sessions we also recorded 'The Lady Wrestler', written around the same time as 'Hall Of Mirrors'. I think I had a Pop Art thing going on for a while – Peter Blake's 'Babe Rainbow', a silkscreen that he based on a cover of *Marie Claire* magazine, was the influence behind the song.

Peter had said of his creation, 'A fictitious lady wrestler, she is 23 years old and has broken her nose in the ring. She was born in New Cross, London, and wrestles mainly in Europe and the USA.'

O'Connor: Whereas other bands of greater experience and professionalism might have done a whole album in the same time, our output was much smaller. 'The Lady Wrestler' was a good song, but even if we had the master tape, it wouldn't have appeared on *Tracks From The Vaults*,

motorway madness

you handled the car like you handled a gun;
as we headed towards the city; we were on the run.
confident you knew a way wed fool them yet.
happy as a trigger, cool as death.

deaf to the tearing of steel on steel;
insensitive to bodies beneath our wheels;
we tore away from that seaside town,
lovers locked together until after dawn.

in the grip of motorway madness.
motorway madness can whip you to your grave.

the east was brightening like a movie screen.
the city lay before us and we knew wed seen
the last of trawlers and fishmongers wives.
wed be lucky to get out of this with our lives.

deaf to the sirens growing near;
insensitive to promises, hopes and fears;
we tore along that old grey road,
the whiskey shared not as thick as blood.

in the grip of motorway madness.
motorway madness can whip you to your grave,

you handled the car like i handled the gun;
as we headed towards the city, we were on the run.
confident you knew a way wed fool them yet.
but you never guessed my name was death.

deaf to your world as it caved in
insensitive to each and every sin.
i know i cant be tricked by (any) road-blocks.
going to keep driving till the engine stops

in the grip of motorway madness,
motorway madness can whip you to your grave,

simply because Sinnott sang the lead vocals on it, so it was always put to one side and not really talked about.

It was hard work, because you wanted it to be so good, but you didn't really know if it was. We did the best we could, and hired in better instruments. I was still playing a viola da gamba-style zither violin with frets and a pick-up. I didn't have a proper electric violin at that point, and it was all a bit trepidatious.

Violin is an awful instrument to play in a rock'n'roll band, but someone had to play it!

October 14: Horslips grace the front cover of *New Spotlight* magazine (below) for the first time.

November 5-6: Trend Studios, Dublin (re-recording and mixing 'The Lady Wrestler').

Carr: We had every intention of putting 'The Lady Wrestler' out as a single, because it seemed to be our most popular live song. Decca agreed to a one-off single deal. We got a contract and, as it was a one-off and we were totally naive, we didn't bother with solicitors. Luckily, I re-read the contract before I added my signature to the others, and became uneasy with a clause that seemed to suggest, against our understanding, that Decca would retain an option to release another single and an album. Technically, we could have been chained to them for a year, or maybe even two, so we tore up the contract.

Devlin: Junior Campbell had just left The Marmalade and was getting a solo career together, and somehow Decca seemed to think he'd be the right producer for us. We had serious doubts, but I was so wrapped up in the idea of becoming a famous rock star that I'd have signed with a chicken farmer, so I'm grateful to Eamon that he had such wisdom.

Carr: In our stupidity, we'd already sent Decca the master tape. It disappeared and we didn't have a copy, because we were very disciplined about keeping our

costs to a minimum. Still thinking that we'd get a release for this somehow, we went back in to re-record it. Unfortunately, we were unable to recapture what we considered to be the magic inherent in the performance and mix of that recorded version. The second version was the one we mimed to on TV, and that, along with the footage, also disappeared, making 'The Lady Wrestler' the Holy Grail amongst rare Horslips recordings.

Unknown to us, Jackie Hayden, an astute A&R man from Dublin's Polydor office, had attended one of the events we staged at Galerie Langlois. He arranged company funding for a demo tape to present to the London office. We re-recorded 'The Lady Wrestler' and one or two other tracks, and I was dispatched with the tape to London. Meeting their executives was a dispiriting exercise. Clearly we weren't what Polydor UK were then looking for and, as our repertoire expanded, 'The Lady Wrestler' dropped out.

Only a scratchy cassette copy of that Polydor demo remains, and it's what prompted Philip Chevron to record the song in 2011 for The Radiators From Space album *Sound City Beat*.

Polydor wasn't the only company to show interest in the band during 1971. We were invited to meet record chief Phil Solomons, with a view to signing with his Major Minor label. But we agreed among ourselves that it was much too early to consider committing to a label. Later, we came to the attention of Charisma,

"The band set their sights on being an international touring act ..."

when enlightened company people met us at a concert in Cork. Again, we realised that we were on a steep learning curve.

Mick McDonagh tried to sign the band to Transatlantic Records. He checked us out, and then brought company founder Nat Joseph to see us play, in the Mansion House Round Room in October '71. Those discussions with Mick and Nat were hugely beneficial, although our innate hunch was that if we went with Transatlantic, we might get lumped in with the folk crowd, and we weren't that easy to label, let alone market. We were aware that our music still needed to develop.

Deeny: Transatlantic were very keen to sign Horslips. But the band set their sights on being an international touring act, and didn't want to be restricted by a purely Irish-based career. It was therefore important to partner with a record company who would share the same ambition. We all believed that being on Transatlantic would be too limiting. All of this happened before we decided to pursue our own independent route, which we felt would be more suitable in that it afforded us complete artistic freedom.

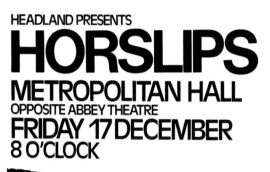

Late December: Horslips launch one of their many characteristically tongue-in-cheek PR campaigns.

Devlin: There were only about six music journos in Ireland back then, and we thought it'd be a real hoot to send each of them a miniature of whiskey wrapped up like a Christmas cracker. As Christmas drew near, *New Spotlight*'s hip writer Donal Corvin, who eventually became a big champion of the band, took a critical swipe at us. He said that if Horslips – whoever they are – were to spend less time parcelling up presents for journalists, and a bit more time practicing their instruments, they might do really well.

Carr: Our approach to manipulating the Irish media was like Malcolm McLaren before Malcolm McLaren, and I have to put my hand up here. Being a fan of rock'n'roll culture, I was aware of all the publicity stunts that went on, such as what Tony Secunda did with The Move, and the antics of Andrew Loog Oldham and Derek Taylor, plus I was a friend of BP Fallon, for goodness sake.

I had a slight understanding of how to maximise the fun level, and the episode about our first gig being banned was an affirmation to me that the press would play ball. Naturally, we kept the editors in the loop, because we knew we weren't going to be anything like Fairport. These guys were serious. We had to attract attention a different way.

Devlin: Apart from Jimmy, none of us were from Dublin, which is a strange curiosity. But even Jimmy's parents weren't Dubliners. I have a northern accent ... and Charles isn't even Irish. It ensured that no one really knew us when we emerged on the scene, and that gave us an enigmatic quality that was actually quite useful.

I played the 'Tigger' role: constantly enthusiastic, bouncing around. Eamon was much cooler; he knew how to stay aloof and tease people. And he was very good at controlling the image. Eamon was, and still is, a very complex human being, and the most extraordinary travelling companion, because he's widely read and supremely intelligent.

CHAPTER 3

HAPPY
TO
MEET

January 16-17: Horslips revisit Trend Studios to record 'Johnny's Wedding', 'Flower Amang Them All' and 'Knockeen Free' with Fred Meijer. When Michael Deeny (pictured opposite) finds it difficult to find an appropriate record label for Horslips, he and the band decide to form their own: Oats Records.

Deeny: Horslips' recording career began just as the industry was changing. Until the late '60s, bands would sign to record companies, they would be sent into a studio, told what to record and have little or no say in the production, packaging or marketing. The Beatles started to change the landscape when they independently founded Apple Records in 1968, but even though they were taking control of their own music and publicity, EMI still released their product.

When we launched Oats Records, my contribution was to ensure that every decision was made by the band. Horslips had the ability to not only create the music, but also handle artwork and design through Charles, and publicity through Eamon [Horslips formed an internal PR 'machine' called Mouthpiece Promotions], and look after all the other important factors between them while I concentrated on the business.

Oats gave us all immense satisfaction and Horslips really knew their stuff. When you pooled their experience in advertising and graphics, their appreciation of R&B, blues and pop, and their knowledge of traditional music, what you had was a real force to be reckoned with. It meant we could do everything. So all we had to do was hire a pressing plant for the records, a printer

BARRY DEVLIN   CHARLES O'CONNOR   EAMON CARR   DECLAN SINNOTT   JIM LOCKHART

for the sleeves and a distributor – in Ireland it was Mick Clerkin at Release Records.

Carr: Release had a huge distribution spread, not just in record shops, but into hardware shops and filling stations. These guys knew how to sell records.

O'Connor: Michael then sent us to his parents' country house, Sessiagh Lodge in County Donegal, to get

ourselves in better musical shape and come up with the arrangement for 'Johnny's Wedding'. It was a very large bungalow in Donegal, on a lake that had a monks' haven island in the middle, and we always had a really nice, relaxed time there because we treated it like a working holiday. We'd ride out on the lake, go to the pub, then walk back at night, get the instruments out and maybe entertain some local musicians who visited. We used that house for the next couple of years, whenever we had an album to write.

Later on, we would rent other places around Ireland to get new songs rehearsed. The normal idea would be to rent a pair of thatched cottages – one to live in and one to store the equipment – with a pub that was within crawling distance. The idea was always to just escape from Dublin for a while, the girls would come and cook, and we would work in an undisturbed environment.

February 28: Horslips receive their first major press attention outside of Ireland when Lindsay Mackie writes a feature on the band's progress for the *Daily Express*.

March 17: Michael Deeny throws a launch reception at Dublin's new hamburger joint, Captain America's, to celebrate and promote the release of Horslips' début single 'Johnny's Wedding' / 'Flower Amang Them All' on Oats Records (MOO 1). 'Flower Amang Them All' – one of many Northumbrian tunes imported by O'Connor – later becomes the theme for RTÉ Radio's popular '301' show. On this very same St. Patrick's Day, the five members officially turn professional.

Lockhart: When Captain America's opened in Grafton Street in 1971 it became our hang out whenever we were in Dublin. Kevin Myers of the *Irish Times* once described its attraction as being that the staff looked as though they might have had sex at some point in their lives, as opposed to anywhere else in Ireland that you might have gone for a meal.

Carr: The release of 'Johnny's Wedding' was the flashpoint. Until then, we'd been this curious, arty collective that had done some TV and a few interesting gigs. But it started to gain momentum. We had started to pick up a following and were regularly hiring an Avis truck to get us to an increasing amount of gigs.

O'Connor: By early '72, I had moved to another agency, O'Connor O'Sullivan, but combining the day job with what was becoming a busy gig schedule was compromising. I'd be returning home at five or six in the morning and going to work only a couple of hours

later. The guys I worked with knew what was going on, and suggested that maybe I should leave and concentrate on the band.

Up until the end of the previous year, we didn't really have a distinctive look. In fact, some of our photos made us look like truckers. And we were now conscious of this, so instead of resembling The Grateful Dead, we wanted to glam up in T-Rex fashion. At least most of us did. Declan wasn't so keen, but I always found him hard work. I was constantly questioning why any band would want to walk out on stage with their everyday scruffs on, to play for a paying audience who are used to seeing glamorous images of pop stars.

We had to get some flashy stage clobber made and the solution was literally on our doorstep, because Eamon and I were living in Sandymount under the same roof as Jackie McNeill, a seamstress. Jackie and Sue [Calvert] made our first suits, out of any material we gave them. There would be ocelot skin from the local furriers, leather and snakeskin, and even curtains from Clery's – whatever we could get our hands on that would make an impression. The band seemed to just like dressing up and, being the band's fashion guru, I was the ringleader.

Carr: Jackie's husband was Jim McNeill, a very famous boxing correspondent who came from Glasgow and lived in Dublin. He drank Scotch from the bottle and was about as masculine as you could ever imagine. But Jim would return home from work to see these boys poncing about in front of the mirror in high-heeled boots, wearing what appeared to be women's clothes. The look on his face said it all.

Shakespeare was a great believer in the 'buskin boot', and I think [for us] platform shoes and high heels were very much the buskin boot. We couldn't get any

"Instead of resembling The Grateful Dead we wanted to glam up in T-Rex fashion ..."

wolfskins, but it was the next step to being survivalists.

O'Connor: At one time I was buying my high-heeled shoes from Sex, the shop run by Malcolm McLaren and Vivienne Westwood in the King's Road, Chelsea. I've always had a thing for footwear and, to me, it's not strange for a straight guy to wear outlandish shoes and boots.

Lockhart: We weren't just appealing to an audience of shoegazing hippies; we tapped into a teenage glam market made up of kids who had no interest in traditional music. They saw the way we dressed and for a lot of them we were their Bolan, Ferry or Bowie.

Devlin: I think it was good for the fans to see a home-grown band glammed up in a way that was similar to what they might be looking at on 'Top Of The Pops'. We were The Darkness long before The Darkness were even thought of, although their clothing was made of much better and more expensive fabric!

Lockhart: Away from the wardrobe department, we

were getting serious about writing material by then. Charles had a copy of 'O'Neill's Music Of Ireland', the early 20th-century collection of old fiddle tunes and airs, and we also had Edward Bunting's 'The Ancient Music of Ireland'.

In between gigs, Charles and I would go through them, trying to find and dissect tunes that we could borrow from to use for a new song. 'The Ace & Deuce Of Pipering' was one that we played around with as early as the 'Fonn' TV series, and we felt it was an approach that no one was trying. It was indigenous, and not an attempt to follow trends.

March 23: 'Johnny's Wedding' makes its Irish chart début. The single will spend three weeks in the chart and peak at No. 10.

April 3: Rescheduled from the previous day due to rain, the band star as 'the pop group' in

Right: Live work and song choices in the first half of 1972.

Bottom: Scenes from the Mirinda ad shoot.

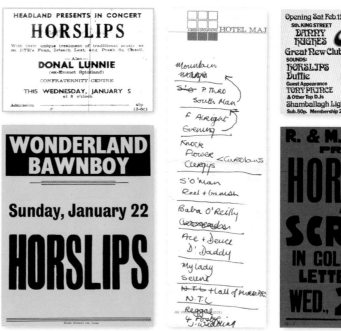

a TV commercial for soft drink Mirinda, shot at a specially-organised Easter Monday concert at Ardmore Studios, Bray, in front of a 'groovy audience'.

O'Connor: I was 'the lead singer' and it still slightly haunts me. I mean, come on, it was so tacky that it was off the Richter scale of tackiness. How did it go? '*Hey Mirinda, orange Mirinda, hey Mirinda, sparkling with flavour.*' Obviously this was not an Eamon Carr lyric.

Carr: Unknown to us, an advertising agency had taken some shots of the band and our audience at a free concert we played in Blackrock Park the previous summer. From these they constructed a cinema commercial demo for their client, who liked the proposal.

The agency then contacted us and asked if we'd make ourselves available to play a free concert in the grounds of Ardmore Studios in Bray, and appear in the commercial. The bad news was that they wanted us to mime to a jingle that had already been written and recorded in Germany. They would stage a free festival gig at which all of the support acts, including Chris Davison/de Burgh, would get a fee, and the audience, some of whom were well-placed models, would be supplied with free bottles of Mirinda – the new orange

soft drink from PepsiCo – plus ice cream and crisps.

We were dead against it at first. Imagine the Rolling Stones singing 'Hey Mirinda' at Hyde Park ... they'd be bottled off stage. But when they started talking about decent money, it was like, 'Okay, so how does that jingle go again?'

We were dependent on hire companies for our PA equipment, but frequently had problems with availability and transportation. To own a PA to our specifications that would cater for our unique requirements was a dream. The Mirinda fee now made this a reality.

As you might expect, the debate about whether we were selling out was intense. But the equation seemed simple enough to me. While we risked looking foolish miming to a jingle by some German session players, we were going to headline a great outdoor free festival on a great stage with other bands, and as part of the trade-off get to own our own rig.

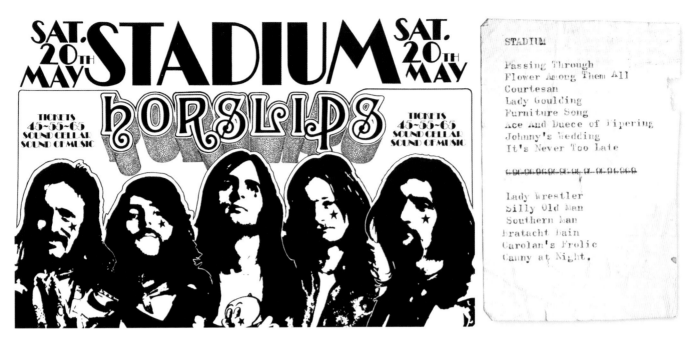

STADIUM

Passing Through
Flower Among Them All
Courtesan
Lady Goulding
Furniture Song
Ace And Deuce of Pipering
Johnny's Wedding
It's Never Too Late

Lady Wrestler
Silly Old Man
Southern Man
Bratacht Bain
Carolan's Frolic
Canny at Night.

The set list and poster for Horslips' first headlining show at the National Stadium, Dublin.

I'd seen those early ads The Beatles did for Lybro jeans. And the Stones and other bands had recorded radio commercials for Coke. I may even have had a premonition that one day Dylan would endorse a line of lingerie, so Mirinda was a doddle. Money for someone else's old rope. I'm still waiting for the Devil to get back to me on a price for my second-hand soul.

Overall, the Ardmore affair was a hoot. The festival and the timing of it was a great boost for a new, young band that just happened to have a début single creating a buzz on radio and in the charts.

May 20: The first Horslips headlining gig at the National Stadium, Dublin, with Chris De Burgh playing support, dressed in a satin stars'n'stripes suit. Although the show is a success, tensions within the ranks leads to Declan Sinnott leaving the band just a few weeks later.

Carr: The Mirinda commercial had unhinged Declan's motivation or ideology. He wasn't having any of that. We'd come back from rehearsing in Donegal, ready to rock on the back of a very popular first single,

but by the end of that next run of gigs, Declan was gone.

Devlin: Declan taught me how to be a bass player, so I owe him that much. I know he doesn't have many positive things to say about us and, conversely, I wasn't very enamoured with him as a personality, but I wouldn't deny him his place in the band's history. He must have liked the band enough at the start to be in it. We wouldn't have got the band together without Declan – he made a big contribution in that early period, especially as he and Eamon were the two people who had previously been in bands and had an idea of how all that works. He was – and remains – a very good guitar player.

Lockhart: [Sinnott] wasn't happy being in the band, and we weren't happy with him either. It was a relief when he was gone, but filling the vacant position permanently looked like it was going to be a problem.

In an interview with Joe Jackson of *Hot Press* some years later, Sinnott does not pull any punches when asked to explain his reasons for quitting:

'[Tara Telephone] were a bunch of guys doing something that was really esoteric and interesting. It was the

Lead guitarist Gus Guest (second from right) with Horslips in August 1972.

same when Horslips began but then it got into, "You have to wear this shiny suit, we have to sing this ...", and to me it soon fell apart. By that stage they suddenly became... well, we'd done an ad for an orange drink, for God's sake!

'I felt that as a musician I was becoming less of a craftsman in Horslips. We tried to be a rock band but we were so bad we had to do something else. "Johnny's Wedding" probably was the first [Celtic Rock record] and then everybody began doing it! I remember saying to Eamon Carr one day, "we'll be found out" ... that's really how I felt about it.'

Sinnott will temporarily abandon his music career and move to London to take up a job as a trainee postman. In later years, he will join such

bands as Gandydancer, Homegrown and South-paw, before forming Moving Hearts with Donal Lunny and Christy Moore.

His position is immediately filled by Gus Guest. Born in Dublin to British parents on December 26 1948, Guest joins after spending several years on the road as lead guitarist with bands including The Kinda Blues and Pye signing The Deep Set.

Guest: I had been living in Paris for some time, and as a result I was a bit out of touch with the music scene in Ireland. Almost as soon as I returned, in the middle of '72, I was asked if I fancied playing with Horslips. I didn't really have a clue about these guys, but they talked a good talk, and after asking around I soon realised they were a happening band.

on the road for years before I joined them and it really showed, because they were one of the tightest bands I'd ever played with.

Devlin: The Deep Set were a seriously good pop band, with very tasteful musicians. One night in 1970, I saw them in Zhivago's nightclub playing the *Abbey Road* album in its entirety, with note perfect accuracy. The lead guitarist did his parts so beautifully and so when Declan left, I remembered him and tried to see if he might be available. By then, however, Gus had replaced this guy and it was one of his tapes with the band that we heard. It impressed us enough to make some enquiries.

Guest: Horslips had more equipment than any band I'd ever seen and, of course, the get-ups they wore were pretty extreme! I was like, 'What's all this?' It was like being a member of The Glitter Band – they insisted that I wear knee-high boots, white trousers and a dress as a shirt. I could see why my predecessor might have had a issue with the wardrobe department. Being essentially a bluesman, I would have been more comfortable in jeans but, you know, these were Horslips fashion rules!

Barry and Michael Deeny were the ones who approached me first. They'd listened to a recent tape of my playing, and I think that's how my name got in the frame. Gigs were approaching fast in the diary, so very quickly we went up to Donegal to rehearse for a couple of days. I thought we sounded a little rough, but getting on the road would sort that out soon enough.

Carr: I had seen Gus with The Kinda Blues some time in the mid-'60s, and they were a good Kinks/ Animals/R&B-type band. I remember that Gus impressed me with his use of a fuzz box on the Stones' 'Satisfaction'.

Guest: The Kinda Blues was my first taste of a fairly serious band. The Deep Set were based in Dún Laoghaire, and they were a great band. They had been

The feedback from the audiences was fantastic. The music was different to what was going around at the time, and the thing that struck me most about them was their absolute tunnel-visioned focus on being successful. They knew exactly what they were doing and where they wanted to go.

Carr: Gus brought Pink Floyd albums on to our radar. Apart from *A Saucerful Of Secrets*, I hadn't been listening to much Floyd. Gus had all that *Atom Heart Mother* stuff and, like Charles, he was very much into Frank Zappa.

"The thing that struck me most was their tunnel-visioned focus on being successful ..."

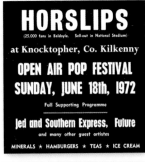

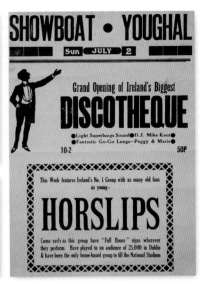

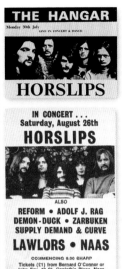

By the time Gus arrived on the scene, we were ready to make our second single, so we went back up to Donegal with him to rehearse and arrange two new numbers. Basically we were trying to work towards the album that we were planning to do in the autumn.

June: Horslips are boosted by the arrival of three road crew members: Robbie McGrath, Joe O'Neill and Kevin 'Skee' Dietrich.

McGrath: I was a serious Horslips fan right from the start, because I got excited by the way they fused the Irish traditions with rock'n'roll. They were the first band I knew of who had done that and, being a great lover of rock music, with Irish music running through my gene pool, it ticked all the boxes for me. I would see them whenever I could, and it was one night in Galway that I met the band properly.

Eamon's bodhrán had been stolen and, being a tough 18–year–old, I went hunting for it around a local camp site and a few other dodgy places, and was willing to take anyone on to get it back. Sure enough, I tracked it down and returned it.

About a month later, while working as a jeweller at Hopkins & Hopkins in O'Connell Street, I was going out for some parts when I saw Eamon walking towards me. He told me the band had a great tour of the ballrooms lined up, and asked me if I'd be interested in helping with the equipment. He gave me Michael Deeny's number, and that was the start of an amazing episode in my life.

I was joined by Joe and Kevin, a general grafter who owned a van. I was looking after backline, but my role on the crew varied over the years, from driving, mixing sound, booking hotels and paying bills to organising freight for overseas tours in North America, as I would do later. I was also in charge of looking after the band's outfits, getting them ironed and ready for gigs. So I did a bit of everything, which was what roadies would do before they became specialised. I didn't even need a driving licence in those days!

June 21: Horslips arrive at Dublin's Trend Studios to record 'Green Gravel', 'The Fairy King' and one other unidentified instrumental track with engineer Fred Meijer. The tracks are mixed on June 26.

July 9: While topping the bill at a festival in Bally-vaughan, Horslips are impressed with the talents of a young lead guitarist …

Lockhart: On the bill were Skid Row and another very good band called Jeremiah Henry, who also played

Neil Young's 'Southern Man', only better than us. They had a tiny guitarist strapped on to a red Gibson 335 that he'd borrowed from Brush Shiels [whose Skid Row were also on the bill]. It looked huge on him, because he was such a small, skinny kid, a bit like an even younger version of Jimmy McCulloch [of Thunderclap Newman and Wings fame], and he was a really tasteful, fluid guitar player.

We were all there nodding and grinning at each other in agreement that he was quite brilliant. And his name was Johnny Fean.

Nobody got paid for anything, apart from us. Fortunately, our tour manager, Mick Reilly, was a hard man. Told there would be no fee, he tied one end of a length of cable to the centre pole of the marquee and the other to a tractor, and threatened to pull down the place. At which point, he was handed some money! We thought, 'Ah, that's what our tour manager's there for!'

August 25: Coinciding with a gig in Ballyhaunis, Horslips' second single, 'Green Gravel' (MOO 2), is rush-released. A traditional song about the untimely demise of a young, beautiful girl, 'Green Gravel' is backed with 'The Fairy King', **an ancient harp melody coupled with the Welsh tune 'Blodau'r Drain' (Flowers Of The Thorn). Recorded with Gus Guest at Trend Studios, the single hits the Top Twenty in its first week.**

Guest: I'd recorded at Trend with one of its first clients, a band called This Village, so I was familiar with the environment. On the day we arrived to record 'Green Gravel' and 'The Fairy King', I bought a Les Paul from a friend who was emigrating, and I played it on the session. Up until then, I'd been a Strat man, but the tone of the Les Paul seemed to suit Horslips.

September 30: The Hangar, Galway. Gus Guest's final appearance with Horslips.

Guest: I had a great few months with Horslips. They were all wonderful company and we shared many laughs together on our travels, but I think it became apparent very early on that I wasn't settling in very naturally, and that perhaps I wasn't the right guitarist for them. I had no problems with the lads personally, but as a player I was at the jazzier end of the blues style, and at that time in Horslips' career, I don't think that's what they needed.

Lockhart: Gus was a very experienced musician, with a good six or seven years of playing live behind him. He'd probably developed more of a session muso vibe about him that doesn't always suit some bands who aren't quite so together in their approach. I suppose Gus was like a Chris Spedding figure – more of a professional musician than this bunch of guys who were chancing their collective arm.

Guest: I'd been playing with them for about six weeks when, one night after a gig, they asked me if I wanted to join the band. It seemed a little puzzling, because I thought I was already in the band. I hadn't realised up to then that I was essentially standing in. In my experience, that wasn't how bands worked. I'd done plenty of deps, but I didn't accept the Horslips gig on the basis of it being a dep. I'd never heard of musicians doing trial periods, so in my mind I began to think that this wouldn't be lasting too long.

Devlin: We knew we'd be doing an album, but we needed a different kind of guitarist, and I suppose in a semi-conscious way we were keeping one eye open for a replacement. I would have continued with Gus, because I've never been one to make the hard decisions.

Later moving to North Wales, Gus Guest will go on to form a variety of bands, including Overnight Bag, The Dublin Blues Band and Stagger Lee, and play jazz residencies in the Dominican Republic, before ill health prompts him to downscale his music career.

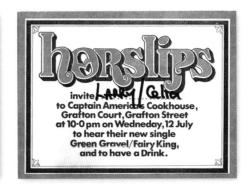

Johnny Fean with Horslips at the Savoy Cinema in Cork for his first 'photo op' with the band.

October 1: A crucial day in the Horslips timeline. The classic line-up is established when Johnny Fean joins as the band's new lead guitarist.

Devlin: After the Ballyvaughan festival, Johnny was very much on our minds. We briefly considered asking Chris De Burgh to be our lead singer, because none of us were great singers, and Johnny was initially brought in to teach Chris lead.

Fean: Chris was already an accomplished acoustic guitarist, and Michael Deeny asked me if I'd give Chris some lead guitar lessons. I think I gave him about nine or 10 lessons, but I don't know if he'd ever have been a candidate for the lead singer role in Horslips.

O'Connor: I went to Shannon in a taxi with the aim of bringing Johnny back to Dublin, and I ran up a huge fare – something like £35, which was extortionate then. I looked around for him everywhere in pubs and shops. And then someone who knew Johnny pointed me in the direction of where he lived. So I knocked on his door, but he wasn't in, and I returned empty handed.

Fean: My brother Donal told me that Charles had come knocking for me while I was in Lisdoonvarna. I thought he was winding me up, but Donal was very persistent and my mother confirmed it was true, so I then started to take all of this seriously. Fortunately, Charles left a phone number, so I called him and, sure enough, they wanted me to audition.

A day or two later, I arrived at Jimmy's house in James's Street. He'd borrowed a guitar and an amp, so we started jamming for a bit, with Jim on the family piano. By the end of the day, Barry came over with Michael Deeny, and Michael took me aside to ask me there and then if I'd join the band.

I'd seen the band in Ballyvaughan and was quite impressed with them – I didn't realise it was mutual. When I first heard 'Johnny's Wedding', I had no doubt that they'd be a huge success. So being asked to join them was mind-blowing, and it completely changed my life.

O'Connor: Guitarists are normally the ones who throw the wobblers and shake their hair around. But Johnny has always been a quiet, well-mannered lad, and it was an absolute pleasure to have him onboard. We headed over to Donegal to rehearse the live set with Johnny and it went brilliantly. He'd obviously done some homework.

Johnny lived with me for about a month until things settled down. From that moment it felt like a proper band, because Johnny was such a vital ingredient that it knitted together as it should have done but had never quite got there before. There was a definite feeling that Johnny was in for the long haul.

October 8: Horslips appear on the RTÉ radio programme 'All The Wild Sweetness'. Produced by Gene Martin, it is described by the *Sunday Press* as 'a loose musical documentary series that has already dissected the Dubliners, Clancy Brothers and Chieftains'. Repeated in June 1973, the programme is notable for its original soundtrack, recorded by the Sinnott-era Horslips in early 1972.

Lockhart: In 2012, a tape turned up in RTÉ's archives of a programme that was already out of date by the time it went on the air, because no one really knew about Johnny joining us at that point. Sinnott had long gone. As well as about 14 tracks of music, there are also separate interviews with each of us on the tape – two are with Barry, who did an extra one in place of Sinnott.

The music is interesting: there's a very early, non-reggae version of 'An Bratach Bán' on the tape, and a sweet acoustic number sung by Sinnott [with Eamon Carr lyrics] called 'Traps', on which he sounds not unlike Nick Drake. Some of the performances are good, some are pretty weak, but there's definitely historical interest value attached to the tape, and there could be an argument for giving it a commercial release as it's about an album's worth of material.

October 10: Red Barn Ballroom, Youghal, County Cork. Johnny Fean plays his first Horslips gig, followed two days later by his second at the Savoy Cinema in Cork.

Fean: The Red Barn and Savoy dates were really low-key warm-ups for a much bigger affair the following Saturday. The rehearsals in Donegal had gone very smoothly, but we needed to get out in front of an audience as soon as possible to make sure everything gelled on stage.

October 14: Within two weeks of Fean joining, Horslips headline at the National Stadium, Dublin, performing material from their forthcoming album along with covers of The Beatles' 'I Saw Her Standing There' and, appropriately, Chuck Berry's 'Johnny B. Goode'.

Fean: At the time I joined, the band were most likely not very aware of my musical background, other than being in Jeremiah Henry. But I had notched up about seven years of playing in bands and, although I was the youngest member of Horslips, I would have had more experience than the other members, with the exception of Eamon. I'd spent a long time honing my onstage guitar sound, and I was able to meet the demand of learning an entirely new set of songs and tunes, playing a major concert at the National Stadium, and preparing for the very first Horslips album to be recorded.

It was a huge leap for me to play at the Stadium so early on, and I was pretty nervous, but I left no one in doubt when I stretched those guitar solos that I was here to stay. Getting to know the band was really the first step. My top priority from the start was to make it appear as if I had been there from the beginning.

I also got to play some tenor banjo down at the front of the stage when we did 'Happy To Meet, Sorry To Part' and a couple of other traditional pieces, with Charles on concertina, Eamon on bodhrán and Jimmy on the whistle. It was a fantastic night.

Carr: Johnny's a very quiet lad and he came over as being incredibly shy at the start. He's almost like Mick Taylor, never pushing. It must have been tricky for him coming in, because he was a younger lad.

The band had been building for two years and we were bigger in Ireland than Lizzy because they'd moved to England. Johnny just walked into that. He might have felt intimidated, but it didn't show in his playing. By the end of the year he had cemented his position.

McGrath: It was right into the deep end for Johnny. The guitar solo for 'Furniture' went on a lot longer than planned and the band were looking down at me as if to say, 'Fuck, when's he gonna stop?'.

O'Connor: There were certain moments when you were on stage and you would go, 'Yeahhhh! This is great!' and that Stadium gig, the first one with Johnny, was one of them. But I had a problem when it came to make a poster, because when we announced the gig, Johnny hadn't joined. Gus had just left, so we didn't have a current photo of the band. Using the clowns' heads was an arty way of getting around the problem.

Even though it was a bit of a scuzzy venue for music, the [2,500 capacity] Stadium was the biggest gig in town and if you headlined it, as we did, you knew you were heading for the big time. The feedback from the crowd was sensational – to a lot of them it suddenly felt like Ireland had caught up with the rest of the planet at last. We had a lighting rig, smoke machines and a pretty pokey PA system, and it blew a lot of people's minds.

The National Stadium headliner marks the début of Peter Clarke as Horslips' new lighting man.

Clarke: After abandoning a career in hotel management, myself and a few pals from Dalkey and Dún Laoghaire, one of them being Bob Geldof, went over to the UK and got some student work. I became a tea boy on a construction site on the M23 near Gatwick.

I had fallen out with my parents and ended up crashing at my friend Gregory Brown's pad. He was the archetypal space cadet hippie, known in social circles as Ashtar From Mars, and he was Horslips' first serious lighting man.

"My top priority was to make it appear as if I'd been there from the beginning ..."

HORSLIPS at the STADIUM

Sat. Oct. 14th.   Tickets 55, 65, 75.   Sound of Music, Burgh Quay · Sound Cellar

Ashtar [who would become part of the influential Krishna Lights company] was such a character. He used projections, strobes, effects discs and liquid oil wheels that projected exploding patterns across the band. On odd occasions, Ashtar would invite me to Horslips gigs and I would lend a hand, mostly setting up lighting for the support bands.

In September '72, Ashtar said that he wanted to go to South America to chase spaceships, and Michael Deeny offered me a job if I could get some lights together. So I bundled together some of the cash I'd made working on the motorway, and Michael added some extra funding to enable me to buy a Rank Strand lighting system in London, through Ashtar's acquaintance at Optikinetics, Keith Canadine. I loaded it all into my Transit van and returned to Dublin, thinking all the way there that I didn't really know what to do with this kit! But I'd already decided to drop Ashtar's projection style and concentrate on straight stage lighting.

November 3: Horslips begin work on recording their début album, the elegantly-packaged *Happy To Meet, Sorry To Part*. The sessions are held at Longfield House in Cashel, County Tipperary, the former home of Bianconi, the man who had introduced the first commercial transport system to Ireland centuries earlier. Alan O'Duffy is hired as the producer and engineer along with the Rolling Stones Mobile.

Devlin: There wasn't a 16-track studio in Ireland and although we could have gone to England, Michael Deeny and Eamon suggested the Rolling Stones Mobile that had been in France earlier in the year to record the Stones' seminal album, *Exile On Main Street*, and in Switzerland to record the *Montreux Jazz Festival*. It came over on the ferry for us and it was such a big deal.

As soon as we started rehearsing for the album at the Deeny family holiday home – Sessiagh House near

Dunfanaghy, County Donegal – all the Irish newspapers were curious about how we were progressing with the sessions, and ran unusually big stories. This kind of attention was like Beatlemania all over again! The Dublin *Evening Herald* even published pull-outs after despatching a reporter to Cashel to get all the gossip.

Later, the sessions attract the first coverage from a major music weekly, when *Melody Maker* journalist Mark Plummer arrives to soak up the heady atmosphere and interview the band for a feature (published on November 18).

Plummer: Michael Deeny phoned and said that he managed an Irish band who were recording with the Stones mobile, and asked if I would be interested in coming over to hang out and write a story on it. I love Ireland and the idea immediately took my fancy, but I thought that it might be a hard thing to sell to my editor. To my surprise, he was all for it.

When I arrived, the house was dimly lit by candles. The excessive amount of equipment had blown the fuses. Despite the blazing log fires, it was very cold in there, but there was kind of a romance about being in this fantastic, beautiful building. They soon worked out that while they were recording, every single amenity had to be turned off in order to preserve power.

The first people I bumped into were Eamon and Robbie McGrath. Eamon and I hit it off immediately. I could tell that he was a tremendously smart guy and a great storyteller. By the time I arrived, I think they had laid down most of the rhythm tracks and were into the overdubbing stage, so Eamon, Robbie and I hung out that first night and got to know each other while the rest of the band were busy.

On the second day, Jim needed a couple of new reeds for his uilleann pipes, so Robbie and I went on this wild goose chase, visiting several reed makers, interspersed by numerous shots of whiskey. It was super relaxed, but also very surreal, because we were so stoned. We must have seen four or five people before we got what we needed.

It was extraordinary to witness this album being created. I'd obviously known of bands who styled music by borrowing from disparate sources, which is why I think Deeny called me. It was a smart judgement call.

I stayed at Longfield House for about a week and what I heard knocked me for six. Some of the melodies they were using were quite familiar to me but I couldn't work out why. I didn't know the names of these tunes – I guess they'd just been in the air for hundreds of years.

Working on *Melody Maker*, we each used to write three or four feature stories a week, and I filed my Horslips article as soon as I returned to Blighty. It was the first major feature on the band published outside of Ireland and I was very pleased about that.

The producer/engineer responsible for helping to create the definitive Horslips sound on record, Alan O'Duffy had worked at Pye Studios before Rolling Stones manager and Immediate label owner Andrew Loog Oldham persuaded him to accept a tape operator job at Olympic Studios.

Ian Stewart, the Stones' pianist and manager of the band's cutting-edge mobile studio, is credited by O'Duffy as the matchmaker between him and Horslips.

O'Duffy: Ian kindly recommended me to Michael Deeny who asked if I'd produce and engineer this band I'd never heard of. Richard Branson suggested that I go freelance and on the same day I drove to Ireland and arrived in Cashel to work with Horslips. Apart from the Chieftains and the Clancy Brothers, Irish traditional music was not in commercial vogue in the early '60s but it was part of the background to the music of Horslips. I was perhaps more familiar with that musical culture than most people thought.

As a Dublin-born boy, I was introduced to a wealth of Irish music through my parents – Dad [Michael O'Duffy] was a world-famous Irish tenor, with whom

Above and opposite:
Recording *Happy To Meet, Sorry To Part* at Longford House with producer/engineer Alan O'Duffy in November 1972.

I sang harmony. I had a cousin, Gerard McHugh, who would bring Telefunken tape machines to our house to record my Dad, and for the early '50s this was going some. We had a harmonium and a piano in the front room in Clontarf. This was all before I was 10.

By the time O'Duffy starts on *Happy To Meet*, he has notched up some enviable credits, with Slade ('Mama Weer All Crazee Now'), Procol Harum, Humble Pie (*Smokin'*), Blind Faith, Traffic (*The Low Spark Of High-Heeled Boys*), Amen Corner, Deep Purple, Manfred Mann ('My Name Is Jack'), the Stones (*Let It Bleed* and *Sticky Fingers*), scores of TV ads and film soundtracks, and the hit cast recording of *Jesus Christ Superstar* – a No. 1 for six weeks in the United States.

Lockhart: *Happy To Meet* was recorded on a shoestring budget. The reason that Alan O'Duffy made it work for us financially was that he was both an engineer and a producer. Michael was very good at spotting these benefits and it meant that we weren't too exposed on the expenses front.

O'Duffy: Horslips wanted the modern facilities of a London studio but didn't relish the idea of rigid hours, so working 'on location' with a great mobile was an enormously fun way of making their album. I was the first soundman in Ireland with a big-time multitrack recording studio – a Studer 16-track machine, way ahead of anything on the island.

I needed drapes to turn the front room into a studio and our runner, Paul McGuinness, borrowed the stage curtains from the Trinity College Players' theatre in Dublin.

We recorded in most of the rooms, and did some overdubs in the cellars and the library, which was good for vocals. We did stuff I would not even dream of doing today like buying bales of straw and hay from a local farmer to baffle and provide separation for the multi-miking style of recording. Just to think of covering a beautiful Georgian lounge with straw is quite mad, especially with everyone smoking.

A party scene was recorded one night. The band decided to play a set of tunes and everyone in the house was invited to take part by shouting, whooping and clapping, and I captured it all with microphones around the hallway.

O'Connor: That was 'Scalloway Ripoff', so called because it included 'The Scalloway Lasses' and 'The De'els Take The Minister'. Mick Reilly, Robbie McGrath and Alan's assistant engineer [Jeremy Gee] got everyone up to join in the jolly japes, including Mark Plummer and his wife, who were staying with us.

Carr: There might even have been some ghostly presence on that track and others, because the house was allegedly haunted. Mark's missus had psychic tendencies and she believed that she saw the infamous 'Lady in White' out of the corner of her eye one day. I don't think any of the rest of us experienced anything odd, but there were many stories of sightings.

O'Duffy: My first meeting with the band was right there at Longfield House, and my first impression was of a great bunch of talented characters who were masterful with the media. They were great to interview and

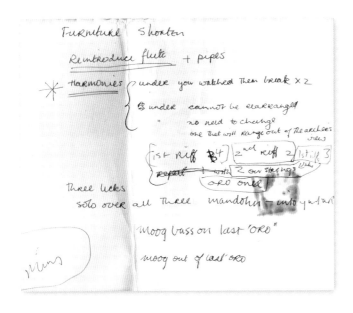

Furniture — shorten

Reintroduce flute + pipes

* Harmonies { under you watched them break x 2
{ B under cannot be rearranged
" no need to change
one that will range out of the archers view

[1st riff B⁴] [2nd riff 2] [1st riff 3]
repeat with 2 ow strings?
ORO once

Three licks
solo over all three mandolin — into guitar

"moog bass on last 'ORO'"

moog out of last 'ORO'

Times out of mind

B♭ c D♭ D₇ C° Gm B♭ F D₇ E♭⁶ F

intro 2x bass + piano
2x Johnny's lick
2x jim Charles ——— jim organ 8ft flute,
1x intro "Times o M
{ verse
{ 3x chords
Repeat into
Chorus   Slow vib
into solo x6
into Chorus   Poss flute
and into final solo.

Tunings.

• Hall of mirrors	6:00	✓	W
Furniture	5:00	✓	TM
#. D Daddy ✓	5:00	✓	—
Comb your hair ✓	3:40	✓	—
• Ace + Deuce	3:45 ?	✓	F
Clergys	5:25 ?	✓	F
Times out of mind	3:40	✓	S
Musical Priest ✓	4:35 / 4:30	—	
g leantanna	3:35.	✓	T
Bratach Ban	2:30	✓	TM
• Johnny's Wedding	3:00	✓?	W
Flower	2:26	✓	S
Scallawa'	1:50	✓	T
Happy to meet			S✓
	50:00		

Technical notes from the *Happy To Meet* sessions, including an arrangement guide for 'Times Out Of Mind', a song that fails to make the final album selection.

• •

could present stories that PR guys would've died for. The influences behind the songs, all the old yarns could be brought out and delivered to every journalist, and they loved it. The band traded on their talent to talk, amuse and entertain, and they ran circles on rivals who were basically less interesting to interview!

Devlin: One of Alan's secret weapons was a tape echo machine that he kept close to his person. I guess it was his calling card. He'd never explain his techniques, but Noddy Holder's vocals all went through it for the big Slade singles, and with us it got used on 'Dance To Yer Daddy' and 'The Shamrock Shore'.

Fean: For me, those sessions were a fantastic intro-duction not only to professional recording, but also to working with the band properly. I'd made some demos in Limerick with Jeremiah Henry, but they were very basic. This was on a much bigger level and Alan seemed like a magician, a master of the art.

We knew this was the start of something massive; it was all happening so fast. I suggested a few ideas, but the songs were already fully formed. I was playing existing parts, although I was able to mould them in my own style. My contributions as a writer would come later.

When I knew I'd be joining the band, I got myself a 1970 Gibson Les Paul Deluxe Goldtop, which I played on *Happy To Meet* and *The Táin*. During *Happy To Meet*,

I used a lovely Guild D-35 jumbo for all the acoustic guitar parts, most notably 'Ace And Deuce'. It was one of a few instruments brought in for the album, because I didn't own an acoustic at that point. But early the next year, I bought myself a Yamaha SJ-180 acoustic and played it on every studio album that followed.

Everything that had inspired me – like the octave style that I discovered through Wes Montgomery and played on 'Hall Of Mirrors' – eventually worked its way into my guitar style, resulting in something that embraced folk, jazz, classical, rock and blues, and I've been able to pull out different references whenever a song required it.

The tapes are mixed almost immediately at the place of O'Duffy's former employment, Olympic Studios in Barnes, south-west London.

Carr: This was real big time stuff. The Eagles were recording when we were at Olympic. Johnny had his 21st birthday during those mixing sessions, and he met Jimmy Page who was passing through. He was gobsmacked, like all of us! Johnny Halliday and the Stones' sax man Bobby Keys came into the control room to check us out. Keys was particularly enthusiastic.

December 4: Bearing an elaborate, concertina-shaped sleeve designed by Charles O'Connor, *Happy To Meet, Sorry To Part* (MOO 3) is released in Ireland. Featuring the classic 'Furniture', it will remain Ireland's fastest-selling album until ABBA reach their commercial peak in the late '70s.

Lockhart: The lyrics of 'Furniture' started out as a poem that I'd written about my parents and how tolerant they were about me abandoning my academic career in favour of playing in a band. It's a very metaphorical song in the vein of 'Whiter Shade Of Pale' in the sense that you would really need to know the background to understand what the hell it's about.

Carr: 'Hall Of Mirrors' was largely written in our semi-pro days, while I was sitting at my desk supposedly devising ad campaigns. 'An Bratach Bán' is a Scots Gaelic song that was introduced to our set after Jim heard Seamus Ennis singing a version of it. We thought of how to make it sound really different, and going down the reggae path definitely achieved that. It's got a couple of other tunes woven into it – 'Rolling In The Long Grass' and 'Kitty Got A Clinker Coming From The Races' – and Alan suggested we add the percussion. Jimmy's voice was absolutely perfect for that number.

The rhythm section parts didn't happen by accident. Every song to a certain degree, from 'An Bratach Bán' through *The Táin* and later, was very carefully worked out in rehearsals before we got to the recording stage. It was never a case of bish-bang-crash. The drums and bass did a job, and there was always space left for the other instruments to do their thing. We were always very conscious of that.

As John Waters describes in his book 'Race Of Angels, Ireland And The Genesis Of U2', 'An Bratach Bán' was '... not merely a rocked-up version of a traditional tune, but a reinvention of the medium for a different version of history. It was as though we were being given a glimpse of what the radio might have sounded like if the past 800 years had happened differently.'

A hint of O'Connor's childhood environment in the north east of England is heard in 'Dance To Yer Daddy'.

"The release of *Happy To Meet* became a national event ..."

Carr: Charles introduced me to sea shanties and whaling songs. I learned a version of 'Reuben Ranzo' by AL Lloyd from a Topic sampler. I drove Charles mad trying to get him to play it in the Horslips set, but to no avail. 'Dance To Yer Daddy' was quite enough!

'Bím Istigh Ag Ól' is included on the album after the band receive a fan's wisdom …

Carr: We had been playing the instrumental 'Comb Your Hair And Curl It' live for over a year when a woman from the audience came up to us at the end of a gig in the west of Ireland, just before we were about to start the album.

She said, 'I really liked your version of "Bím Istigh

Ag Ól"' Jim asked, 'Which one was that?' and she sang it. He said, 'Ah, you mean "Comb Your Hair And Curl It"?' She said, 'Do you not know the song? There are actually lyrics; it's a song called "Bím Istigh Ag Ól," which translates, "We do be inside drinking".'

The woman could only remember the first verse but she knew an old man in a pub who would sometimes sing the full song. We told her that we'd be at Longfield House and if she found all the lyrics, maybe we'd record it. Luckily, she came up trumps.

Devlin: The release of *Happy To Meet* became a national event. Ireland now had its own rock stars, even though we were just big fish in a small pond. It was very flattering to be recognised on the street.

O'Connor: *Happy To Meet, Sorry To Part*'s concertina never existed in the flesh. I only had a five-sided concertina, and that shape wouldn't have worked for the record – it had to have eight sides and Eric Bannister, who we had all known at Arks, co-ordinated the artwork and matrix for the sleeve, based around my drawings.

The Small Faces' round sleeve for *Ogdens' Nut Gone Flake* and Family's TV-shaped *Bandstand* album had both been difficult to manufacture, but they proved that anything was possible.

Stacey Print, the manufacturers, had never been pushed very far with LPs, before but all we were asking for was a concertina-shaped bit of cardboard with punched holes. Why couldn't the Irish printers do the same as the English? Well, they could, and they did it very well, but it took a lot of time and the format for cutting that shape had to be quite elaborate. There was no margin for error.

We must have scared the pants off them because we were also asking for a gatefold sleeve. There was a Monty Python look about our photos, that you see through the holes in the front of the sleeve. Of course, the band weren't too thrilled with me at first for spending so much money on the design – probably more than we spent on the recording – but it actually helped to sell it, even though record shops had problems fitting it on their shelves because of the odd shape.

We had to do a lot of gigs to cover the expense of pressing up our own record. In fact, the technical problems raised their head once again with the digipak CD version, which was just as challenging a project as the original album, and I think we were quite successful at recreating the artwork. The problem with downsizing to that degree, however, is that it becomes almost impossible to read the sleeve notes. Creativity can sometimes bite you on the arse!

Carr: Having scored a hit with our first single was astonishing enough, but it was staggering when our début album on an indie label and with a strange sleeve made a massive dent in the charts, because Irish rock bands didn't have hits in Ireland at that point. It caused a stir across all age groups. It was bizarre.

We instantly shifted 35,000 copies in the first wave. In Irish terms that amounted to quadruple platinum back then. It became the most wanted present that Christmas, and people clamoured for a copy, very much in the same way that they might these days for the latest games console at that time of the year.

At the time of *Happy To Meet*'s release, Horslips' future business manager, Shay Hennessy, is working as a sales representative for Solomon & Peres, a Dublin record distributor for various labels, including Oats.

Hennessy: It was absolute mayhem in Dublin, because everybody wanted a copy. No one had seen or heard anything like it before. Subsequently, stock ran out very quickly and there was a long wait until after Christmas to get the numbers to meet demand. There was serious competition between us and our rival distributor, Irish Record Factors, when those additional copies surfaced. We did pretty good business over that winter.

Lockhart: The album was a fantastic lift off. However, a lot of the folk purists that had now started to become aware of us were righteously apoplectic. They were fiercely protective of the tradition, and viewed what we were doing to 'their' music as vandalism, like we were drawing a moustache on the 'Mona Lisa'. But equally we saw that we were bringing this music to an audience who were never likely to hear it, let alone embrace it.

The harping tradition was fading out by the end of the 18th century, and in 1792 there was a famous convocation – the *Belfast Harp Festival* – that was called by a gentleman's society to bring together as many of the surviving old harpers that could be found. A young clerk named Edward Bunting was employed to transcribe a lot of their tunes for posterity because they were in danger of extinction. But we have no idea what this music would have sounded like.

Ó Riada tried to recreate what it might have sounded like by incorporating the harpsichord into his band, Ceoltóirí Chualann, in the early '60s, but the tradition was very weak on its feet. When I was a kid, you could count the number of thriving pipers on one hand, and in real terms what the purists were protecting had been fairly debased anyway by the cacophony you'd hear in pubs. Their attitude was very indicative of the closed, conservative country that Ireland was around the time that Horslips began. It's very hard to imagine that now, with the proliferation of shows like *Riverdance* that celebrate tradition, and the fact that thousands of people around the world are now learning to play the Irish music that was so guarded back then. It's now incredibly popular and arguably the strongest branch of world music – it's everywhere you look.

But Horslips started as a rock'n'roll band. We didn't feel we had a cultural responsibility to incorporate the traditional content; it just evolved. We would be at parties and Charles would get out his concertina, I'd grab my tin whistle and Eamon would join in on his bodhrán, and we might knock out a tune that originated from Lough Neagh or wherever. Gradually, those tunes began to inform the way we played rock'n'roll, and that was only one step away from blending the two genres together, and writing about subjects that connected with our homeland. Obviously, when we began to realise what we were doing, we would create this fusion more consciously, but it was never the case that we had a master plan.

When Charles and I went to Abbey Road Studios to remaster all the albums in 2000, it was the first time I'd heard this stuff in 10 or 15 years, and I was amazed at how brave and adventurous we were. But because we didn't all have that pre-experience of being in rock bands, we didn't know there was stuff we shouldn't do or try, so it felt like anything was possible. It's sometimes true that knowledge can be a great inhibitor of creativity, and I think that being blue-eyed and inexperienced was our strength at the beginning.

In our defence, I would argue that we did more than most musicians to knock the dust from traditional music and frame it in a way that was able to gain the attention of the young person on the street in 1972 or '73, who was listening to Deep Purple, Yes or T-Rex. If what we did turned them on in some way to check out the origins of the tunes we incorporated into our music, then we served that tradition very well, and possibly gave those tunes an extended life that may not otherwise have been possible.

We received equally good and bad responses from people. While a lot of the staunch traditionalists were very tetchy with us, we did have our allies who would come to us with tunes that we may have overlooked, because they could see beyond the glitter boots and silver paint.

O'Connor: There was never any disrespect from our side towards the trad brigade. We were like punk folkers without really knowing it, and I think that really appealed to young people who loved seeing these old timers getting wound up.

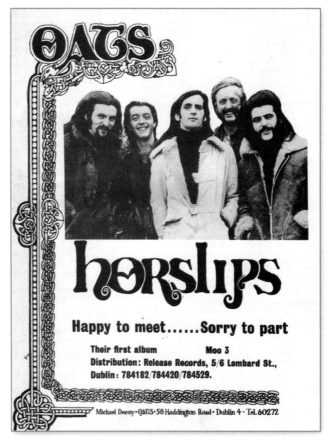

Devlin: Our first album was making headlines at the same time as Decca's hugely successful release of Thin Lizzy's 'Whiskey In The Jar' [which reached No. 1 in Ireland and No. 6 in Britain]. Even though they weren't initially keen for that track to go out as a single, it got them on 'Top Of The Pops' and instantly made them a household name.

They had moved to London and toured with Slade, but by the end of 1972, I think Philip was ready to throw in the towel. If 'Whiskey In The Jar' hadn't been such a monster hit, the band might have ended fairly soon after.

December 16: Horslips perform at the grand opening of the Fillmore West (formerly the Arcadia Ballroom) in Bray, Co. Wicklow.

Lockhart: One of the big effects of The Troubles was that bands from overseas stopped touring in Ireland, and you can hardly blame them. Emerson, Lake & Palmer were one such band, who pulled their plans to play at the launch night at the Fillmore West after a highly publicised spate of serious attacks and killings. When they cancelled we took their place.

Fean: The Fillmore West was set up to be a proper rock venue. Jim Fitzpatrick contributed murals for some of the walls, and the venue generally had a completely different vibe compared to most other places we played. There was a circus atmosphere on that opening night, with acrobats brought in from Fossetts' circus and lots of different side show acts. It was completely over the top.

February 13: Introduced by TV presenter Tony Johnston, Horslips are filmed in concert at the National Stadium, Dublin, by RTÉ for its series 'The Music Makers', broadcast on May 28.

Peter Clarke: I didn't have enough kit to do such a big show. So it was handy that RTÉ were handling the main lighting for filming purposes. I sometimes wonder how I never got fired very early when they sussed that I didn't know what I was doing. But Michael Deeny was a chancer himself in the most professional way, and I think he was willing to give another chancer a try.

Robbie, however, knew exactly what he was doing, and he was a real gentleman in the way he covered for me and helped me to get my act together. Robbie and I carved out a very successful career, thanks to Horslips allowing us the freedom to prove ourselves.

McGrath: At the time I joined the crew, we were using two WEM PA columns at each side of the stage, and I was mixing on a small eight-channel mixer. The WEM Audiomaster mixer was then regarded as high tech, and it was a real coup when we finally invested in two of them, as well as additional PA columns, just ahead of the Stadium gig.

Fean: Due to the filming, the lights were a lot brighter than they would normally have been at the Stadium. In fact, I think the occasion suffered slightly for it, if you believed the press reviews. Generally I felt the vibe wasn't as 'up' as my first Stadium gig with the band, but it was still a good show.

April 19: Conway Hall, Holborn, London WC1 – the band's live début in England (supported by Riff-Raff). Horslips' confidence in the magical qualities of their musical fusion is now growing by the day, but they still question their appeal among non-Irish audiences.

O'Connor: It was some time before we reached outside of Ireland with our music. The home crowd had made us feel so justified, but there was a big world out there. We had to do a lot of gigs to cover the expense of pressing up our own record. It took until early '73 for Michael Deeny to manage to get us to play in London, on the college circuit.

Carr: Before they went completely acidy, The Grateful Dead were playing Appalachian tunes alongside R&B, but it didn't seem so schizophrenic then. In the beginning we felt that we fitted into that loose bag, as opposed to being clearly defined with a

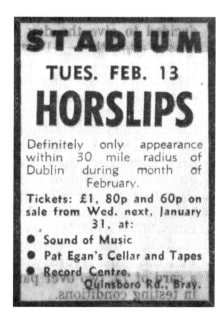

nicely packaged image, which we weren't. A lot of A&R guys came to check us out, because there was a buzz about us, but they'd shake their heads and say, 'Mmm, I can't really see this happening.' It wasn't what they were used to.

O'Connor: It was very fashionable at the time for Irish bands to travel to London in search of glory, but it meant an incredible amount of work to do it right, and we were an unknown quantity. Lizzy always had a hard time putting their tours together, because going to England was effectively going abroad, and there was a lot to organise.

Fean: The college circuit audiences were very receptive but we knew we had to get bigger gigs if we were going to make it. The first couple of years were very difficult, particularly as we were hardly making any money.

Lockhart: There was no doubt that we wanted to be the next big thing. It was just a question of how long it was going to take, and the strategies involved. Our début London gig at Conway Hall was well received and we actually pulled a reasonable-sized crowd. Word must have been spreading around through people in the Irish community who had previously seen us playing at home.

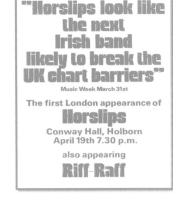

"Horslips look like the next Irish band likely to break the UK chart barriers"

Music Week March 31st

The first London appearance of

Horslips

Conway Hall, Holborn
April 19th 7.30 p.m.

also appearing

Riff-Raff

Clarke: Robbie and I would go and see other bands' stage presentations. We were particularly impressed by Curved Air, but there was more of an urge to be original.

The Conway Hall show is the catalyst for an international deal with Atlantic Records, reportedly worth £1,000,000 – the biggest ever offered to an Irish act at this point.

Deeny: *Happy To Meet* became a very expensive showcase demo that I shopped around. RCA were very interested but they weren't offering real money. However, I saw that they could probably represent us well in the UK, and that was what we agreed. It did us a lot of good because I the necessary ammunition to look further afield, internationally.

I felt that Atlantic Records would be perfect for America and the rest of the world. It took a while to get to Atlantic, because they had Led Zeppelin, the Stones, Aretha Franklin and many other premier acts, so a little Irish band had to wait in line. But I was determined to move things forward and realised it would be easier for them to see Horslips in London than in Ireland.

Johnny Fean recording the classic guitar riff for 'Dearg Doom' at The Manor.
Opposite page: Alan O'Duffy in session; Mitch Mitchell and Eamon Carr talk drums.

Dave Dee [formerly of Dave Dee, Dozy, Beaky, Mick & Tich pop fame] was representing Atlantic in the UK, and I persuaded him to come to the Conway Hall gig. Dave really liked Horslips, and encouraged the Americans to sign them. I then flew over to New York to do a deal that was quite heavy going, because I insisted on retaining control of our product, whilst taking a substantial amount of money from Atlantic.

I was dealing more with Nesuhi Ertegün – who ran the international business – than his younger brother [co-founder] Ahmet, who looked after the American market. Nesuhi and Jerry Greenberg [then VP of Atlantic A&R] protested quite fiercely over the cover of *Happy To Meet,* because of the cost of faithfully reproducing the die-cut design and shape. I explained that it was fundamental to remain faithful, as it was designed by one of the band and it was part of the group's appeal.

Eventually we came to an agreement for an inter-national deal, excluding Ireland and the UK, but when *Happy To Meet* first appeared in America, Mick Jagger flew into a rage when he saw the sleeve. He had jumped through hoops with Atlantic over the Stones' wish to feature a zip on the cover of *Sticky Finger,* for which they had to pay production costs in cash, and wondered how 'this cockamamie Irish band got a sleeve like that'.

There is always a packaging deduction from royalties, but how much is a matter for negotiation. We had an advance against royalties, so if *Happy To Meet* had been a big hit, once we had recouped the advance, a deduction of 10 cents per unit would have then happened. But it wasn't the big hit in America that we'd hoped for. At that point it was too traditionally Irish-sounding for American radio to embrace.

To be fair to Atlantic, they had never released an album remotely like *Happy To Meet,* so we were very impressed with the risk they were willing to take.

Devlin: We heard from some people at Atlantic that maybe they should have signed Michael instead of us, because he was the real genius! We were never richer than we were then.

Late April: Horslips begin new recording sessions with Alan O'Duffy at Richard Branson's newly-built, state-of-the-art residential studio, The Manor in Oxfordshire. During their stay, the band are treated to a preview of one of rock music's seminal works.

O'Duffy: When we finished at 3am, a young lad there called Michael Oldfield would come in and play until we started up again next morning.

Devlin: It was as if this Mike geezer was doing the night shift, and it took a while to work out what he was doing there. Occasionally we'd hear little snippets of what he'd been recording, and it was all quite interesting. Little did we know that this album he was working on would be so famous.

O'Connor: He called it *Opus One,* and he'd already been working on it for about a year. I think he was pleased to play it to fresh ears, because I got the impression that everyone else at The Manor had grown a little sick of Mike's album by then. It was later retitled *Tubular Bells* and became the first release on Richard Branson's Virgin Records. The rest is history.

Fean: A visit from Mitch Mitchell of the Jimi Hendrix Experience was a bit of an event. He seemed to be into what we were doing and he spent a lot of time sitting in a corner talking with Eamon about drums. You couldn't get a word in edgeways!

April 30: 'Dearg Doom' / 'The High Reel' is a new Irish single release (MOO 4). Recorded during the *Happy To Meet* sessions, 'The High Reel' is added to later pressings of that album. 'Dearg Doom' is a classic in the making that will reach No. 8 and spend seven weeks on the Irish singles chart.

May 28: National Stadium, Dublin. For the first time, Horslips present extracts from their forthcoming album, *The Táin*. The concert is rescheduled after the original May 22 date is postponed.

Carr: When we played *The Táin* live for the first time at the Stadium, we printed a broadsheet programme that included a hint of the future album artwork, along with lyrics and an explanation of the story. The audience were intrigued, and there was great anticipation in the air about the project after that show. We added a little more to our special effects arsenal that night to ensure that our in-progress album went off with a bang ... literally. But maybe we overdid the smoke bombs.

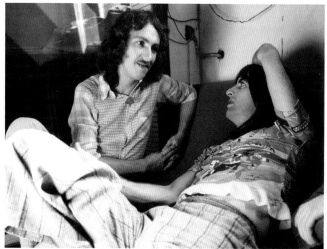

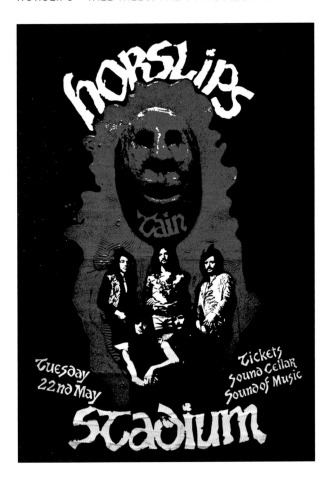

July 20: In the wake of a short British tour, along-side bands including Family and Brinsley Schwarz, Horslips release their first UK single – 'The High Reel' / 'Furniture' (RCA OAT 1).

August 5: *Peace Party*, Phoenix Park, Dublin. All dressed in white, Horslips headline a bill that includes Chips, Terry & Gay Woods, Peggy's Leg, Rodeo, Trench Band and Dave Murphy. Conor McAnally of the *Irish Independent* reports:

'The band started with a bang – a huge firework exploded on stage and throughout the act rockets, flares and smoke bombs went off as the group performed part of their mini rock musical "The Táin" based on the legendary story of the Táin Bó Cuailnge.'

Lockhart: I acquired an English-registration Mini that summer, but it didn't last long. After the *Peace Party*, I was driving with Charles through South Wales, and wrote it off in Port Talbot on the way to taking it to sell in London. We're really lucky to be alive, because I drove it under a tanker that was full of nitric acid. The road was slippery and I managed to get into a skid on the approach to a roundabout. My seatbelt wasn't working, so I didn't wear it and got thrown out of the driver's door, arcing about 30 feet into the centre of the roundabout, but only had a tiny scratch beside my eye to show for it.

Charles bumped his head and sustained a broken nose, for which he needed hospital treatment. When we were eventually discharged, we got a lift to London, where Dave Dee, our then A&R man, met us and took us down to a session in Kent.

Mid-August: Horslips record backing tracks at Escape Studios in Kent, a residential studio in a converted barn run by Teddy Roffey.

August 22: *Edinburgh Pop Festival*, Empire Theatre, Edinburgh. Horslips and John Martyn play one of 10 concerts promoted by record store chain owner

Horslips at the *Peace Party* in Phoenix Park, Dublin.

Bruce Findlay, who has been asked by Lord Provost of Edinburgh, Jack Kane, to organise the city's first-ever pop festival. In 1978, Findlay will discover and manage Simple Minds.

October 1: Recording session for BBC Radio 1's 'Top Gear', produced by John Walters. The tracks recorded are 'An Bratach Bán', 'Dearg Doom' and 'Maeve's Court' (listed as its source tune 'Knockeen Free' on the session files).

Carr: John Walters was a great guy to work with. He handled the incoming bands in a very friendly, professional and respectful manner. We were conscious of using the same studio in Maida Vale that other people had been in the week before, and quite often we'd have listened to those sessions. But we couldn't dwell on that, because we had to get in, set up quickly, try to get a good sound, and then deliver. Those sessions were always done in a hurry, although the studio engineers had recorded Hendrix, Bowie, Floyd and Bolan, so we were in pretty safe hands.

October–November: Horslips' first full UK tour includes support dates with Steeleye Span & Suzi Quatro. The conceptual structure of the forthcoming album *The Táin* has a significant bearing on the way Horslips present themselves on this tour and at subsequent concerts.

O'Connor: We weren't really Celtic rockers in the glam sense, but we had some interesting, theatrical ideas for sets, which was always my domain because I was responsible for just about anything connected to the look and presentation of the band. There would be backdrops emblazoned with Celtic motifs, and we'd come on stage kitted out in snakeskin and leather.

Clarke: The Steeleye Span tour was a massive education for all of us. Maddy Prior and her band were doing very well with their Top 30 album *Parcel Of Rogues*, and the UK venues were all sold out. It was an introduction to the big league. Horslips had to fight every night to win the attention of the Steeleye fans, and they saw it as an opportunity to blow the headliners off the map. I think they won a lot of fans.

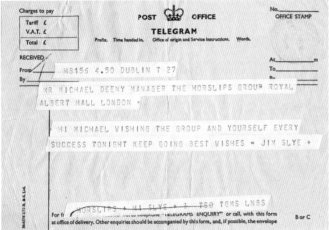

of *The Táin*, occasionally inserting some instrumental passages that were left over from the album. Some of the tracks were studio creations that we couldn't have reproduced very faithfully on tour with the technology that existed then. These days it would be a different matter.

Being invited to play on Steeleye Span's tour was a godsend for us, especially at the Albert Hall, which was probably the most fulfilling gig I ever did in London. We were tagging along, but we made the best of it and had a whale of a time.

McGrath: The Suzi Quatro date we did [Nottingham Uni, October 13] was a completely different vibe. It went from a folk-rock to a teenybopper audience. Suzi had put out a couple of massive hits ['Can The Can' and '48 Crash'], and obviously most of the crowd were there to see her in the leather ... I wasn't complaining!

October 19: 'Dearg Doom' / 'The Shamrock Shore' (RCA OAT 2) is released as a UK single.

November 16: Horslips and Michael Deeny are involved in a head-on road collision near Kilkenny in which 37-year-old local farmer Michael Piert is killed. All of the band suffer injuries but only Deeny and O'Connor are detained in hospital. Several concerts are postponed.

Even though we weren't headlining at the Royal Albert Hall gig [October 8], we thought that we'd made it, because it's on every band's wish list. So Robbie and I were very proud of our own situation, and the Steeleye crew could see that we were very good-natured and professional in the way we looked after the band. We came in for a bit of verbal at the start of the tour, but once they realised we could give as much as we could take, the camaraderie between both parties was fantastic.

Carr: We would include generous extracts from *The Táin* [a live 'extended sequence' is included on the digipak CD reissue of the album, recorded at My Father's Place, New York, in 1974], but we never played the full album. We tended to link 'The Clergy's Lamentation' from *Happy To Meet* on to the end of 'You Can't Fool The Beast' as a dramatic way of exiting that section.

Over time, we developed a kind of orchestral version

Carr: We were on the way to play a midnight gig in Kilkenny when we had the crash. I was knocked out, and woke up over the back seat of the Range Rover on top of the guitars. When I woke up everything was dark, but then I saw the headlights of the farmer's Hillman piercing through the steam. The lads were out of the car by then, but I quickly got my senses together and jumped out, fearing that the car might suddenly blow up.

I went off to have a go at this stupid driver who had nearly killed us, but the firemen wouldn't let me anywhere near his car, which had concertinaed. They told me it wasn't a pretty sight back there, and that's when I realised he had died.

A few weeks earlier, we had each been given a miniature clay ceramic head as a talisman gift. They were based on *The Táin*'s inner sleeve figure that Charles had created to echo ancient Celtic stone figures of heads, some of which have a face on both sides. No one understands what they mean, but perhaps Charles thought that a reference to them would fit the package. The monks who transcribed 'The Táin' inserted a coda at the end that essentially said anyone who fails to re-tell this story accurately will be cursed. I was quite satisfied that with the research I put into the album, we were being faithful.

While we were standing there at the scene of this road crash, Barry produced his little Táin head out of his pocket and flung it across the field. He said, 'It's obviously the curse of "The Táin".' I decided to keep mine, and many years later I gave it to my friend, Myles Lally. But that idea of the curse was a hot topic for a while.

Charles was in the front seat and, although he had a seatbelt on, he broke his nose, again, and had to have it straightened. My hip got bruised and damaged, so I had to go for an X-ray in Dublin the next day, and Roger Armstrong, who had been the social secretary at Queen's University in Belfast, came down to collect the wounded at Michael's request. For the next few weeks, I was hobbling around with a walking stick.

Lockhart: I've had a few scrapes with cars over the years, but this one was really frightening. I suffered from headaches for a time and I became a very nervous passenger to be with. I didn't want to get near a steering wheel for quite a while.

November 23: Release of *The Táin* (MOO 5), a musical documentation of the Táin Bó Cuailnge (the Cattle Raid of Cooley), one of the most infamous legends of early Irish literature, dealing with the 500BC conflict between Ulster and Connacht over a prize bull. The songs tell the story from the perspectives of Cú Chulainn, the possessive Queen Maeve of Connacht and Ferdia, among other characters.

After rehearsals in Donegal and sessions at Escape Studios, the album is completed at The Manor in Oxfordshire.

Devlin: The thing with most new bands is that by the time you get to record your first album, you've probably been playing most of the material for some time, and by releasing it, you're actually freeing yourself to get on with the next step. That was certainly the case with Jethro Tull on their first album, which for obvious reasons got titled *This Was*. It was exactly the same with us.

Carr: We first looked at *The Táin* during 1971. Jim and Barry had been members of the Cumann Drámaíochta,

the Irish-language drama group in UCD, and some of the people that they had been involved with – specifically Sean O'Briain – decided to stage a dramatic interpretation of 'The Táin' at the Abbey Theatre. It was kind of experimental and they wanted music. We thought we'd like to try it, and so we started to attend rehearsals with the troupe, but the show never ran.

Devlin: Although Eamon would have had some lyrics and jottings floating around, because he worked fast, the music that we made for the album came much later.

Carr: After all the fuss surrounding *Happy To Meet* died down and we were thinking about what to do for the next album, I suggested that we might revisit some of the sketches that we'd discussed for the Abbey Theatre project, and maybe focus on 'The Táin' as a big piece.

There are several versions of 'The Táin', the most famous being Thomas Kinsella's contemporary interpretation with Louis le Brocquy's beautiful wash drawings. Purposely, I didn't refer to Kinsella's translation because it was too current. I preferred to go back to different source materials and take out my own highlights of the story to try and set up little pivotal action points.

Initially, I dragged in various versions and re-tellings of the yarn. Among the devices I employed were attempts at weaving in strands of a Cú Chulainn narrative as described in the plays of WB Yeats – whose son, Michael, was very generous in ensuring that we had permission to use the marvellous quote by WB on the back of the original album sleeve. It helped explain why I felt the story might have a contemporary resonance. This was a time when concept albums were hip and happening, so it didn't seem like a bad idea.

O'Connor: When we were planning our first album, we thought about doing a conceptual piece, although it didn't happen until *The Táin*. Barry and Jimmy were into pop/rock, Johnny and I were interested in the traditional elements, as was Jimmy, and Eamon was the poet. We found that organising a conceptual album was a way of pulling five people together and harnessing strengths. We were delighted that the album's eclectic flavour captured our true essence.

Carr: Before 'The Táin' there was no clear definition of young Ireland. Coming from County Meath, where you have Newgrange and all the mythological sites, I was very conscious of Ancient Ireland. But allied with that, I was also into reading Marvel comics, and Stan Lee was a huge influence. And I was very much aware of all the traditional Irish mythological superheroes.

The merging of those two cultures was the kind of stuff you used to see in Oz, and it only took a simple leap of imagination to visualise how these legendary tales might be placed into a musical format.

For many, the urgency of Johnny Fean's guitar playing on 'Dearg Doom' ensures it remains Ireland's greatest rock anthem. The iconic riff is later incorporated into 'Put 'Em Under Pressure', the Republic of Ireland's official FIFA World Cup 1990 single, inspiring a younger audience.

Some have argued that Fean's blues-tinged guitar motif overshadows its original, traditional source in the collective consciousness.

Fean: I had learned 'O'Neill's Cavalry' on tenor banjo with Ted Furey one day in Lisdoonvarna. Nearly three years later, I was with the lads over at Jimmy's pad and started playing the tune on the banjo, thinking that maybe it would work as an electric guitar intro.

"We were delighted that the album's eclectic flavour captured our true essence ..."

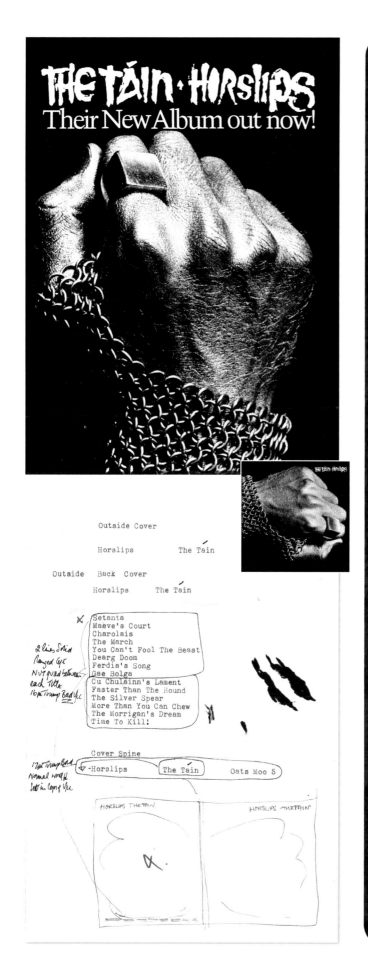

O'Connor: We were considering using a Louis le Brocquy ink splodge illustration from Thomas Kinsella's translated publication of 'The Táin', but then we thought we would have to pay a sizeable sum to reproduce it, and so I came up with an alternative idea.

The Táin wasn't as complex as *Happy To Meet*, but it had its own manufacturing difficulties. It's probably our most iconic design, because the fist is such a strong Celtic image, with male aggression suggested by the chain mail. That was actually a British-style demiglove and not medieval or Celtic. But as soon as I spotted it I saw its potential for cover art.

That's my fist. We didn't realise that by spraying my hand silver and dressing it with the chain mail, it would look as silver as it does on the printed sleeve. The texture against the black background was just perfect.

We got a lot of use out of that image – on the album, on T-shirts and on the front and side of our twin-wheelbase Transit van. When we drove into town we had an instant presence. Kids would say, 'I've seen the van, I've seen the van, they're coming ...', and it was a thrill for us to know we created such excitement.

The square, silver ring I'm wearing in that image was mine. My then girlfriend, Sue Calvert, bought that for me and I loved it, but somebody stole it from the dressing room at one of our gigs in Cashel and I was very upset about that. I hear that it's currently residing somewhere in Galway.

I wanted something that wasn't a regular typeface for the title graphics. The range of fonts that we had available in 1973 was tiny compared to the wealth of choice we have today, so it was hard to be original. We also wanted a very Celtic-looking font as a way of maybe paying homage to le Brocquy, and his ink splatter lettering informed our approach.

One of Eric Bannister's colleagues, Sean and I sat down one day, and I scribbled my idea for this typeface as a guide. Billy Moore then hand drew the lettering, and in doing so he created what has now become our definitive logo.

sleeve notes

The next time we were rehearsing, I got the riff going on my 1970 Goldtop, and Eamon jumped up from behind his drum kit, and asked, 'What in God's name is that?' I explained the background and he asked me to play it again. So I did and everyone was looking around in amazement. It was like we'd hit gold and by breaking up the tune into a few parts, then with Charles singing Eamon's brilliant lyrics, we suddenly had a great song.

Carr: I was shocked by how fuckin' powerful and immediate this riff sounded, as if I'd been smacked around the face. The arrangement didn't take very long to get together but it was some time before we achieved the right feel. We tried a number of different rhythms and accents, and it still wasn't setting up the guitar properly. Alan O'Duffy had the solution, and maybe there was some hi-hat influence from Isaac Hayes' 'Theme From Shaft'.

O'Duffy: I couldn't get away from thinking it should be a Motown groove behind Johnny's riff. It took a while to get it right and I think we met in the middle. 'Dearg Doom', for me, was a great achievement, and I got a lot of pleasure from watching it grow in the studio. It made me realise how influential the bodhrán was on Eamon's drumming style.

Fean: Alan also took a lot of time over Barry's bassline when we were at The Manor. He pushed for a much more funky approach to syncopate against the guitar. It probably wasn't what Barry would naturally have played, but once the drum pattern was set in stone it was killer.

Lockhart: Turning the riff into the basis for a song was a challenge – part of the solution was to effectively double the length of the riff by changing the chords for the repeat, which gave you better options for the melody line.

Carr: I knew straight away that the riff was so strong that it had to be a central part of the album's narrative, and therefore probably had to be about Cú Chulainn. We felt it should be vaguely superhero-ish, through which you would define a character. What is he? Who is he?

Left: Working with Alan O'Duffy at The Manor.

There was a great anti-hero in the Marvel comics called Doctor Doom, who was the nemesis of the Fantastic Four. And then, there was this 'Dearg' being red, being Ulster's bloodied red hand, so it fell together as 'Dearg Doom' – The Red Destroyer – and it just seemed to stick. It had a cabalistic resonance.

The lyric, in a funny way, may owe a debt to Muddy Waters and Bo Diddley, kind of 'I'm The Man', the strutting of one's stuff. We also took some direction from the old Irish poem, 'The Song Of Amergin' ... and perhaps a sly steal from Yeats to boot.

The parallel was there between the Celtic and the Marvel comic heroes. But it wasn't a glib thing and you couldn't treat it lightly, otherwise it would have come out like Hawkwind. It had to be approached properly and fortunately I had studied Old Irish at college, so it was a case of delving back into these subjects and doing a lot of research, like I was preparing a thesis.

Getting deeper into the story behind 'The Táin', I discovered things that they never taught us at school. Eastern philosophy had infiltrated into rock'n'roll, possibly through George Harrison's interest in the Maharishi, but now I was examining Western mystery traditions and it was taking Horslips on a new journey.

Devlin: 'Dearg Doom' has earned a reputation over the years as the song that can turn a wedding reception into mayhem if the DJ puts it on just before the last record of the night. It's equal to a war dance if you've got the right crowd.

O'Duffy: It will be interesting in, say, 50 years from now, to see if young people learn to play 'O'Neill's Cavalry' as 'Dearg Doom', such has been its popularity.

During interviews with Maurice Linnane for his documentary _The Return Of The Dancehall Sweethearts_, U2's The Edge pays tribute:

'Horslips tapped into this hunger for something authentic in music that was Irish. And I think that 'Dearg Doom' as a song, for instance, is a wonderful combination of rock'n'roll and traditional Irish music that stands up as one of the great rock songs of all time.

'Horslips and Thin Lizzy were the two bands that everyone I hung out with spoke about. Rory Gallagher as well. And because they were all Irish they kind of stood alongside Led Zeppelin or the Stones or The Beatles in terms of stature.

'In everybody's head they were the five biggest groups in the world. We'd argue about who was the best and who was the biggest.

'Probably because we didn't really see any of those bands live, it was really about records in those days and along with _The Dark Side Of The Moon_, _The Táin_ was one of the five great records that everybody had – if you didn't have it you borrowed and taped it.'

Above: Original handwritten lyrics for 'More Than You Can Chew'.

O'Duffy: We started work on *The Táin* in the spring, about 18 months before I did *Venus And Mars* with Wings in New Orleans.

Although I'd suggest harmony parts, chords, arrangements, rhythm feels, percussion and backing vocals, I wanted the sound of the band to be them at their best, and I think we achieved this every time.

I would often add third part harmonies to backing vocal mixes which would add something special to the sound and make the albums a little more commercial.

The female backing vocals on things like 'More Than You Can Chew' were sung by Kay Davis and Jo Collins who, with Mary Ward, went on to form Chicken Shed, a world-class theatre company for children of all talents, having a non-discriminatory approach to handicapped performers.

demonium subsides as O'Connor's sweet concertina ushers in 'Maeve's Court' and the tale begins.

Lockhart: A lot of discussion went into how we were going to start the album. 'Setanta' begins with me playing dissonant sounds on a cheap Italian organ while Alan applied effects. 'Cú Chulainn's Lament' was originally my setting of Stevie Smith's poem 'Not Waving But Drowning'. It was later one of the surprise highlights of *Roll Back,* with a cello part I wrote for Aisling Drury Byrne to play on it.

Carr: We had to cram a lot of narrative detail into some of the songs. The lyrics for 'Cú Chulainn's Lament' were from a poem I'd written called 'Love's Lament', which was about suicide. It's as dark as Nick Cave ever was. The trick was that, whilst we were dealing with mythology, I needed to make these words seem personal.

The Táin's introduction, 'Setanta' (the birth name of Cú Chulainn), sets the scene with a disturbing, chilling backwash of sound. Fading in from Lockhart's wispy, psychedelic organ glissandos, Carr attacks his snare drum with stereo-panned military angst as Fean's echoed lead guitar triplets settle into a stern low register riff. The pan-

Horslips are now mastering their fusion of age-old jigs and reels with original rock – another fine example is the use of 'The March Of The King Of Laois' in the uilleann pipe breaks of 'More Than You Can Chew', while 'The Morrigan's Dream' is a reworking of 'Old Noll's Jig'.

Above: Lyrics for 'Charolais', written on the back of a Mouthpiece Promotions letterhead.

Revived for their arena shows in 2009, 'Charolais', the album's first vocal track, is another instance of a traditional tune being used as the basis for the main melody. Here, it is 'Rosc Catha na Mumhan' (The Battle Hymn Of Munster), which reappears in 'The March' – the track that forms a bridge to 'You Can't Fool The Beast'. Again, Fean's guitar work is exemplary as it wraps itself around Lockhart's fluttering flute and proud organ lines.

Eamon Carr explains 'Charolais' during an interview for BBC2's 'Second House' arts programme in 1974:

'Because the original Táin saga is quite witty in places, and a bit far-fetched in fact, we stuck our tongues firmly in our cheeks and wrote "Charolais". And the thing is, the Charolais is quite an expensive animal. It was only introduced in these islands maybe 12 years ago, and the lyric content of the song "Charolais" basically just sets the earlier scene; the story. It refers to Queen Maeve having a quarrel with her husband.'

Other highlights include the dark, prog rock menace of 'Ferdia's Song', the slow-paced 'Faster Than The Hound' (with a descending chord pattern reminiscent of The Beatles' 'Dear Prudence'), O'Connor's upbeat fiddle hoedown 'The Silver Spear', and finale track 'Time To Kill!'

which, as well as showcasing O'Connor's mandolin rendition of the hop jig 'The Humours Of Whiskey', bows to psychedelia with its reversed cymbals and otherworldly a cappella coda.

Carr: Someone had edited a piece of tape backwards on to the end of 'Time To Kill!' by accident. It was a naked piece of harmony vocal that now, peculiarly, sounded like weird poltergeist language. We were just listening to a playback at Olympic. It sounded so eerie that, in terms of radio drama, it just seemed to suggest some sort of conclusion.

'Time To Kill!' features Fean's lead vocal début with the band, and will later inspire Irish novelist Jennifer Johnston to title her book 'Shadows On Our Skin'.

Fean: The lead vocal parts on *Happy To Meet* had already been allocated, but when we were recording *The Táin*, the guys thought they'd try me out on 'Time To Kill!' and it seemed to work, so it then seemed natural to think of me for the occasional song or two. Our decisions on who would sing lead were always about what best suited a song. Alan was an absolute master at helping to create really good blocks of vocals and encouraging us to stretch ourselves as singers.

Above: 'Time To Kill!' – another lyric sheet salvaged from the studio floor.

November 29: National Stadium, Dublin – supported by Monroe.

O'Connor: We were constantly asked if we'd play *The Táin* as a big, stand-alone production piece with an orchestra and all the trimmings. It was always proffered and it was a shame we didn't. After the album came out, we featured extracts from it in our set for a few years and at this Stadium gig, as a nod to the narrative, we had sheep skulls painted gold and cattle skulls on long sticks with flashpowder pots in them that would smell of burning meat whenever we set light to them!

I'd never seen another band try as hard as us to do something that visually exciting before, and the kids appreciated it. It would have been good to become more like the cultural ambassadors some people expected us to be. We had a lot to offer in that respect and also as a more theatrical rock act, along the lines of what Alice Cooper did later with *Welcome To My Nightmare*, and it was a missed opportunity.

December 1: Savoy, Cork.

O'Connor: Peter Clarke was a little over-zealous here with the amount of flash powder he used in two of the flashpots and consequently the stage went up in flames. He ran from the lighting desk with rubber-soled clogs on his feet and started to stamp out the fire. But the rubber on his clogs set alight and there was this amazing spectacle of our lighting man doing what appeared to be a dance with his feet on fire. The band stopped playing.

In his panic, Peter pulled one side of the lights down and the audience were in raptures over this impromptu dancing. Far out! Could this have been how Michael Flatley got his idea for *Feet Of Flames*?

He also had a predilection for using cherry bombs that accounted for the vast clouds of smoke that would envelope us on stage. At one dancehall we played, Peter set off a cherry bomb in a dustbin, backstage in the dressing room. What he didn't know was that the venue

manager had gone in there to count the box office receipts. The thing went off and the dressing room door flew off its hinges. All the money floated up in the air and there was this poor guy looking like a war victim. It was like a scene from a 'Carry On' film.

December 5: Horslips appear on 'Musikladen' performing 'The High Reel'. Filmed in Bremen, the show is the German equivalent of the UK's 'Top Of The Pops'.

Carr: The New York Dolls were on the bill with us. Bassist Arthur Kane was wearing a basque, women's tights and leather boots, with an oversized baby's dummy around his neck. Not wishing to be outdone, I decided to take this red body suit out of my case.

The detail was probably lost on the TV audience, because there was red snakeskin coiling up and around the body, over the hood and down over the eyes. Somebody must have spiked our drinks. It wasn't such a great idea though – it was pretty damn sweaty inside that suit.

'Did ye hear the one about the broken glass table top?'

An outtake from Ian Finlay's photo shoot for *Dancehall Sweethearts*, summer 1974.

105

CHAPTER 4

MAD PAT'S GOING BACK ON THE ROAD

January 15: Following a string of dates in Ireland to open the new year, Horslips record their classic live TV performances of 'Dearg Doom' (bottom) and 'Faster Than The Hound' for 'The Old Grey Whistle Test' at BBC Television Centre in London.

Carr: The 'Whistle Test' studio was a very cold place, slightly intimidating and not at all glamorous. Of course, the backdrop was familiar, but 'Whispering' Bob Harris was nowhere to be seen. We were playing to a backing track in front of a bunch of cameras, just as bands before us had done. From some time in 1974, bands tended to play live. The Wailers were a revelation. But in 1973 it was usually live vocal to backing tracks.

O'Connor: We were taking the album cover a little too literally because I got someone – I might have done it myself – to spray my hand silver with car paint for that programme. The idea was to reinforce the macho chain mail demi-glove I was wearing. It looked great on TV but it was a bugger to play with it on ... and get off!

January 17: UK press reception for *The Táin* at the Irish Club in Tudor Street, London.

Mark Plummer (Melody Maker): Just before the reception, I'd been having a drink with Michael Deeny in a nearby pub. As soon as we left in his car, two police cars followed us. Deeny had Irish number plates and as a result of recent IRA activity, the coppers weren't taking any chances.

Suddenly, Deeny got seriously paranoid and shot down a one-way street the wrong

way, took a left, then a right, and finally eluded these coppers. At that point he told me that his boot contained several Lucozade bottles full of poitín and he was really shaken up because you didn't want to get caught with this hooky stuff. It had been illegal for centuries.

O'Connor: Holding our press bash at the Irish Club ticked all the boxes, because it was inexpensive, it was in the heart of the city, and we were promoting a very Irish-themed album. Everyone got blind drunk on Michael's poitín – it's absolutely lethal stuff.

We emptied one of the bottles into the punch bowl without knowing that Eamon had done the same thing already. So the punch contained at least two bottles of very potent stuff. One particular well-known journalist fell victim and his magazine called us to ask where he'd gone. He had vanished somewhere in the country for a few days and we heard that a young lady had picked him up and given him a good seeing to over a weekend.

Devlin: Of all the people who succumbed to the powers of poitín, I'd say that Horslips were amongst the worst affected. I have an indelible vision of Jim Lockhart with a permanently stupid look on his face as he tried to reason with a journalist about all things mythological. Despite all this we were sensible about alcohol; we were always sober on stage. After the gig was another matter.

January 18: *The Táin*'s UK release by RCA Records coincides with the start of *The Táin* 1974 UK Tour, with support act Rab Noakes. Ending on February 9, this will be Horslips' last tour with Peter Clarke in charge of their lighting.

Clarke: Once Horslips had completed their run on the previous UK tour, I carried on with Steeleye until the tour finished about a month later. I then did Thin Lizzy's Christmas '73 tour of Ireland, and one more tour with Horslips. After that I relocated to London and ended up working with Dr Feelgood.

The Steeleye crew referred to us as 'The Micks' and because I tended to have the biggest mouth, I got the nickname 'Supermick', which I think was a back-handed compliment. The joke extended to the lighting company I founded in 1976 – I called it Supermick!

McGrath: When we toured with Steeleye, they were carrying a Midas mixing console and a Martin Audio PA, and it sounded astonishing compared to the gear we'd been working with. We knew we'd have to spend some wedge to keep up. I went to see Clive Davies at Colac [Colosseum Acoustics], the PA company that looked after Steeleye, and it transpired that all of their gear had returned to Colac's rental stock following their late '73 tour. So we did a deal with Clive and bought this entire system for the next major tour in the UK.

That console was the first made by Midas. It represented a quantum leap for live sound, and people at home were amazed at how good we now sounded.

Reviewing Horslips' show at London's Imperial College on January 26, journalist Tony Stewart gives a balanced appraisal of the shape of the band's repertoire and performance in early '74:

'Horslips have everything going for them right now. Their gig at the IC on Saturday was remarkable not only for their excellent performance, and the subsequent crowd reaction, but for the number of people who attended. And this all goes to show that this Irish band have grown in stature.

'What is more important though is that the music has improved ... and the effect is quite devastating, with huddled groups of young souls flying through the motions of a calaidh [sic] dance to the music of "Johnny B. Goode" and "Talkin' 'Bout You".

'In spite of their heavy rock aura, there is still a tremendous amount of reels and jigs and strong melody in their music. If you want my honest opinion, Horslips are one of the best outfits currently touring England.'

February 2: University of East Anglia, Norwich. Horslips also record a daytime session for BBC Radio 1's 'Top Gear' with producer John Walters at BBC's Studio T1 in Kensington House, London W12. They record 'The Silver Spear', 'Charolais', 'The March' and 'You Can't Fool The Beast'.

February 12: At Mayfair Studios in London, producer Fritz Fryer remixes 'Dearg Doom' and 'More Than You Can Chew' for a single in Germany (Atlantic ATL 10 436), where it hits No. 1.

Born David Roderick Carney Fryer in Lancashire in 1944, 'Fritz' was always destined for a life in music. His composer grandfather, Herbert Fryer, had more than 2,000 hymns to his name, and by the late 1950s, the young Fritz was playing guitar with his first group, The Fables.

Renaming themselves The Four Pennies, they reached No. 1 in 1964 with 'Juliet', co-written by Fryer. He later moved into production, working with CBS and MCA artists.

Fryer: After Alan O'Duffy completed his work on *The Táin*, the band wanted to remix some tracks for singles, and my name was mentioned. They were so pleased with my results that they asked if I'd like to produce the next album. I'd recently had my first major success with a version of Neil Young's 'After The Gold Rush' by Prelude, which put me in good stead at the time, because I think Horslips were big Neil Young fans and really liked that version.

Eamon Carr has a more colourful explanation of Fryer's arrival into Horslips' world ...

Carr: I mean no disrespect to Fritz, because he was a good guy but, commercially, we may have made a big mistake in 1974 by rejecting Tom Dowd as a producer, because we heard he was seriously into the idea.

Atlantic loved 'Dearg Doom' and its powerful mix of a catchy trad riff with rock'n'roll and a very danceable four-to-the-floor beat, and they wanted more of it. To them it probably sounded like Irish disco! Unfortunately we mistook good advice for interference, which was often the case. So the word came that Tom Dowd, the legendary cornerstone of Atlantic's success, with

stellar credits from Ray Charles to Cream, wanted to produce us. Despite all this, we doubted whether he would be able to relate to what we were doing.

Meanwhile, someone in England had told us about Fritz Fryer, who also wanted a piece of the studio action. The answer to this dilemma was to give 'Dearg Doom' and 'More Than You Can Chew' to both Tom and Fritz, ask them to each remix the tracks and see what they came up with.

The results were interesting. There was nothing wrong with Tom's mixes, but they were too smooth to represent what we were. In contrast, Fritz's mixes seemed more energetic, and we were wedded to the theory that we needed to capture that slightly elusive excitement of the live performance. That was a Holy Grail thing for a lot of artists and it was why bootlegs were all the rage.

There was a serious discussion, obviously, but we decided to pass on Tom.

Just after we completed *Dancehall Sweethearts,* I heard Tom's production on Eric Clapton's new album, *461 Ocean Boulevard*. It was lively, sweet and melodic – all the things I liked. It returned Eric to greatness, and it then troubled me that we might have cocked up. Would Tom have managed to pull that stroke with us had we decided to work together? Conceivably, yes, but you don't know what you lose in gaining something else.

February 14: Horslips travel from Harwich to the Hook of Holland as they embark on their first European tour, with Finbarr Quinn newly installed as lighting man. Their dates span the Netherlands, Germany and Switzerland. A month later, they briefly visit Canada.

O'Connor: We went over with a view to penetrating the North American market. The Canadian tour did us a lot of good and we had a great time, but to organise a proper tour of the States was going to be a different ball game, because it's such a vast place.

March 29: Fritz Fryer's remix of 'More Than You Can Chew' is coupled as a UK single (RCA OAT 3) with 'Faster Than The Hound'. Legendary broadcaster John Peel files a guest review for *Sounds* **...**

'Horslips' chosen brief is a difficult one to fill, despite the acclaim given to their ambitious *The Táin*. I'm yet to be convinced that they are filling it. They may well in the future, the signs are certainly there, but this single, like the curate's egg, is excellent in parts – and that's not enough.'

April 14–May 2: Irish tour, including dates at the National Stadium, Belfast's Ulster Hall and Cork City Hall.

May 4: Horslips return to the UK and, as they play the Roundhouse in Dagenham, a pre-recorded Horslips are seen performing extracts from *The Táin* **on BBC2's arts show 'Second House', introduced by Melvyn Bragg, later of London Weekend Television's 'The South Bank Show' fame.**

Carr: For our spot on 'Second House', some interviews and footage of kids dancing were shot in Dublin, while we were filmed at Ardmore Studios in Bray, where they set up risers in positions that were very unnatural to us.

As with 'Whistle Test', I had pads on my drums because we were playing to a backing track, but I still had to hit cymbals and occasionally there would be some bleed from the kit into the live vocal mics, and it sounded like tin cans in the background.

At one stage, the camera panned over some of Le Brocquy's drawings and sure enough, there were some black swans. I may have used that image as a trigger for writing 'Time To Kill!', but I have no memory of it.

Opposite page: Horslips on the road in spring 1974.
Below: Devlin's John Birch custom 'shamrock' bass, designed by O'Connor.

May 5: Headlining an all-day show at Round-house, Chalk Farm, London – supported by Good Habit, Clancy & Isaac Guillory. *Sounds'* **Robin Katz is in the audience.**

'Horslips are one band whose musical success on stage is still best judged by their audiences. Anyone who can pull a zonked-out crowd like this to its feet [at the end of a seven-hour programme] deserves five stars and a free supply of Guinness.'

The tour, which ends on May 18, includes shows at Barbarella's in Birmingham, Nottingham University and St George's Hall, Liverpool.

Carr: Artistically, Liverpool felt like my second home because of the amount of times I travelled there in the '60s to visit the Cavern and immerse myself in the bubbling poetry scene. So to return and play that venue with some old poet friends in attendance, including Roger McGough and Mike Evans [Liverpool Scene], was really lovely.

Late May: Barry Devlin takes delivery of a new, shamrock-shaped bass guitar that is set to become a long-standing Horslips icon.

Devlin: It's a very manly instrument with a wide neck that was built for me by John Birch from Charles' thorough working drawings. John also custom-built amazing guitars for Mud, ELO and Wizzard, as well as the Super Yob for Dave Hill of Slade.

I dearly love the 'shamrock'. You wouldn't choose to play for a whole gig because, being made from mahogany, it's frighteningly heavy, so I used my Fender Jazz for the lion's share and pick up the shamrock for encores. All these years later, I still have this beautiful instrument and can report that it's in good shape.

In 1974, Devlin plays through an Ampeg 100 watt amplifier stack, while Lockhart uses a modified Leslie Pro 900 rotating speaker for his Hammond organ and a Marshall 100 watt stack and Schaller Rotor Sound effect for his Diamond 800 keyboard. He plays a Yamaha flute, Generation and Clarks tin whistles, and uilleann pipes made by Liam Weldon.

Along with his Les Pauls, Fean is currently touring with a Marshall 100 watt amp and 4 x 12" cabinet, a Vox AC30 combo and a WEM Copicat echo unit. Carr's touring drums consist of a Ludwig Super Classic kit with Paiste and Avedis cymbals, and custom bodhráns. O'Connor's stage tools are a Grimshaw custom solid electric mandolin, a Dan Armstrong-converted Victorian fiddle, and Wheatstone and Crabb concertinas.

June–July: Recording sessions at Rockfield Studios, Monmouth, with Fritz Fryer.

July 5: *Buxton '74 Festival*, Derbyshire, sharing the Friday bill with Man, Lindisfarne and headliners Mott The Hoople.

July 8: 'King Of The Fairies' (MOO 6) is released as a single in Ireland, and will spend five weeks on the chart, peaking at No. 7. 'Phil The Fluter's Rag' is on the B-side.

A July–August Irish tour is interrupted by the band's slot at the *Santa Monica Festival* in Italy on July 28, where they share the line-up with Alvin Lee's Ten Years After and The Strawbs.

August 9: A UK single from the band's upcoming album, 'Nighttown Boy' / 'We Bring The Summer With Us' (RCA Victor 2452), becomes a popular 'Powerplay' on Radio Luxembourg.

September: A tour of Germany, including support dates with Nazareth. In 2004, Barry Devlin will recall the tour in a radio interview with Francie Quinn …

'Nazareth were hard Glaswegians and you wouldn't want to upset them, but they were actually the nicest guys we ever toured with. Their bass player Pete Agnew and I were in a nightclub after a gig in Germany, and he explained to me the ins and outs of contract law. He said, "I'll tell ye what a contract is, Barry. A contract is when you've been on stage for 15 minutes and the money's in your shoe".'

Devlin: Germany has a very easy circuit for rock bands to play; it's probably easier than Britain. And they loved us because we played this odd traditional music and were hairy. So we went over there often.

The ladies were of a different breed compared to those who came to see us in Ireland. They were so incredibly upfront about extending international relations, but we never knew what they were saying, so who knows what was going on in their minds? Maybe they wanted to cook us a meal or wash our smalls. But perhaps some of us had an idea of what was really on offer.

O'Connor: It was a brand new country for us, so it all seemed very fresh and exciting. The language barrier was obvious from day one, and it was hilarious watching the road crew struggle as they asked for directions, speaking English in a daft, fake German accent. We ended up touring in Germany several times, and as it became more familiar, we found ourselves going into 'German mode'.

In England, we were seen as a college touring band, and it was hard work but fun. Germany, on the other hand, was very rewarding. The audiences were less reserved. It lacked rock'n'roll sparkle sometimes, and that surprised me, because we expected the country to be a lot more rock-orientated. The attitude towards

Fun and games
on tour in Europe.

getting everything just right and in its place seemed to be of utmost importance, and that could appear slightly sterile at times. Despite the squeaky cleanliness, however, there were always surprises.

I was in a bar in Tuttlingen, having just played another great gig, and the barman said there was a girl who would like to see me. He said, 'Her name is Petra and she will be along in five minutes.' So in she walked: a very well-figured, beautiful woman in a billowing blouse and tight leather trousers.

'Hello, I saw you on stage,' she said, looking me up and down with a hungry look in her eyes. It's important to note that I had been wearing high heels and effeminate stage garb, so I might have looked a little gay. Petra continued, 'When I told my teacher that I was a lesbian, she said I should not admit to this until I have checked out a man, and so I have chosen you.'

This may not have happened in England. In Germany, a different set of rules applied and the people were very matter of fact about everything – 'First we will go to the gig, then we will smoke some hash, then have some drinks, then we will have some nookie before going to a nightclub.' It had to be laid out like an itinerary.

I had a feeling about how this night would progress.

I was sharing rooms with Barry then and tried to get him out, but he wasn't playing ball, so Petra and I went out on a late night tour of building sites, ending up at the local railway station; we found a train parked up on the line and proceeded to climb onboard and occupy the back seat of the end carriage, giving it what-ho. Big time. She was a very game lass, and we lost all track of time.

We were right in the middle of doing whatever we could in the name of international relations when, suddenly, the train starts pulling out of the station. It was 7.30am and all the commuters were lined up along the platform. 'What the fuck was that? Holy fuck, the train's moving … oh my God!'

Trousers were briskly fastened and we jumped out of the train as it moved, thankfully, at about 4mph. That was the last I saw of Petra.

Our deals were always for two albums with options to continue if it suited the label. I always set the subsequent advance at quite a high level, which worked to protect the band, because the last thing we wanted was to be with a label who didn't want to put any effort into marketing a third album if they had been disappointed with the first two. Atlantic wouldn't have wanted to exercise an option under those terms, so we broke free.

But *Happy To Meet* and *The Táin* had done quite well in the UK, and this encouraged RCA to extend our deal internationally after we left Atlantic. By then, the label had become a little more fashionable. On a trip to New York, I met RCA's president, Ken Glancey, and he convinced me that his company really wanted Horslips onboard, so the deal went ahead and we released *Dancehall Sweethearts* with them.

Devlin: We felt that *The Táin* had a very monochrome sound, that was emphasised by the cover artwork. We wanted to add colour to our next offering, which is where Fritz came in. I loved working with Fritz; he was a lovely guy. But he walked into a room full of fellas who were already fairly set in their ways, when what we really needed was someone to kick the shite out of us. Overall though, I think he did well.

September 27: With Fritz Fryer onboard as producer to influence a more commercial approach – assisted by engineers George Sloan and Paul Watkins – Horslips' third album, *Dancehall Sweethearts* (MOO 7), is released. Still on their own Oats label at home in Ireland, the album is the band's first to be released internationally as part of a new deal with RCA Victor. It marks the beginning of the previously elusive crossover into the American market.

Deeny: It was unfortunate that *The Táin* didn't sell enough for Atlantic to renew our contract. When you sign a deal, the contract usually contains options that are biased in favour of the label. But if the artist has good management, it should cost the record company more and more to exercise each option. They would only tend to do that anyway if the artist has been successful.

***Dancehall Sweethearts* maintains the conceptual approach introduced on *The Táin*, with songs documenting the story and travels of the 17th-century blind harper and composer Turlough O'Carolan (Toirdhealbhach Ó Cearbhalláin).**

Born in 1670 (d. 1738) near Nobber, County Meath, O'Carolan was one of the last Irish harper composers and a significant number of his 'planxties' (tunes) survive in single-line melody. Although possessing well-honed skills as a harp player, it was O'Carolan's gift for composition

and verse, not to mention his travels across Ireland, that brought him lasting fame. It was around the age of 18 – after O'Carolan contracted smallpox and lost his sight – that he started on his journeys.

Dancehall Sweethearts is also notable for its inclusion of brass instruments – a first for the band and a move that Fryer encourages.

Fryer: Horslips understood the need to be commercial but in doing so I don't think they ever lost their integrity. There was a confidence in the band that gave them more of a sense of musical adventure, and that seemed to reach a peak when we made *Dancehall Sweethearts*.

Most of my work had been album stuff rather than commercial pop single productions, although I always retained a commercial sensibility. In my time I've covered pretty much every style from Stephane Grappelli to Motörhead. So few ideas ever really shocked me, and when it was suggested to add a brass section to Irish folk-rock music, it didn't exactly grate.

They were very intelligent guys, and they knew that everything was a transition to something else. I think that *Dancehall Sweethearts* was seen as a vehicle for broadening Horslips' appeal, and they all seemed to embrace the commercial possibilities, and went for it. I was probably very guilty of encouraging them to do that.

Just prior to these sessions, I'd worked with composer/producer/arranger Ray Russell and I asked him to write the brass arrangements and bring in his regular session players, Harry Beckett and Henry Lowther.

Lockhart: I don't think those brass parts worked in the way we thought they would. I think the 'lurch' was wrong. If you give most jazzers a straight piece to play they'll automatically dot it, but what we needed on 'Nighttown Boy' was for them to play it exactly as it was written out.

Located in Monmouth, Wales, Rockfield Studios is a choice made by the band's new producer.

Fryer: I had been producing the Roy Young Band at Rockfield. Being in a very rural environment, without the distractions of London, it meant that everyone was very focused and got on with it. I started to sharpen up my engineering skills there, working alongside George Sloan, and it ended up being my studio of choice. Rockfield was ideal for the Irish musicians I would later work with – like Donal Lunny, The Bothy Band and Clannad – because it was a convenient journey away from the Fishguard port, so when the Horslips gig came up, everyone agreed it was the perfect studio.

Carr: The studio we used at Rockfield was the 24-track in the renovated stables, where Dave Edmunds had recorded 'I Hear You Knocking'. The success of

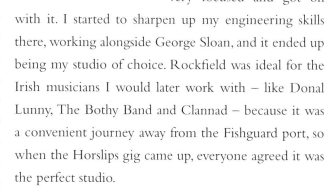

"Horslips understood the need to be commercial, but they never lost integrity ..."

Laid back at Rockfield Studios, summer 1974.

that recording was the bedrock upon which the rest of Rockfield Studios was built.

Fryer: When we convened in Monmouth in the summer of '74, they brought in a stack of songs that had mostly been written on tour, and the thing I remember was that the sessions clashed with the World Cup, so the TV was often switched on between takes! I loved working with the Irish as a rule anyway, because of their passion, and I have so many fond memories of my time with Horslips.

Fean: We weren't afraid of pursuing the concept idea after *The Táin*, and although *Dancehall Sweethearts* wasn't conceptually as strong, it reached a slightly wider audience because it was more commercially accessible.

Carr: *Dancehall Sweethearts* was something of a road album. There were parallels to be drawn between the rock'n'roll lifestyle that we were leading and someone like the womanising Carolan, who'd collapse drunk into bog holes. We used to laugh and say, 'If he could see us now!' So on that album, it was easier to just rattle off a set of tunes.

To follow *The Táin* with an equally conceptual album might have led to a narrow view of what we were about. We didn't want to be seen doing the same thing twice, so if some of the songs suggested using brass, strings or a choir, then this was seen as an opportunity.

The album title itself was a pun. I mean, the photo on the album sleeve showed us looking pretty sick and weary, and the idea of describing ourselves as dancehall sweethearts was a laugh in itself. It could've been a drawing of a dead, blind Irish harper on the cover, but RCA in England were already getting nervous!

Lockhart: Record companies don't understand bands most of the time. They don't exist to understand music – they run a business – and Horslips was just one of many bands caught up in that system. Once you appreciate that this is a given, you'll have a much happier life.

It wasn't ever the case that we gradually drifted into being a rock band. We were constantly experimenting and considered ourselves to be mainstream, but with Irish influences that were sometimes more upfront. *Dancehall Sweethearts* may have started with the O'Carolan theme, but we curbed its dominance. Motifs ebbed and flowed, and 'Nighttown Boy' demonstrated our aim to become more ballsy.

Fritz wasn't trying to drag us into a sonic area that we didn't think was suitable. It was quite the reverse. We overruled him on occasion if we felt strongly about some elements. In some instances we probably overloaded the arrangements, and Fritz didn't want that because it would complicate his mix. So I point the finger inwardly.

Dancehall Sweethearts' sleeve notes include the now-famous line, 'These tracks have traditional airs concealed about their persons'. Those elements include: 'Follow Me Up To Carlow' ('Sunburst'), 'How Much Has She Got' ('Mad Pat'), 'Fhir a' Bháta' ('The Blind Can't Lead The Blind'), 'Thugamar Féin an Samhradh Linn' ('We Bring The Summer With Us'), 'Saint Anne's Polka' ('The Best Years Of My Life') and 'Bill Harte's Favourite' ('Nighttown Boy').

Lockhart: The singers on 'The Blind Can't Lead The Blind' were from a choir called Cantairí Óga Átha Cliath (The Young Dublin Singers), and they were shipped over with their choirmaster. They were such a lovely bunch to work with. I wrote a special arrangement of 'Fhir a' Bháta' ('The Boatman'), a 19th century Scots Gaelic song written by Sìne NicFhionnlaigh, and the girls did well.

Eamon's lyric for 'The Blind Can't Lead The Blind' – *'Well you can move to Boston / Take a job in a small hotel / But that won't be the answer / You'll still hear St Patrick's Bell'* – starts out referencing O'Carolan and broadens out to a lyric about loss and leaving. Meanwhile, 'Fhir a' Bháta' is written from the viewpoint of a woman who is hoping her man will return when the boats come back ashore. The two different stories are happening simultaneously.

The album's masterpiece is arguably 'King Of The Fairies'. A live favourite to rival even 'Dearg Doom' in the hearts of many fans, it is a drastic reinterpretation of the age-old tune that Carr had performed with his school band. Featuring O'Connor's fiddle as the lead instrument, 'King Of The Fairies' also showcases Lockhart's tin whistle and Fean's under-acknowledged skills as a banjo player.

Carr: We worked on the arrangement for 'King Of The Fairies' in rehearsal at Unit Studio in Kings Cross, London, during the February. The bass drum is four-to-the-floor and with the snare I settled on something that had a piledriving feel, playing on the first beat of each bar instead of the [conventional] second. It was a million miles away from what was expected from 'folk-rock' at that time.

Fean: 'King Of The Fairies' was well known to most of us, because it was a popular tune that you'd learn in music lessons at school. Our idea was to place it in a rock format. It was a given that people would know the tune, in Ireland at least, and so we had a head start. Charles' fiddle part was a fairly straight reading of the original tune and I added the guitar solo and banjo section, but we experimented quite a bit with the beat and Jimmy's use of the Moog synth.

Lockhart: I used a Mini Moog on 'King Of The Fairies' and multitracked it because it was monophonic. That was a common technique. I never owned a synthesiser in the band, because back then you couldn't rely on them being in tune on stage. So we hired one for the whole duration at Rockfield, and it crops up here and there as a sweetener.

Fryer: I thought that 'King Of The Fairies' was a tremendous victory for contemporary folk music. All my acquired rock'n'roll skills as a producer were out in force to achieve the rawest possible sounds. For me, it remains one of the most powerful examples of Horslips' abilities to fuse musical genres.

'Nighttown Boy' is highlighted in John Peel's *Sounds* review ...

'The feeling once the record has finished, is that the boys are on the verge of doing something fine. It starts with strident electric guitar, slips into a modest glitter beat and then changes again in the twinkling of an eye into a more ambitious little thing, with overtones of Bowie/Ferry, et al.'

Carr: 'Nighttown Boy' was written between *The Táin* and June '74, during a hectic and exciting touring schedule. While not wishing to demystify the song in any way, I could at last celebrate being part of a curious demi-monde that had fascinated me for years, particularly since I began reading stories of The Beatles in Hamburg's Reeperbahn.

Around that time, it seemed that certain rock bands were writing directly about their lifestyle experiences. But there were other motifs swirling about. Thanks to Joyce, I had a convenient location, simultaneously Irish and international, in which to place the teenage rebel with his vigour and his braggadocio. I was attempting to reflect stuff I'd been witnessing first hand that seemed, to me, to have an air of desperation. The lyric was intended to be somewhat sinister, not altogether pleasant.

The imagery of bird flight is found in 'Sunburst' and will be a running theme in Carr's lyrics, from 'Dearg Doom' through to his 2008 book, 'The Origami Crow'.

Carr: Since Tara Telephone, I had been toying with what I considered to be mutant renga [linked verse in the Japanese style] in different syllabic patterns, neither haiku nor tanka, as a means of expression. There were a number of writers whose work made a powerful impression on me – Basho, Issa and also the little-known Tachibana Akemi.

We arrived for sessions in Rockfield with some material unfinished. I had found that the three-line verse concept fitted one of the emerging songs ['Sunburst']. The closest Japanese form would probably have been the folksy katauta. A series of linked images weren't sufficient to create a proper song structure, so Barry helpfully contributed a middle section. He also proposed the last triplet – *'You wait for me to take you / And make you a hunter like me / When we're flying free'* – which tidied the piece up by suggesting an ending.

'Blindman' had originally been written by Carr for *The Táin*.

Carr: Unsure of how best to tell the Táin story, I over wrote, and much of the stuff quickly became redundant as the narrative jigsaw pieces slotted together. 'Blindman' went into the live set almost as soon as it was written and remained there. The Blindman [in Yeats' 'The Death of Cú Chulainn'] had been in Maeve's tent and the 'Scarecrow', my pun on the Morrigan, was his Fool. The 'Late Late Show' verse was probably a device to briefly represent the present, but it may just have hinted at something dark.

To prepare for the recording sessions, Horslips rent a nearby farmhouse for their rehearsal base and temporary living quarters.

Tiffany Murray (pictured centre), who will later become Fritz Fryer's step-daughter, observes the band working at close range, and will base her novel 'Diamond Star Halo' (Portobello Books, 2011) on her childhood experiences in a musical environment.

Tiffany Murray: My mother, Joan, was trying to make ends meet. One morning she sat at the kitchen table and wrote an advertisement for *The Times*: 'Country house available. Rehearsal space for bands. No heavy rock.' Mum had tried foreign students, but they never paid. The next logical step must be moving us into the barn and renting out the house to rehearsing bands. This made sense to her.

Our barn wasn't some luxury conversion. This was the English/Welsh borderland of the mid-1970s. It was rats and wet walls, not the World of Interiors. That first night the room smelled of riverbanks. My bed was a mattress on the flag floor. It was so cold I wore clothes. Cleo, my Great Dane, slept with me, and my pet bantam clucked from a shoebox at the foot of my bed.

Mum hated the barn. She hated the rats and the fact that men who could quite easily sleep in the back of a tour bus were inside our glowing house, using her Egyptian cotton sheets. Men called 'roadies' had my attic bedroom: these men didn't sing, they carried things. I felt like Baby Bear. I wanted to point and yell, 'What's that hairy man doing in my bed?'

There was a rule: if I annoyed the bands I had to go away. The next lot arrived in a line of Mercedes with funny number plates. 'Irish,' Mum told me. When hairy men stepped out of the cars, she asked, 'You're not heavy rock, are you?' 'Ah no,' a man said. 'We're a little folk band.' The men laughed.

Horslips were Ireland's leading rock group of the time. They kept the windows open and the music loud. By the second week the police were knocking on our door. The combination of electric guitar and Irish number plates, just down the road from the SAS base, had alarmed the authorities, and Mum had to convince the police that these men were musicians, and in no way linked to the IRA. The evidence of guitars, amps and the sound of Horslips themselves didn't seem to be enough.

I liked Horslips. They were family men and they called me 'Tiff'. I loved to watch a man called Jimmy walk up and down along the high gallery, playing his flute. The day they arrived, a black-and-white dog trotted into our barn, cocked his leg and peed on Mum's onions. 'Who's sodding dog is that?' Mum screamed.

A man with Jesus sandals and a beard popped his head round our barn door. 'Sorry about that.' He was Horslips' producer, Fritz Fryer, though he wasn't German. Fritz was from a place called 'the north'. Fritz told me his real name was David, but because he'd worn a balaclava to school like a German, they'd called him Fritz and it had stuck.

Mum didn't like him; he had Horslips play loud electric guitar out on the lawn. I was also fascinated by his dog, which was in turn fascinated by my Great Dane. Mum had to turn the hose on that dog most mornings.

When Mum's boyfriend disappeared, it seemed the house would, too. Luckily, my mother's food was popular; she was asked to follow these bands, and we moved to the now legendary Rockfield Studios in Monmouth.

One night I woke with dreadful earache. Mum was washing up in the kitchen, but I could hear electric guitar. I tiptoed outside, towards it. I pushed the thick studio door, into a musty control room. Here the noise was so loud my ear roared; men with fantastic moustaches and beards sat on black sofas. It was Horslips.

A man at the mixing desk turned the sound down. It was Fritz Fryer. 'What's up?' he asked. 'My ear hurts.' That night I slept on an Irishman's lap. Heavy guitar and an Irishman's voice banished my earache. I knew I'd marry an Irishman, and years later I did.

A year later, Fritz moved in with us and became my father. Fritz taught me how to swim, fish, ride a bike and make a proper fire. Fritz taught me how to coil a microphone lead and when he played in the local pubs, I was his roadie, aged nine. He would try to teach me guitar, but he'd have more success teaching me about music and the bands he produced: Horslips, The Bothy Band, Smile and Motörhead.

I now see that house, filled for two summers with half-naked male musicians that my mother fed, was a houseful of different fathers. I still can't believe our luck that we found Fritz.

Fryer: After we'd finished at Rockfield, I mixed the album at Kingsway Recorders in London. I was satisfied with the result – as a third album it demonstrated that Horslips were a very well-rounded band.

Fean: The 'Mr. Togog' credited on *Dancehall Sweethearts* was Ger Tuohy, an old friend of mine from Limerick who was a driver for us in Ireland, the UK and Europe between 1974 and '76. He also helped out when we were recording at Rockfield. He was a great one for keeping our spirits up, because he always seemed to be in good humour.

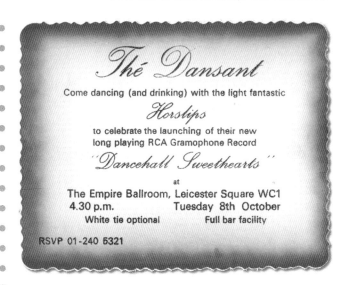

October 3–November 10: UK & Ireland tour.

October 8: RCA hosts a launch reception for *Dancehall Sweethearts* at the Empire Ballroom, Leicester Square, London WC1.

October 20: Top Hat, Spennymoor.

McGrath: I have a horrible memory of the Top Hat gig. Halfway through the set, Eamon suddenly vomited

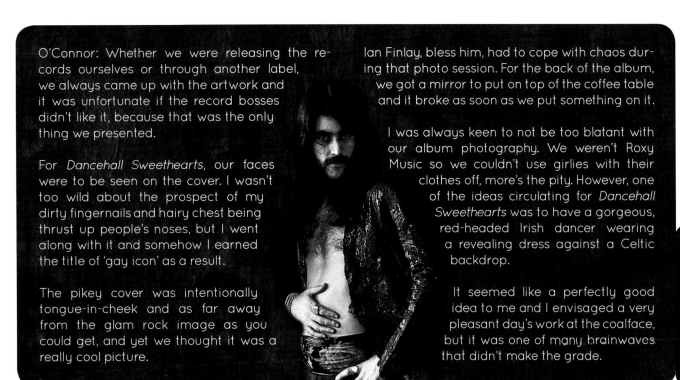

O'Connor: Whether we were releasing the records ourselves or through another label, we always came up with the artwork and it was unfortunate if the record bosses didn't like it, because that was the only thing we presented.

For *Dancehall Sweethearts*, our faces were to be seen on the cover. I wasn't too wild about the prospect of my dirty fingernails and hairy chest being thrust up people's noses, but I went along with it and somehow I earned the title of 'gay icon' as a result.

The pikey cover was intentionally tongue-in-cheek and as far away from the glam rock image as you could get, and yet we thought it was a really cool picture.

Ian Finlay, bless him, had to cope with chaos during that photo session. For the back of the album, we got a mirror to put on top of the coffee table and it broke as soon as we put something on it.

I was always keen to not be too blatant with our album photography. We weren't Roxy Music so we couldn't use girlies with their clothes off, more's the pity. However, one of the ideas circulating for *Dancehall Sweethearts* was to have a gorgeous, red-headed Irish dancer wearing a revealing dress against a Celtic backdrop.

It seemed like a perfectly good idea to me and I envisaged a very pleasant day's work at the coalface, but it was one of many brainwaves that didn't make the grade.

sleeve notes

all over his drum kit and had to be taken off stage. He might have eaten a dodgy Chinese meal earlier and it didn't agree with him. So, being a drummer myself and knowing the material like the back of my hand, I was able to fill in for Eamon. However, I hadn't realised just how much he'd puked. Every time I hit the snare drum or the hi-hat or a tom, I got a splashback of sick on my face, shirt and up my arm!

November 4: Horslips are at the BBC's Maida Vale Studios to record both a 'Top Gear' session for Radio 1 (aired on November 19) and a 20-minute soundtrack that includes 'Oisín's Tune', a later version of which will be released as the B-side of 'Daybreak' in 1976. The music is featured in an hour-long radio drama, 'The Great Debate', produced by Paul Muldoon and funded by RTÉ and the BBC. Described by Muldoon as 'a souped-up version of "Agallamh na Seanórach", it examines the Christianity-induced changes in Ireland through the beliefs of St Patrick and Oisín, as played by actors Patrick Magee and Norman Rodway.

November 9: Rainbow Theatre, Finsbury Park, London – supported by Ducks Deluxe & Gary Farr. Although unfounded, it is later reported that a camera team was present to film Horslips' 'most successful English concert to date' for US television. The *NME* is present to witness a classic performance …

'When Horslips came on stage, oo-ee-oo, the Rainbow's roof nearly lifted off. Horslips have a following whose devotion is obvious; absolutely riotous applause after each number, the kind that normally happens after the end of a show, and knowledgeable attention while they're playing. I was in the presence of a phe-

nomenon – one I'd been unaware existed. 'King Of The Fairies' was one of the numbers that received a deafening applause that drowned out the intro to the next title. Hell, the entire set had the audience frothing at the mouth.'

For many Anglo-Irish musicians living in north London, the Rainbow '74 gig proves to be an inspirational catalyst.

Philip Chevron (The Pogues & The Radiators From Space): I know Shane McGowan was a Horslips fan, and so was Johnny Rotten, and that whole generation of London/Irish musicians who grew up as that sort of one step removed. For pretty much that whole generation, Horslips offered the possibility that there were ways of playing Irish music that were different from the way they were prescribed, and that reached as far as America and Canada and certainly England.

Carr: As we were now touring in England fairly regularly, it became apparent that we needed a handy base in London, so we found some short-lease properties in Chesham Street, in the middle of embassy land in Belgravia. I lost count of the mad nights we had and how many guests came to crash.

The Laune's Arms was our little pub and the local was The Antelope, opposite Lord Lucan's house. We were there in November 1974 when Lord Lucan disappeared. It may even have been the night we played the Rainbow.

One Sunday lunchtime, I popped out to buy the newspapers on Sloane Square. When I opened the front door, a young guy was looking at the doorbells in a suspicious manner. A family saloon car was outside, with a baby seat in the back and a middle-aged man in the driving seat who looked like a detective. I freaked, because God only knows what was going on in the house the previous night.

So I delayed my return, peeping around the corner as I got near the house. The car had disappeared. I came in and said, 'The law have been checking us out.' Everyone thought I was being paranoid, but at seven o'clock the next morning there were 14 armed police officers and dogs in the fuckin' house.

Everybody raced out of bed and went down to the kitchen. We were treated politely, but at the same time there was no mistaking how serious this was. They demanded to see passports and driving licences, and we tried to explain that we were a band. We were asked what we were doing on a particular night, and I kept a diary so I could tell them exactly what we were doing. A policeman accompanied me to fetch it. I found the page and took a deep breath. 'We were in Portlaoise.'

Of course, Portlaoise is a notorious prison in Ireland where many IRA prisoners were housed, so I had to emphasise that we weren't there, but at St Mary's Hall, Portlaoise. 'We were gigging, you can check!' Anyway, we had some albums with us, so we could prove who we were, and everything cooled down.

The rozzers told us we'd been under observation for the last five days, as part of their investigations of the Guildford bombings that October. There had been two identikit photos published in the *News Of The World*, and these two villains with black hair and moustaches didn't look too dissimilar to Robbie McGrath and Martin Mulligan. One of the fuckin' neighbours had decided it was them, and told the police.

McGrath: It turned out that Special Branch had spotted our truck in the vicinity of Guildford, which was quite probably as we'd done a gig at the University of Surrey around then. They ran our number plate through their system, and landed on our doorstep. We got the impression that they were just out to point the finger at anyone who was in the wrong place at the wrong time.

Carr: Between the autumns of 1974 and 1975, it got particularly nasty in England. I heard the explosion of the Green Park tube station bomb that killed a young guy, and the Birmingham pub bombings and the Balcombe Street Siege were also around that time.

If it's at all possible that anything good came out of those troubled times, it was that anger and frustration could be channelled into music. Irish bands like Stiff Little Fingers and The Undertones were formed by young people who had grown up through the constant

"The next morning there were 14 armed police officers and dogs in the house ..."

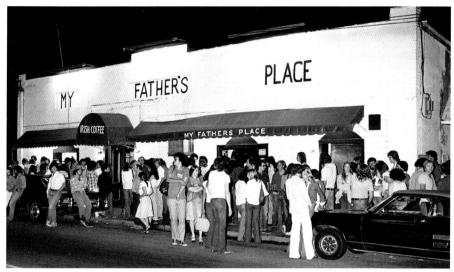

threat of violence, and that had an effect on what they wrote. It was punk in the purest sense. Not necessarily always lyrically, but certainly in the way the music was performed, loaded with intent.

November 11: Horslips leave Ireland to begin a four-week Canadian tour, during which they play in Newfoundland with disco icon Sylvester. Eamon Carr and Jim Lockhart are also guests on Canada's popular rock music TV show 'Boogie'.

Carr: Whenever we weren't gigging, we would do anything we could to promote the band in Canada and the States, and that often meant doing radio and TV. But because there were so many stations across a vast distance, we would implement a 'divide and conquer' strategy, meaning that two or three of us would do an interview with one station while the others did another, several hundred miles away.

On this particular day, Jim and I agreed to appear on 'Boogie', this general music and chat show, and allowed ourselves to be interviewed by someone who obviously hadn't done any research. 'So you guys play Gothic Soul, huh?' he asked us. Jimmy and I looked at each other and decided in that moment to just go along with this guy, who probably felt a little silly by the end of it when, off camera, we whispered, 'It's Celtic Rock actually.'

December 10: The tour moves across the border, and Horslips make their US début at My Father's Place, Roslyn, New York. Owned and run by Michael 'Eppy' Epstein, the venue is known by its regular local audience as the 'cultural capital' of Long Island.

O'Connor: We couldn't wait to get over to the States. My Father's Place was a good rock'n'roll venue and we made some recordings there that have ended up as bonus tracks on our CD reissues. Things had started rolling after we did some press in New York, which helped pave the way for our subsequent dates there towards the end of '74.

Because what we were marketing was so different, some of the Americans couldn't work us out, but it was no more of a struggle than reggae had to deal with. Fortunately, the Irish community went bonkers for us and it became contagious, filtering through the college network.

December 21: Horslips are included in several end-of-year music polls. Colin Irwin of *Melody Maker* includes *The Táin* amongst his favourite six albums of 1974. In the same week, *Sounds* magazine's Robin Katz features *The Táin* in her Top 10 Best Albums selection.

SALUTING THE ROAD WARRIORS!

HORSLIPS
CREW
PAST AND
PRESENT

Robbie McGrath

Peter Clarke

Pat Maguire

Kevin Dietrich

Steve Iredale

Paul Verner

Bob DeJessa

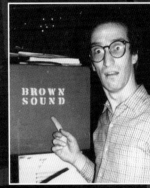

Barry Mead

Alan McKenzie

Sue 'Duchess' Iredale

Liam McCarthy

John Willis

Not pictured:
Joe O'Neill, Mick Reilly, Gregory 'Ashtar From Mars' Brown, Ger Tuohy,
Martin Mulligan, Finbarr Quinn, Billy Louth, Maurice Linnane,
Gerry Brady, John Heffernan, Chris Somers, Ciara Davey and Mary McCarthy.

Horslips on the set of RTÉ's 'Aimen High', March 1 1975.

January 24: RCA releases 'King Of The Fairies' / 'Sunburst' (RCA Victor 2505) as a UK single.

March 1: Horslips appear on RTÉ's pop music TV show, 'Aimen High', presented by Aimen Cannon and produced by Ian McGarry.

April 1-21: After completing new recording sessions with Fritz Fryer, the band embark on a new Irish tour.

April 11: Written largely while secluded in a rented cottage in Puckane, County Tipperary, Horslips' fourth album, *The Unfortunate Cup Of Tea!* (MOO 8), is quickly released, once again produced by Fritz Fryer at

Rockfield Studios, whose facilities have now been upgraded to enable 24-track recording. Coming only seven months after the release of *Dancehall Sweethearts*, *The Unfortunate Cup Of Tea!* is recorded by five people burned out by constant touring and the psychological difficulties of coming to terms with yet another change of record label.

Fean: We didn't give ourselves enough time after the previous album to write new material and make a wise selection. *The Unfortunate Cup Of Tea!* was our attempt at a pop album, but it was made when we were at a low ebb. No one seemed particularly interested in making it and for the first time recording felt like a chore. It was just a collection of songs with one or two good moments, like 'The Snakes' Farewell

To The Emerald Isle', but generally I'd say it remains the least inspiring of all our albums.

We were in a college town in Nova Scotia in late 1974 when I wrote the basis for 'The Snakes' Farewell'. I was playing around with a melody that had been in my head for a few days, and it suggested a very different kind of arrangement to what we'd been doing.

There's a Latin influence on this track and perhaps Santana's music had some effect on the way I played the guitar part with the '52 Goldtop that I purchased in late '73, although Peter Green probably also had some influence, as did George Harrison on the choppy rhythm guitar track. It was quite a departure, not least because I had a firm idea of how the bass part should be, and Barry just told me to play it.

It was Eamon's idea to randomly call it 'The Snakes' Farewell To The Emerald Isle'. It's a humorous reference to the myth that St Patrick banished snakes from Ireland. He never did, of course; it's been said that the story is symbolic of driving out the old pagan ways.

Devlin: The album was lambasted by the critics, and there was good reason. But in revisiting it more recently, I found that there was actually some really interesting stuff going on. 'Turn Your Face To The Wall', 'Ring-A-Rosey', 'Everything Will Be Alright' [incorporating the tune 'The Trip To Durrow'] and 'Flirting In The Shadows' are nice songs played well. I can hear Bill Payne [Little Feat] influences in Jimmy's keyboard parts.

Lockhart: We'd usually take a fortnight off, rent a cottage and get the new songs written and rehearsed in advance of recording, so that we didn't waste expensive studio time. We ran a very tight operation, financially speaking, so the rule was to never leave it to the last minute to write new material. *The Unfortunate Cup Of Tea!* was the most obvious exception to this rule, and what the album really lacked was road-testing prior to the recording. I can't think of a single song from that album that was played live before we went to Rockfield.

Jim Lockhart and Fritz Fryer in the Rockfield control room.

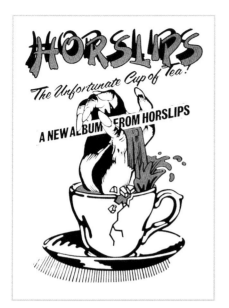

Devlin: We were too stressed out. It was our most 'unfinished' effort and it certainly lacks the 'big song' that other albums had. Some of the tunes were to some extent doodles that needed more attention. It was probably frustrating to Fritz that he never had the time to impose a moral authority on the band. Given a different set of circumstances we could have made a seriously good record with him, because he knew his stuff, but we never got that opportunity.

Hindsight defines what is or isn't a good album, or perhaps sales, and we always did our best at the time. *The Unfortunate Cup Of Tea!* is the album that divides our fans. Some hate it, while others can't see what all the negative fuss is about.

Carr: The album played to a similar sense of the ridiculous and the haphazard principles of 'found art' as The Beatles' 'Being For The Benefit Of Mr Kite!' – complete with exclamation mark. It was a new, different challenge. Conceive, arrange, record and package an album in a tight time frame. The loose theme offered the possibility of a complex set of dramas or, at least, a reading of suggested dramas.

Introduced by a stern grand piano motif from Lockhart, the title track – a lift from O'Neill's collection – is a traditional reel known either by the same name or, in some parts, 'An Cupán Tae'.

O'Connor: That was our music hall melodrama, and it actually informed the cover design.

McGrath: I was forever 'Monster McGrath' after that. You could tell what religion I was with that bastard costume on!

Devlin: We imagined the couple abandoning their cup of tea for something more in-the-ear whispery and then ... eek, a monster!

Carr: It was very 'Victorian drawing room scandal meets silent movie via Spike Milligan'. The chatter and noises you hear on this and also 'High Volume Love' are us just having a laugh late one night – that's Jim as the husband and myself as the wife at the start of the song, believe it or not. We were worn out, make no mistake, but our humour was intact – as indeed it always was, even in the darkest of situations.

Devlin: The album was full of ironies, and a song like 'High Volume Love' was our own double entendre on turning up the volume – possibly to 11 – and Prince's exhortation to 'come on, baby, let's make some noise'. Every rock'n'roll cliché was thrown into that song. The lyrics were a sort of continuation of 'Nighttown Boy'.

It was around then that we were spending time in Berlin, where Romy

Haag, and Müller and Schultz had lots of pale girls – or guys, you didn't look too close – dancing in the shadows. It has overtones of fishnets and dungeons, except we were Catholic boys, so it didn't have any of the danger of a Stones track like 'Little T&A'.

Fryer: Jimmy Lockhart always had a knack of pulling the odd gem out of the bag, like his flute on 'The Snakes' Farewell' – the only track I can remember well, mainly for non-musical reasons.

There was an equipment problem at Rockfield. They'd just refurbished the studio and we lost a lot of level, so we had to re-record this track at around 7.00am, having worked all night against the odds. It had been raining all night and water was draining into gullies in the stud yard. Jimmy was recording his flute with the doors open and we could hear all this running water from his live microphone. It was so atmospheric, romantic even, and yet borne out of a cock-up – one of those typically magic moments that you could never plan.

I accepted that our relationship would have its natural span. I got the impression that they wanted to take the traditional elements of their music as far as they could, from album to album. Having seen the treadmill of their daily touring routine, I knew they were working so hard that it was knocking the spark out of them. They never had the chance to recover, either creatively or spiritually, to take a step back and see where they were going. On reflection, I think *The Unfortunate Cup Of Tea!* was aptly named.

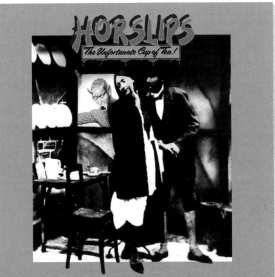

O'Connor: I used to collect 3D stereoscopic cards from all manner of sources in Ireland, and I later discovered that Brian May of Queen is also a massive collector. I had a series called something like 'Irish Villagers' or 'Scenes From An Irish Life', showing things like women knitting, and one of the cards depicted a lad courting a girl. There was a cup of tea on the table and an open window.

We decided, after succumbing to the effects of too much tea I would guess, to use this very folky image for the album … and it was all Eamon's idea. We used to rummage through the O'Neill book and look for daft titles of tunes.

'The Unfortunate Cup Of Tea' was one of the more wonderfully bizarre titles that we found, and it just stuck. While it was a great image, it still lacked something.

The front room window was dying to have something happening in it … like shoving a green monster through it from the other side by the band, maybe? That was my daft idea.

The two cottages we were renting in Puckane ahead of the sessions looked quite similar to the house in this stereoscopic card, and so we 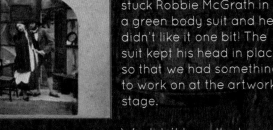 had a photo taken of us for the back cover. We stuck Robbie McGrath in a green body suit and he didn't like it one bit! The suit kept his head in place so that we had something to work on at the artwork stage.

We didn't have the luxury of Photoshop, but we did have Geoff Halpin, who ended up working for Hipgnosis. He was a master at this kind of thing and also came up with the lettering, while Tom Griffin drew the monster and cup illustrations.

sleeve notes

The author's interview with Fritz Fryer for this book was to be the producer's last. On September 2 2007 he would sadly lose his life to cancer.

Tiffany Murray: Fritz died a few precious months before his 63rd birthday. Both my mother and I were with him. I held his hand and whispered to him about Boggle, his dog. Like the best of fathers, Fritz led by example: he died without fear and without self-pity.

April 21: Horslips play the National Stadium, Dublin, which is re-opened after a £55,000 refurbishment programme. The show is filmed for the RTÉ TV series, 'On Stage At The Stadium'. Maurice Linnane, a 12-year-old fan who many years later will become Horslips' documentary maker, is in the audience.

Linnane: The Stadium was an absolute tip of a venue back then – nothing like the arenas we have today – but it came over well on television. None of that mattered to me. As soon as the band hit the stage, with the smoke, the flashing lights and all the excitement, the venue was transformed into this magical place. I was dizzy from the sheer energy of it all. It was the most extraordinary experience for me, and it would be a long time until I'd be so affected by a live show.

When I was growing up, the Irish music that made up the sonic landscape was a constant stream of drivel that only served as a reminder of boring, wet Sunday afternoons, and it was enough to make you break out in

a rash. Everything was about suffering and being second best. So when Horslips came along, it was our moment. People go on about 'Whiskey In The Jar', but it didn't hold a candle to the revolutionary sounds I heard on *Happy To Meet*. This band made me feel proud instead of pathetic.

May 3: At London's Imperial College, long-time fan Liz Bean (née Moorshead) meets her heroes.

Liz Bean: So what attracted an English girl to Horslips? Probably 'Arthur Of The Britons', a TV show starring Oliver Tobias that was aired when I was at an impressionable age and which portrayed Celtic leaders as rock stars. So what better to discover than a group of rock stars who portrayed themselves as Celtic leaders? When I bought a copy of *Happy To Meet*, a love affair for life was born.

As a geeky physics A-Level student, I was desperate to gain some culture cred by running a poetry society at my sixth form college, and one of our finest hours was managing to engage the services of Seamus Heaney to read for the apparently crippling fee of £12.

The charming Mr Heaney insisted that I should knock on the dressing room door at the next Horslips gig, and introduce myself face-to-face with his brother-in-law, Barry Devlin. Astonishingly, I did so at the Imperial College in May and filled my diary with my account of the evening, which included being invited, post-gig, to the band's Chesham Street haunt and learning that, really, all you need to get on with Barry is a bottle opener on your key ring when no other is to be found.

May–June: European tour.

July: A new Irish tour is memorable for a sinister experience at Carndonagh's Lilac Ballroom.

Devlin: 'The Republic of Donegal', as it's known, is geographically the most northern county in Ireland, but politically it's in the South. We often played the huge Lilac Ballroom in Cardonagh, which is right at the tip of the map. And there's a rule when you play ballrooms like that: if a fight breaks out, never look or draw attention to it, because everyone else will start looking or worse, get involved. So you look everywhere else and just carry on playing.

This night it was packed and the punters were having a great time, but then we suddenly noticed that everyone was lying down on the floor. We looked at the door and there were three men in balaclavas carrying semi-automatic rifles. You never knew in a situation like that if you were going to walk out of the place alive. They glared balefully around for a while, fired some shots into the ceiling and then they left.

Throughout all of this, we continued playing 'China Grove', and our only concession was that we couldn't get out of the middle eight. After the gunmen vanished, we kind of petered out, as the confused and alarmed audience began to rise to their feet and dust themselves down. There were sounds of pursuit from outside.

We took a short break and then returned to finish the night. Afterwards we discovered that these guys had come to rob the box office, probably thinking that with 2,500 people in the hall, there'd be a fair bit of cash to be had. But our crew chief Joe Wynne, had somehow been tipped off that this was going to happen, and had been going down to the box office every 10 minutes or so, taking the ticket money out to hide it.

There was nothing to steal and the gunmen got incredibly cross, ordering the box office staff outside. They got them to lie down and fired shots into the ground beside their heads. That's when they came into the ballroom and fired into the ceiling, in a fit of pique, I guess.

A moment of incredibly high comedy followed. Their car wouldn't start, so they pulled a courting couple out of their Cortina and took off into the night. What they didn't know was that the car had a flat tyre, and so they were forced to abandon it and went off on foot, only to be captured by the rozzers soon after. I can only imagine it was like something out of 'The Keystone Cops'.

Of course, we were nervous, but we took the view that we weren't going to be coerced out of the North, and so we continued to play. Charles plays it down, but he was the most affected by all of this.

O'Connor: I'd inherit a Dublin accent when I spoke, which might have sounded half-authentic because

Above: On tour in Germany, 1975.

my Teesside accent is slightly nasal. But if I was in the North, I tended to keep my mouth shut. You never knew who was eavesdropping. It's only looking back that I can see that we took a lot of risks, but I didn't think about it at the time.

July 13: While on tour in Germany, a new single, '(If That's What You Want) That's What You Get' / 'High Volume Love', from *The Unfortunate Cup Of Tea!*, is released in the UK (RCA Victor 2964).

McGrath: I still have some of my old tour itineraries and they are a scream to look at. They'd give the date and say 'Berlin', but very rarely would you get any more information. Phone numbers were considered heavy detail. You'd have to look for a poster that told us where our gig was, and I'd book the hotel straight out of the Michelin guide. I see guys nowadays complaining about their crew catering. They don't know they're born.

July 31: The Miami Showband massacre. Five members of the Dublin-based band are killed in the early hours as they travel home after performing at the Castle Ballroom in Banbridge, County Down. The tragedy sends shockwaves throughout the Irish touring fraternity.

Devlin: Although the North was hot and heavy, it didn't scare us too much until the Miami tragedy. Up until then, we all figured that musicians and bands, unless they were overtly political, were immune from sectarian violence, but it was now evident that they were going to shoot the piano player after all.

The band were travelling home to Dublin in their minibus after playing in the Castle Ballroom, when they were stopped just outside Newry by what they believed was a UDR [the British Army's Ulster Defence Regiment] patrol, because they were wearing genuine uniforms. As they were asked to step outside for ID checks, they noticed two of the soldiers carrying something that looked like a suitcase towards their vehicle, when suddenly it blew up and killed them, and also wounded Des McAlea, the sax player.

"The Miami massacre was like 9/11 for the Irish music world ..."

Above: Horslips on German broadcaster SWF's show 'Pop Shop', and (right) at a TV station in Halifax, Canada.

It transpired that this was a bogus checkpoint. Some of the soldiers weren't with the UDR after all, but were members of the UVF [the Ulster Volunteer Force, a loyalist paramilitary group], who after the explosion immediately opened fire on the band, killing three members – Brian McCoy, Fran O'Toole and Tony Geraghty.

Stephen Travers, who plays with Johnny these days, was seriously wounded by a dum-dum bullet, and he had the presence of mind to play dead. It ultimately saved his life. He says that he was about to be shot in the head when one of the soldiers said, 'Come on, don't bother, they're already dead.'

The RUC deduced that the bomb was intended to kill everyone on board the band's bus. The theory was that if the bus exploded on Republic soil, word would get around that 'the Fenians from the South' are now carrying bombs around. So all bets were off at that point, and fear struck the showband world for some time. In fact, some might argue that it never recovered, and that the Miami massacre was like 9/11 for the Irish music world.

Horslips had previously played the Castle Ballroom, and had a near miss on the way home. A Triumph 2.5 full of fellas came after us out of a side road, trying to overtake us for miles, but we all felt nervous about this and I decided to stay in front. We were rocketing along at 95mph and came into a place called Loughbrickland,

which then only had a single road running through the town, with a 30mph limit. Luckily, we met an Army patrol coming our way, and the fellas behind us quickly turned off up the hill.

We assumed that if they'd caught up with us, we'd have got a hiding, but they may have had other plans. A little later, they got the Miami Showband.

September 20: Horslips begin another short tour of Germany.

October 11: A date at Friars in Aylesbury, supporting Sailor, kicks off a brief UK visit.

Above: During a press reception at Trend Studios, Dublin, in October 1975, Mick Clerkin (front) of distributor Release Records hands a presentation disc to Barry Devlin and Eamon Carr to commemorate accumulated Irish sales of *Happy To Meet, Sorry To Part*. Back row L–R: Fred Meijer; unknown; Jackie Hayden, then with CBS Ireland (organiser of the event); Jim Slye; unknown; Caroline Erskine (the future Mrs Devlin); Evening Press folk music correspondent Gerard O'Grady.

Mid-October: Michael Deeny makes the difficult decision to abandon his role as manager.

Carr: Michael had been watching our sales curve take a gradual dive, and it must have been very soul-destroying for him after all the effort and dedication. There was a buzz on *The Táin* that we'd become big on an international scale. *Dancehall Sweethearts* didn't deliver on that. There was no hit single on it. The follow up made it worse. RCA in the US had absolutely no fuckin' interest in us whatsoever, but at the time they also had very little interest in Bowie, which says a lot about their intelligence.

We agreed to spend a little longer on the next album, and told Michael that we'd carry on gigging, using spare time to write some A1 material and make sure that the next album is a cracker. He said, 'Well, if you do that, you're going to still need a manager to look after you.'

Deeny: RCA weren't going to take up the third album option, so we were stuck. I'd had so much fun with Horslips, but in 1975 I got married, and my wife Maggie and I wanted to move to London. The chances of them attracting another major deal seemed slight, and I had run my course as their manager. In fact, I wanted to drop out of the music business altogether and concentrate on a new interest, screenwriting.

Although the end of the RCA deal dented Horslips' confidence, they didn't want to give up. At the very least, they could continue to make a good living on the Irish circuit, and Jim Slye, who had promoted some of our concerts and was the publisher of *New Spotlight*, took over their management. It was an amicable parting, and I was proud of the way they picked themselves up.

Carr: Jim came on as our manager with an important caveat: he would be Horslips' manager for Ireland, but not for Britain, Europe or America. Jim seemed happy with the arrangement. Part of our restructure strategy involved continuing to tour Ireland to help finance our next few albums.

October 28–November 9: The band visit Canada for a university tour.

Lockhart: While Jim Slye and our agent Arthur Walters were handling business in Ireland, outside the country we were looking after ourselves, and there was a period in which I was tour manager, taking care of per diems and day-to-day 'admin' stuff like that.

November 6: A festive-themed, acoustic album assembled in just four days at Trend Studios during September, *Drive The Cold Winter Away* (MOO 9) is released on the new Horslips Records label. Presenting a dressed-down Horslips bearing their purest folk influences, the album precedes MTV's fashionable 'Unplugged' series by 15 years.

O'Connor: We retreated to take stock and were in no-man's land for a while, falling back on our own resources and seriously re-evaluating our plans.

Carr: We had done our own releases in Ireland and we had the set up for it, so we thought we should avail ourselves of this opportunity. We'd always talked about doing a nice little acoustic album, so what was to stop us? There were a few seasonal songs and the idea was, 'Why don't we do a Spector? Why don't we do a Christmas album?' We had a lovely tune, 'Drive The Cold Winter Away', and named the album after it.

O'Connor: 'Drive The Cold Winter Away' was an odd choice for a song, and indeed the album title, because although it's a drinking song that I loved, it was Cromwellian – and Oliver Cromwell isn't the most-loved character in Irish history, thanks to his army's invasion in the 17th century.

We needed to make an album quickly, so Jimmy and I researched a pile of tunes together with a winter theme. I was keen to include some Northumbrian references on that album, such as 'The Snow That Melts The Soonest' and 'Thompson's'. The sessions were very refreshing, because we'd never worked that quickly and economically before.

Fean: The album was an opportunity for me to finally record with the gorgeous 1916 Gibson A2 mandolin I had acquired in 1973, just before we made *The Táin*.

Lockhart: It was an album we had talked about doing for a long time, but it wasn't the kind of thing we felt

"We refocused on the origins of what Horslips became in the beginning ..."

Five go mad in Niagara Falls, Ontario.

was an acceptable move in the first few years of our studio career, because we were focusing on the harder-edged stuff. So we all enjoyed the process of going back and rediscovering some of these old tunes that we had kind of earmarked. It was a side of Horslips that only a few people had actually heard.

Charles and I put the basic idea together within a couple of weeks, then presented everything to the band for their reaction and made the album in four days at Trend Studio, reuniting with our old eccentric Dutch engineer Fred Meijer.

Drive The Cold Winter Away probably saved our bacon at that point in time, because it earned us a

few quid and we approached it with a low cost, cottage-industry mentality. The album served a good purpose. It got us back to our roots and it was fun to make, but more than anything we bought some time for ourselves by putting it out, because we were already writing material for our next album.

Devlin: Interestingly, apart from a couple of numbers, we never made a feature of the *Drive The Cold Winter Away* album in our live shows at the time. That would take another 37 years! Revisiting the album for our Christmas gigs [at the Olympia Theatre in Dublin, December 2012] gave us immense pleasure and we were reminded of just how enjoyable that album was to make.

O'Connor: The image on the *Drive The Cold Winter Away* cover was an old engraving from a source book of Victorian pictures. Meanwhile, on the back, we had a montage of Sessiagh Lake where we rehearsed with a photograph I'd taken of the mountain in the background and the New York skyline planted on it.

We were represented by characters I found on old postcards. Johnny, Eamon and Barry were portrayed as dancing girls, Jim as a piper and myself as Mickey Mouse. I loved all that kitsch. That's why we had the ornamental shamrock garland framing the front cover. And the 'To' and 'From' on the back was a sweet little send-off.

I'm actually very fond of that cover and the album itself. I was forming ideas for the cover design in my head over our four days in the studio.

November 7–8: Memorial University, St John's, Newfoundland.

December: Irish tour. On the second date, at the Culdaff Arms, Culdaff, County Donegal, on the 6th, Pat Maguire joins the crew.

Maguire: I had been doing the driving for a lot of Arthur Walters' gigs, working with all kinds of top acts like Elton John, Eric Clapton and Fleetwood Mac, and been involved in the business right through the 'sixties, so I learned how shows work. Arthur was partnering with Jim Slye to book tours for Horslips, and it was by chance that I landed a full-time job with them.

The constant late hours and endless travelling had been getting on top of Robbie McGrath, Martin Mulligan and Paul Verner, and they needed a break, so they simply downed tools for a few days. Martin told me the next gig was in Culdaff, and so I organised a truck driver, loaded up the gear and found some locals to help with the humping when we arrived.

I stacked the PA, got the lights up on the bars, and had the backline on stage by the time the band walked in. They were shocked that I was able to do all this, but it's what I did ... and still do.

December 13: The band's National Stadium concert is filmed by RTÉ.

December 31: Red Island, Skerries, County Dublin – a New Year's Eve event that will be repeated for the next two years. In attendance is superfan and long-time friend of Horslips, Myles Lally who treasures his memories...

Lally: Being too young at the age of 14 to be let in officially, I climbed over the beer store wall, found an open window and climbed in. I then tried to look like I belonged in this Temple of Magic, and mingled with the hairies whilst trying my best to appear older as I prepared to witness a life-changing moment.

All the lights went out and everybody chanted 'Hor-slips, cha cha cha! Hor-slips, cha cha cha!' as they lurched forward in anticipation. With the opening strains of 'Mad Pat', magic was in the air and my heart was fit to burst. Red Island gave me a lifetime's worth of extraordinary nights to remember and New Year's Eve could never come quick enough for me.

CHAPTER 5
POWER AND GLORY

 February 6–7: During an Irish tour with Chris de Burgh supporting, producer Harold Burgon is hired to record Horslips at the Pavilion Cinema in Dún Laoghaire, using the same Rolling Stones Mobile that recorded *Happy To Meet, Sorry To Part.*

Shay Hennessy: It was wild. The place was packed to the rafters, both nights, and there was a huge reaction to the band. Charles' electrifying performance fascinated me – his fiddle was on fire. And Johnny sang like an angel.

February 28–March 27: A UK tour features a new set of Celtic stage backdrops, created at Ardmore Film Studios under Charles O'Connor's direction.

April 23: Midway through their second Irish tour of 1976, Horslips release the double album *Horslips Live* **(MOO 10), recorded at the Pavilion Cinema and mixed by Fred Meijer at Trend Studios.**

Devlin: I remember saying to [journalist] Harry Doherty that it's the only Horslips album I won't defend. If someone asked me to recommend one of our albums to a potential new Horslips fan, that would be bottom of the list. It sounds like our recording budget was a fiver. The truth is, when

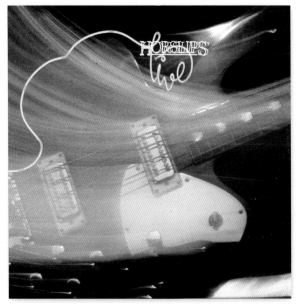

Above: *Horslips Live* producer Harold Burgon.

you're desperate to make some money to fuel running costs, as we were at that point, a live album is normally the default solution.

O'Connor: We generously referred to Harold as the album's producer in the sleeve notes, but it was hardly production with a capital 'P'. He wasn't doing a great deal more than simply capturing the performance on tape.

Lockhart: *Horslips Live* sounded pretty lo-fi and didn't capture the magic of our shows at the time. What I do think, however, is that it drew a bold line between two distinct phases in our career. It was like saying, 'That was the past; here's to the future.' And behind the scenes we were very much working towards our future with an exciting bunch of new material.

O'Connor: I'd designed the Shamrock bass for Barry and it seemed like a good idea to feature it on the cover of *Horslips Live* across the front and back of the gatefold.

We wanted some movement so Ian Finlay shot it at a slow speed as the bass was wiggled about from side to side, hence the out of focus, streamed effects. Geoff Halpin also designed the lettering for the album in the style of wires.

For the inner gatefold, we added some of Ian Finlay's live photography of us playing at the Pavilion Cinema in Dún Laoghaire where the album was recorded.

Also on April 23, 'Come Back Beatles' / 'The Fab Four-Four', a tribute single recorded by Horslips during sessions for *The Unfortunate Cup Of Tea!*, is released under the pseudonym Lipstick (below) by Polydor in the UK (2058 725), in the wake of the first major resurgence of interest in The Beatles' catalogue since their 1970 break-up.

McGrath: At the end of the last Rockfield sessions, the guys fancied a go at a tribute song that had been brewing on tour in Amsterdam. Jim had [another] minor car accident around then and it was a bit of a shocker, but he did eventually come down to the studio. Then Charles left early to go on holiday, so he wasn't there when 'Come Back Beatles' was being finished. They all played on it, but it was done in piecemeal fashion because they weren't all at the studio at the same time.

Fean: My favourite song of all time is 'Eleanor Rigby', and this was our way of saying thanks for the music and happy times The Beatles gave us. We did it with Fritz in the smaller of the two Rockfield studios. Barry and I did most of the vocals, and I played a white Fender Stratocaster through a Vox AC30, both of which belonged to the studio. Harrison had used a Strat on 'Day Tripper', and I wanted to get close to his sound.

Carr: The song was in the same tradition of all those early tribute records by Dora Bryan and The Vernon

Girls during the first flushes of Beatlemania. It was a labour of love. I'm assuming that Barry and I were largely responsible for the lyrics. Of course, this couldn't go under the Horslips moniker – 'Lipstick' may well have been the first word that any of us thought of. And Robbie McGrath was in the photos as an honorary, non-playing member.

We took the track to lots of record companies, who ran us from their offices saying The Beatles were old hat, last year's thing, and that the record-buying kids were now more interested in the Rollers. It was another bright idea rubbished at the altar of commercial reality. Or so we thought.

Months later, EMI re-released all of the original Beatles singles on the same day, and most of them charted. In offices all over London, people remembered the unlikely Irish pop group who'd been touting a song about The Fabs. Offers poured in. Being stubborn, we delighted in telling them all that we'd moved on.

We hadn't approached Polydor, but they rang and didn't flinch when we said it was to be a one-off single by a band called Lipstick. The single was released, and the arbiters of taste in Britain at the time – the playlist panel at the BBC – were split on its merit. Sadly, it didn't make the A playlist, but it was fun while it lasted.

Devlin: I'd always wanted to write a song that incorporated all the big riffs, so I loved doing that single. It's no secret that we're all Beatles fans and were very influenced by them. I think that was quite evident on some of our more acoustic-style songs. I adored them. Every album we recorded had a Beatlesque ditty, like 'The Rocks Remain' and 'Stowaway', with their

suspended D chords, straight from 'You've Got To Hide Your Love Away'.

McCartney was such a hero of mine; he's the Bach of Bass. I loved all those rolls and rumbles he did, and like every member of The Beatles, he knew exactly what to do for a song. What made him play those incredible notes and runs on 'Something', for example? It's the stuff that no one can teach you. 'The Rocks Remain' [working title: 'Mother Of Pearl'] is certainly an example of me taking a leaf from Macca's book, where I play his trademark octave zooms up the neck. But the bass player I've probably admired most is Glenn Cornick from the early Jethro Tull line-up, who never failed me.

On the evening of April 23, Marianne Ashcroft is at the Culdaff Arms to review Horslips' gig for Wessex News, Southampton University's student newspaper. She writes:

'The set included a 25-minute preview of a forthcoming concept album. Horslips fans will probably be pleased to know that the new material marks a return to the *Táin* period that we know and love.

'I met Barry Devlin in the hotel foyer. "Come up to the superstar suite," he said, and showed me into a dingy bedroom strewn with the band's gear. He described a recent gig where many kids were walking home in pouring rain; the group had run a shuttle service and got most of them home safely. To prove his point, Barry drove a friend and myself home after the gig, a round trip of some 10 miles, giving lifts on the way to as many as could be crammed in his big white Range Rover.'

Overleaf: Scenes from Horslips' appearances in 'John Molloy's Dublin'.

Mid-May: A brief tour of Germany includes a show at the Rabensaal in Laupheim and further dates in Nürnberg, Coburg, Stuttgart and at Berlin's Deutschlandhalle, where Horslips share the bill with Rory Gallagher at an indoor festival.

Fean: I never got to meet Rory properly until we played in Berlin. It was a great thrill to be in the company of such an amazingly talented guitarist, whom I'd admired for so long. After the gig, Rory suggested we hit the town and find a club that served good Guinness. We got on like a house on fire because we shared the same love of the blues and, along with the inevitable subject of guitars and our many common influences, that's what we talked about all night. We vowed to meet again, but that was the last I ever saw of him.

June 18–August 22: Irish tour.

July 16: 'John Molloy's Dublin', the Irish entry at Montreux's *Golden Rose Festival*, is broadcast on RTÉ Television.

A combination of comedy sketches and mime by actor John Molloy, the programme features clips filmed during the previous August of Horslips performing 'The Snakes' Farewell To The Emerald Isle' (top) and 'The Unfortunate Cup Of

Tea' in the National Botanic Gardens, Glasnevin; and 'King Of The Fairies' (bottom) on the roof of the Bank Of Ireland HQ – a respectful nod to The Beatles' famous lunchtime concert on the roof of Apple Records.

July 19–21: Horslips rehearse new material in rented cottages in County Limerick.

Fean: We got a lot of arrangements sorted out in those few days for what was to become *The Book Of Invasions*, but it was hard work, because this was in the middle of a famously unprecedented heatwave – then the hottest on record – and we were constantly dripping with sweat!

July 22: The single 'Daybreak (Excerpt From A Celtic Symphony)' (MOO 11) is issued as a trailer for the forthcoming album. Recorded with engineer Pat Morley at Dublin Sound Studios, it peaks at No. 2 during a 22-week stay on the Irish chart, and is pipped to the top spot by Thin Lizzy's 'The Boys Are Back In Town'. The B-side is a version of 'Oisín's Tune' that has been recorded at Avondale Studios with Pat Gibbons.

August 1: Red Island, Skerries, Co. Dublin – the first live concert ever attended by David Evans, a.k.a. future U2 guitarist The Edge.

A promotional shoot for the 'Daybreak' single and forthcoming album, *The Book Of Invasions*.

The Edge: I was about 15, and although there were some kids at school who claimed to have seen a live rock band, it seemed too ridiculous a notion, because full-on rock concerts didn't happen in my world. But, out of the blue, a couple of friends of mine from Skerries told me they were going to see Horslips in Red Island, and invited me along. Now Horslips had been really big news over the last few years, so I jumped at the opportunity and had butterflies in my stomach all the way there on the train from Malahide, where I lived.

The band were incredible! I never imagined so much excitement could be generated by musicians. It was always great to hear the fiddle or the mandolin in a rock'n'roll context, it just adds great extra colour. And they were all great players. All of them are very self-effacing on that level, but when they played live they made an amazing sound.

I could hardly take my eyes away from Johnny Fean for most of the gig. He had this big Marshall rig and was playing a gorgeous Les Paul that was the kind of thing

I'd dreamt about. That first gig was pretty significant for me, because it helped me realise how badly I wanted to be in a band. It was only a month or two later that Larry Mullen put up the 'Musicians Wanted' that led to us forming what would become U2.

August 28: *Rock Circus Festival*, **Rottweil am Necker Stadium, Germany. Horslips appear with Rory Gallagher, Manfred Mann's Earth Band, Scorpions, Baker Gurvitz Army and Alberto Y Lost Trios Paranoias.**

September 2: Horslips perform at Queen Elizabeth Hall in London, during the *South Bank Music Fair 1976* **series of concerts. The band preview their magnum opus,** *The Book Of Invasions: A Celtic Symphony*, **which recounts the 12th-century chronicle of the mystical Tuatha Dé Danann's colonisation of pre-Christian Ireland.**

In a review of the show for the *NME*, titled 'Irish Magic (And Still No Contract!)', Angus McKinnon writes:

'The piece is musically complex … there are quiet, pastoral airs – Jim Lockhart's organ playing has a vaguely churchish feel about it – and full-blooded reels, either delivered straight or wound into the song's entrails. Horslips display an assured energy and abandon that's been found wanting in this field since Fairport disintegrated after 'Liege & Leaf' [sic]. Nonetheless, they're currently without an English recording contract – a poor state of affairs given the audience's reaction at this concert and their own, refreshingly intuitive eclecticism.'

O'Connor: The South Bank gig was a showcase for us, at a time when we needed a new UK label. It was also the first time we had fully previewed *The Book Of Invasions* as a set piece, complete with the backdrop, and we were going all out to exploit this 'breakthrough' opportunity as much as we could. The fibreglass hip-

pogryphs beside Eamon's drums were a good idea. They were based on illustrations found in the Book of Kells. They had lights installed in their mouths that pulsed brightly in time to some of the songs.

One of the people in the audience was Frank Neilson, an A&R guy for DJM Records, the label that would be key to the next stage in our career. We earned some good reviews, and made a good, lasting impression.

October 8–November 1: An Irish tour is punctuated by recording sessions at Dublin's Miracle Studios.

Devlin: Eamon's musical tastes have always been impeccable, and so his job before we set out on any tour was to compile all the mix tapes to play while we were travelling. His choices of black music were inspirational. Around the time we made *The Book Of Invasions*, we listened to a lot of Muscle Shoals stuff. Little Feat and particularly Lowell George also got our attention.

November 6–20: UK tour with support from Alfalpha and (at Nottingham University) the Bowles Brothers Band.

November 12: Recorded at Dublin's Miracle Studios, *The Book Of Invasions: A Celtic Symphony* (MOO 12) is released by Horslips Records. Alan O'Duffy makes a welcome return as producer and Robbie McGrath assists with the engineering.

Lockhart: *The Book Of Invasions* benefited from a much longer gestation period than the previous albums, because we weren't being pressured by a major label to get it finished. We were able to relax and enjoy some artistic freedom to let our ideas mature. We had all the material written, meticulously arranged and well sequenced before we started to record, and had been playing a lot of it on the road from early 1976.

The actual germ of *The Book Of Invasions* came together in the autumn of 1975, when a Canadian tour fell through. A local agent called Ron Boutilier was kind enough to arrange a tour of the Maritimes on the hop, but it took two weeks, so we just hung around Halifax, Nova Scotia, doing the odd gig whenever there was an opportunity. When Ron's alternative tour materialised, we took a sleeper train over to Montreal and a bit of creative magic happened.

It was on that journey that we played bilingual bingo, in French and English, with some old ladies, and conceived the notion of a Celtic Symphony, using three movements: geantraí (When Gods Walked The Earth), goltraí (The Pursuit Of Diarmuid and Gráinne) and suantraí (The Living End). We talked about the kind of tunes that would fit into this piece, and the feel of the music we should write, and the songs seemed to flow very quickly. When that came to fruition at Miracle Studios there was just something about the way everything slotted together so perfectly, and that was a really lovely bit of completion.

Fean: Our initial idea for *The Book Of Invasions* came about when Eamon began researching the old Irish legend of the Tuatha Dé Danann, and in 1975 he began writing some lyrics based around the story. We literally threw ourselves into the project.

Carr: While *The Táin* was the big saga of Irish

A 'comical' session at Miracle Studios.

mythology, *The Book Of Invasions* was about the genesis of the Irish race. We ran shy of it for a while, thinking, 'We couldn't do that, it's outrageous.' But that feeling gave way to, 'Aw, fuck it, let's try.' The three-movement idea was perfect for us; it was a symphony waiting to be written.

Devlin: We always responded well to having something big to aim for, and that was definitely the case with *The Book Of Invasions*. A big piece like that gives a band a common purpose. At the time there were no individual songwriters amongst us as such; we all tended to bounce ideas off each other. The unifying purpose tended to come from the scale of the writing. We were all capable of writing songs, and if we had a big well of songs to pull from, it would give cohesion to a project.

Getting Alan O'Duffy back was the cherry on the cake. He was a brilliant producer and engineer, and he was treated as very much a part of the team, a sixth Horslip in some ways. It was interesting that Alan produced both *The Táin* and *The Book Of Invasions*, both of which I think best reflected what we did.

Lockhart: It was in discussions with Alan that we started to once again value the diverse palette of musical textures that we had at our disposal. Anyone could have brass and string arrangements, but we had a lot more going for us internally. Where Alan was coming

"There was just something about the way everything slotted together so perfectly ..."

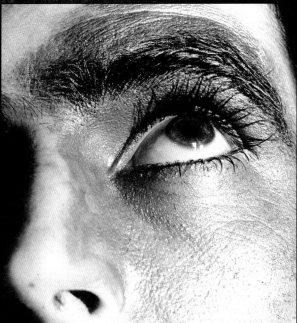

O'Connor: My idea for *The Book Of Invasions* cover was heavily inspired by one particular image called 'The Tears', the female subject of which looks like a silent film actress.

It was taken in the early thirties by the great avant-garde photographer and painter, Man Ray. I really liked the eye because it was looking up to Heaven and the stars, and I imagined a possible Celtic connection.

I emulated that image by asking Evelyn Lunny, a make-up artist at RTÉ and the sister of the famous Donal, to paint my eye silver and flatten my eyebrows for a photo session. I'd already had the idea to cover the cornea of my eye with a Celtic motif at the artwork stage and also to reverse the image for the inner sleeve. At the time I wanted to print the cover on chrome paper to give a silver effect, but it worked well without it.

When it came for Chris Ellis and I to work on the CD reissue, it looked as though we had an underlay of silver ink, but we didn't. The same effect as on the cover of *The Táin* was again present, and it was a happy accident.

On the back of the sleeve, Ian Finlay and I developed this idea of the band's swirling faces. The swirls were done manually with time exposure rather than adding an effect in the processing. We had to sit each member of the band on a chair, give them a 'three-two-one' countdown and get them to move their heads to the left or right on cue.

It took a while for them to relax into it and give us the right effect – Eamon looks particularly demonic – and in the end we had a really lovely set of pictures.

at musically was The Beach Boys and really getting the most from multitrack overdubbing.

Carr: When it came to figuring out how to approach the sound of *The Book Of Invasions*, we realised the best way forward would be to take a direct, logical step from where we were in *The Táin*, as opposed to veering off into any experimental stuff. We saw what we had, with linking passages and ambitions for counterpoints and harmonies, and the spread of instrumentation. And we recognised that Alan had a very good understanding of all that process, how we arrived at it and how it worked. So we were lucky to get Alan back.

O'Duffy: If I were an arrogant man I'd say they were wrong to change to a different producer after *The Táin*, as we had a track record of getting it right – we had a very good partnership in the studio – but I imagine they wanted to see how the rest of the world made records.

They had enormous confidence on *The Book Of Invasions*, much more than they had three years earlier. And Johnny's guitar playing had become so inventive. I particularly loved his tone and sensitivity on 'Fantasia', the instrumental version of 'My Lagan Love'. My father Michael would often sing that song on English radio back in the 'fifties so I felt a warm connection.

Fean: During a trip to London, I visited the music shops in Denmark Street to see if there were any interesting guitars on sale, and ended up buying my first Les Paul Junior, a 1960 model. The Junior features on the main riffs of 'Sword Of Light' and 'Trouble (With A Capital T)'. Everything else was played on the '52 Goldtop, including 'Fantasia', which was done with the front pick-up selected to get that very sweet sound.

Jim played 'My Lagan Love' to us on flute while we were writing the album. The idea was to use it as a repetitive theme to link some of the songs, but also to feature it as a main track, speeding up the tempo of what was usually performed as a slow air by so many artists. Like 'King Of The Fairies', it was a very well-known Irish song, and our challenge was to bring it into the modern rock context.

Lockhart's fanfare introduction is inspired by a film he recalls from his childhood.

Lockhart: I was watching the old film 'Mise Éire', and realised that the featured horn sound must have been at the back of my mind when we were writing *Invasions*, because I'd seen it as a kid. The idea was to have this very basic sound rising out of the mist and those first three notes of 'Daybreak' correspond exactly with the opening notes of the traditional tune 'Níl 'na lá'. The guy playing those notes on trumpet was Ray Moore, a session player that Alan hired and a close relative of Niall Moore from the Horslypse tribute band of recent times.

Left: Recording and arrangement notes.

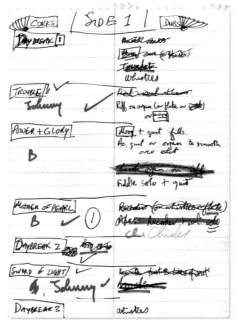

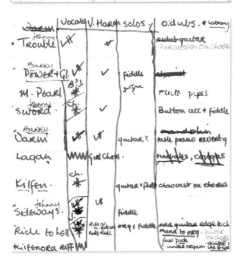

The quieter middle section of 'Daybreak', with the organ and tin whistle, is taken from the melody of a Galway lament called 'Anach Cuan', written about some villagers who set off from the shores of Lough Corrib and were drowned when their boat sank.

Carr: 'Sideways To The Sun' is a favourite of mine. The slow air 'Slán Cois Maigh' is the intro, and then the song follows its own path. In the two verses, as in the title, the 'voice' is of a race we only know from lore and legend, and through intuition. It's that of the inhabitants of another spiritual plane, a place where the normal rules of physics don't apply.

This was easy to visualise, because over the years the band had partly located itself in some quite remarkable landscapes by good fortune while rehearsing. Sessiagh Lake at Dunfanaghy in County Donegal; spooky Lough Gur near Hospital in east Limerick/west Tipperary; and a cottage at the bottom of Knocknarea in Sligo were just some of them. It was easy, even then, to imagine how the other world might view our treatment of the planet.

'Ride To Hell' is a fairytale that was written specifically to provide the album with an epilogue. As I speculated on the Tuatha's decision to go underground, or into a parallel universe or psychic realm, I automatically came to consider the many old folk tales that tell of strange occurrences and happenings at the fairy rath, usually after dark.

Every tribe, society and nation has its own fairy tales. There are plenty of stories of people being tempted to enter the fairy realm. Some came back. Others were lost forever. I wondered what it might be like to be propositioned in such a way. And who or what might offer such enticement? Usually it was the promise of a pot of gold, vast treasures or eternal youth that swayed the individual.

Fean: It was probably the most enjoyable record I'd done with the band so far. The great thing is that every song shines – there are no fillers – and in some ways it's like a 'greatest hits' all on its own. Having more time to work meant that I could concentrate on structuring my guitar parts better. I'm very satisfied with what we did. And the album includes 'Trouble (With A Capital T)', with the riff borrowed from the second part of 'Brian Boru's March', and 'Sword Of Light' which is written around 'Toss The Feathers'. They're still among my big moments live.

I remember playing the 'Trouble' riff to Eamon, and at first he thought it was something by Glenn Miller, probably because of the way I syncopated it. How it evolved was very similar to how 'Dearg Doom' came together in rehearsal. Both songs had these huge guitar riffs, and once Eamon heard me play the 'Trouble' intro in the context of the overall band arrangement he got really excited, and then Jim played the flute part in unison, making it sound more wholesome. When Eamon got excited about an idea it was always a good sign.

Carr: With 'Sword Of Light', we were on intimate terms with the concept of a light sabre more than a year before 'Star Wars' hit the cinemas! The Sword of Light [An Claidheamh Soluis] was engrained in Irish culture and had even featured on a postage stamp. You couldn't pass on something as vibrant and iconic as that.

Incorporating lines like 'I'm a stranger here myself' and 'only lovers left alive' [the title of a 1964 David Wallis novel, themed around generational suicide and social decline] was a fun trick, juxtaposing pop-culture references with detail from the old myths and often discovering that the same stories keep getting retold. There was also an attempt to convey a Bowie-esque whiff of alienation.

Lockhart: 'King Of Morning, Queen Of Day' is based on the 'Kilfenora' jig. It was simply going to be called 'King And Queen', but we switched titles when we got to the art-

work stage. The lyrics unashamedly borrowed from 'A Match' by Swinburne, the last stanza of which reads: *'If you were queen of pleasure / And I were king of pain / We'd hunt down love together / Pluck out his flying feather / And teach his feet a measure / And find his mouth a rein / If you were queen of pleasure / And I were king of pain.'* It's a steal, but a tasty one.

Fean: 'Warm Sweet Breath Of Love' probably got more radio play in the UK than anything else we had done to date. That helped enormously with album sales. You could never account for what worked in some territories and didn't work in others. In Germany, 'Dearg Doom' got the most airplay. We didn't fully appreciate that at the time, but it's obvious now – with the solid beat, to them it probably sounded like Celtic disco!

Devlin: With 'Warm Sweet Breath Of Love', I was trying to write a stylistic response to Thin Lizzy's 'Running Back' from *Jailbreak,* but the Beatle influences really poke through as well, and so it's an interesting blend that shows us at our most commercial.

Lockhart: When we all heard the playback of the completed album, we were all blown away because so many things gelled. We had experimented on previous albums, but while we were checking out possibilities outside of the norm, we realised during our fallow

You'll find him hard to recognise
we were wise oh so wise not given to lies or deceit
juggled secrets at our fingertips wore diamonds at our feet
we showed you ways to play old airs we said we could be friends
but when our backs were turned you got us in the end

THE POWER AND THE GLORY

Into the flash of lightning star-riders are hurled,
see them bumping and grinding bareback on the wheels of the world,
you can see the dawn a'coming or is that the flash of a spear,
ah, the day will come, the dawn will break. the day breaks here.

CHORUS

We've got the power and the glory, we're going to take it from here
you're young enough to take it you can make it or break it; join us
you've nothing to fear; " 2. " " "
People say we've got the power, the phrase I think is heart's and mind's,
Never mind where we come from, we've left our history books behind.
Not so much teachers as fighters, and what we teach is how to fight;
and we're gonna ring the changes, we're gonna ring it right.

CHORUS REPEAT.

with your face to the wind you're
beginning to think of a new life
and you pull tight your cloak
round your throat and the wind
seems to sing
Though we'll both be far from
a place in the sun and its raining
and there's strangers and dangers
and darkness we'll still going
to win

morning ... Day
Evening ... Night
Pleasure ... pain

as the rain starts to fall I recall
how it was in the good times
when the sun seemed to shine and
the wine was a gift from above
but I know that the sun's on its
way and its bringing the
sunshine
So sing me a song make it
long make it all about love

Left: Original lyric sheets for 'Sideways To The Sun', 'The Power And The Glory' and 'King Of Morning, Queen Of Day'.

period that all the raw materials we needed in this vein already existed within the band.

A massive range of sound textures were at our disposal that weren't available to a regular 'two guitars, keyboards and drums' rock band. On *The Book Of Invasions*, we exploited those strengths to the full and reinstated our original direction, while pulling off a highly listenable album that had bags of mainstream appeal.

I was very happy with my keyboard sounds on *Invasions*. I was using an early Roland analogue synth to create some phased textures that sounded a little like a clarinet. A Hohner Clavinet was also brought in for me to play on 'Trouble (With A Capital T)'. I loved the way Stevie Wonder used the instrument, and thought it would work well for the floaty, passing lines underneath the flute and guitar.

Another instrument I loved was the gorgeous-sounding Fender Rhodes electric piano I played on 'King Of Morning, Queen Of Day'. At other times, I tended to use Wurlitzers, but always hired them in. On stage, for the whole duration of the band, I had a Diamond 800, which was a kind of hybrid, two-tier Italian keyboard that I used for piano and organ sounds, as well as the odd freaky sound that I squeezed out of it for things like 'The Clergy's Lamentation'. By the end of the '70s, it came back into fashion, when everybody was playing the tackiest keyboards they could find.

The album was so well planned that only one number was missing from the line-up we sketched out. 'The Rights Of Man', a traditional Irish hornpipe, was destined to be on the album and we'd been playing it live, but as the sessions developed it didn't sit well with the rest of the tracks, so we never got to record it. [A live recording of 'The Rights Of Man' appears as a bonus track on the CD reissue.]

More often than not, whenever we made an album I had to steer clear of it for months, because I'd worn myself out with hearing the same songs over and over again throughout the writing, pre-

Inspecting the final printer proofs of the album sleeve.

production, recording and mixing cycle. *The Book Of Invasions*, however, was the one album I never tired of listening to.

Carr: The album obviously worked, despite the fact that it was an enormous subject to work with. The melodies were always there, and despite sometimes getting into the heavyweight concepts, we still believed in the power of the three-minute song.

Following up his review of the live album preview he covered in September, *NME* correspondent Angus McKinnon concludes: 'Son-Of-Táin this isn't. *The Book Of Invasions* is more ambitious, sophisticated and ultimately more substantial than its forerunner.'

The *Sunday Times* will soon extend the appreciation: 'The music is a magical, muscular mixture of percussion, fiddle, guitar, mandolin, concertina, voices. In beauty, coherance and invention a rare success.'

HORSLIPS

THE BOOK OF INVASIONS
A Celtic Symphony
HORSLIPS

new ACCLAIMED album on sale here!

Nineteen years after its release, noted folk music journalist Colin Harper will revisit the album for an article in *Mojo* magazine, claiming: '*Invasions* still sparkles with more hooks than a shepherds' convention, and in containing perennial anthems like 'Sword Of Light' and 'Trouble (With A Capital T)' is simply essential.'

November 20: Barbarella's, Birmingham. It is here that Robert Aiken gains his first Horslips experience.

Aiken: To say I was stunned would be a gross understatement. As the band made their way through what I now know to be *The Book Of Invasions*, I could not believe the pure magic that they wove, and had never heard anything that approached what they were producing live on stage. By the time that the 'Dearg Doom' riff blasted through Barbarella's, I had fallen for this incredible band, hook, line and sinker. I left the club a fan and converted several friends at parties.

December: After a short tour of Germany and the Netherlands, Horslips finish the year with an Irish tour, which includes dates in Cork, Navan, Ballybofey, Culdaff, Monaghan, Drumshambo and a New Year's Eve show at Red Island Holiday Camp in Skerries.

"Despite the heavyweight concepts, we still believed in the three-minute song ..."

Hanging out at Amiens Street Station, Dublin.

 Nineteen seventy-seven begins with the finalising of a new international record deal. Returning to the Horslips camp, Michael Deeny concludes negotiations with DJM Records.

Deeny: In autumn '76, the band called out of the blue to explain that they'd recorded a new album that they were thrilled with. Jim Slye had tried his best to secure a UK record deal, but hadn't got anywhere, and they asked for my help. They sent me a tape of *The Book Of Invasions* and, although I always liked everything they recorded, I thought it was an extraordinary album that could work internationally.

'Warm Sweet Breath Of Love' sounded like a single the moment I heard it, so there was a pop element, but this was part of a beautifully constructed Celtic Sym-

phony that touched a lot of progressive music fans, and it was wonderful to hear them perform it with an orchestra many years later.

I told the guys that I didn't want to get involved in the ballrooms again, but if they were happy for me to manage their international business, I would return and look for a new deal, so I began playing the album to a few select people. In spite of the failures with Atlantic and RCA, Dick and Stephen James at DJM Records were really enthusiastic about the album. It wasn't regarded as a major label, but they had Elton John, so there was plenty of money for promotion.

This was a world deal [excluding Ireland], because DJM had their own operation on 57th Street in New York City that was run by Carmen La Rosa. They used Lenny Silver's Buffalo-based company, Amherst, to handle the American distribution, and it was a very good partnership.

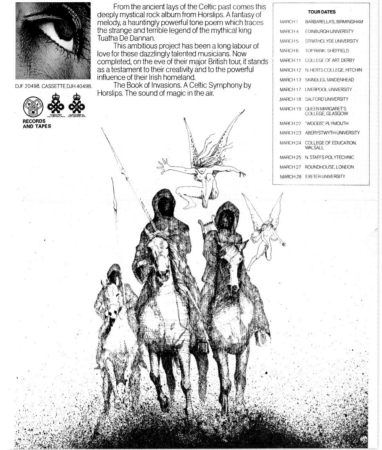

The Book of Invasions
A CELTIC SYMPHONY by HORSLIPS.

From the ancient lays of the Celtic past comes this deeply mystical rock album from Horslips. A fantasy of melody, a hauntingly powerful tone poem which traces the strange and terrible legend of the mythical king Tuatha De Dannan.

This ambitious project has been a long labour of love for these dazzlingly talented musicians. Now completed, on the eve of their major British tour, it stands as a testament to their creativity and to the powerful influence of their Irish homeland.

The Book of Invasions. A Celtic Symphony by Horslips. The sound of magic in the air.

DJF 20498. CASSETTE DJH 40498.

RECORDS AND TAPES

TOUR DATES	
MARCH 1	BARBARELLA'S, BIRMINGHAM
MARCH 4	EDINBURGH UNIVERSITY
MARCH 5	STRATHCLYDE UNIVERSITY
MARCH 6	TOP RANK, SHEFFIELD
MARCH 11	COLLEGE OF ART, DERBY
MARCH 12	N. HERTS COLLEGE, HITCHIN
MARCH 13	SKINDLES, MAIDENHEAD
MARCH 17	LIVERPOOL UNIVERSITY
MARCH 18	SALFORD UNIVERSITY
MARCH 19	QUEEN MARGARET'S COLLEGE, GLASGOW
MARCH 22	'WOODS', PLYMOUTH
MARCH 23	ABERYSTWYTH UNIVERSITY
MARCH 24	COLLEGE OF EDUCATION, WALSALL
MARCH 25	N. STAFFS POLYTECHNIC
MARCH 27	ROUNDHOUSE, LONDON
MARCH 28	EXETER UNIVERSITY

January 1–February 16: Irish tour. At the National Stadium gig on January 4, Horslips are supported by The Verbs, whose line-up includes Johnny Fean's brothers Ray (drums) and Donal (vocals).

Donal Fean: The Verbs were a rock'n'roll revival band, doing rhythm & blues, doo-wop and rockabilly. We opened for a number of well-known bands, including the early U2 in 1978. I'm sure Johnny originally got the idea of doing 'Shakin' All Over' from joining us on one of our gigs, because that was a regular number in our set and he loved playing it.

Ray Fean: On the way to the gig, we got trapped behind a funeral procession somewhere around Nenagh, and arrived late for the soundcheck to find a very irate

Jim Slye. Nevertheless, we were still given our soundcheck slot and went on to play a good set. We were delighted with our association with Horslips and their crew. Our mother turned up for the gig and brought much-needed sandwiches to a happy and relieved bunch of lads from Shannon!

February 25: *The Book Of Invasions: A Celtic Symphony* **is released in the UK by DJM Records (DJF 20498), and peaks at No. 39 on the album chart. Also isssued is 'Warm Sweet Breath Of Love' / 'King Of Morning, Queen Of Day', a new UK single (DJS 10754). It becomes an instant airplay hit on BBC Radio 2, and much favoured by Radio 1's John Peel, Peter Powell and lunchtime show presenter Paul Burnett (who makes it his record of the week), although it will fail to make the Top 40.**

March 1–28: UK tour, during which a tape of Seán Ó Riada's soundtrack for George Morrison's 1959 film 'Mise Éire' introduces Horslips' set. Before the band head out on the road, there are some changes within the crew.

A crucial member of the touring team since the summer of 1972, Robbie McGrath makes the difficult decision to move to London and work with The Boomtown Rats, who are on the cusp of signing a deal with Ensign Records.

Over the next year, he will share 'many a loony night' with Bob Geldof and his band in their communal home at Barwell Court, Chessington, and will later tour as the sound engineer for the Rolling Stones, Oasis, Kasabian and The Stone Roses.

Pat Maguire: Robbie had fallen out of love with the ballrooms and their random technical issues. He wanted to spread his wings. If he had stayed in Ireland there's a chance he'd have given up, so he did the right thing by leaving, and his next phase with the Rats set him up for a great career.

I took over as sound engineer up until the next UK tour, but I didn't have the experience to mix on all the different consoles that we would use along the way, especially in Europe, so I suggested they get a 'proper' sound guy in to take over while I looked after other things. Alan McKenzie came with some good ideas and because he'd toured the world with Jethro Tull, he had a great feel for folk-rock.

April 1–May 1: Irish tour. A new face is seen hanging out with the Horslips crew. Steve Iredale will eventually become a key full-time member of the team and, much later, help steer their reunion shows with wife Sue, a.k.a. Duchess. But in the mid-'70s, he is little more than a willing fan.

Iredale: I loved Horslips from the moment a friend played me their first album over the Christmas of 1972, and it was 'Furniture' that really set my imagination alight. That's really when I got into music in a big way. It opened me up to listen to more bands like Mott The Hoople, but Horslips were more accessible.

You'd see colour pictures of all the supergroups at the time with large productions. They had drum risers, big lighting and PA systems. None of the showbands had this, but Horslips did, and so when they arrived into town it was a big occasion. I became obsessive, not just about how the music was played, particularly, but about the nuts and bolts behind what made all of this happen.

They came with six or eight guys, including Robbie McGrath and Martin Mulligan, who had big beards, moustaches, long hair, flares and tie-dyed shirts, and I wanted to hang out with them. What they did looked really exciting and different, and I suppose I was a bit of a nuisance at first. Any time the band turned up in the west of Ireland and I had parental approval, I tried to be at the venue by 3-4pm when the truck arrived, and give the guys a hand with the gear. My eyes and ears were wide open, and I was paying a lot of attention.

On the day of the Midnight Club gig in Ballaghadreen [April 13], I had just taken one of my mock exams for my Leaving Certificate, and hitchhiked over to help the lads on the crew as I'd done so many times before. This time, the guys dropped me back at my boarding school after the gig so that I didn't get into trouble!

When I finally left school in 1977, I spent that summer following the band around, and I was allowed to travel in the truck. When the crew were back in Dublin for days off, I even slept in a van belonging to the Band Centre on Harcourt Street to make sure I was available.

To justify my constant presence, Joe Wynne got me

O'Connor: There was little continuity between album designs, and the cover of *Tracks From The Vaults* serves as evidence, but does it matter? Eamon liked that Marvel comic idea as one might expect, and I drew the basis of it one night after coming home from a gig, slightly worse for alcohol. This was normal for me if I couldn't get to sleep.

I gave myself the design credit under the name 'Les Lee Superior' and John Webb produced the final print-ready artwork.

We could have achieved a better result if we'd have given the job to a genuine comic artist. Someone from 2000AD would have been ideal, as would Toko Mata style, but we didn't have a superstar art budget.

Some fans have said it's their favourite cover and it's also now a T-shirt, and that's very flattering.

to play records before the band came on. I was often the 'support act', and they'd slip me a few quid, but at that stage I was happy just to play a part.

May 6–10: Songwriting sessions in Ballyvaughan, County Clare.

May 7: *Tracks From The Vaults* (MOO 13), a **Horslips Records compilation of mostly rare tracks, is released to capitalise on the positive reception to** *The Book Of Invasions.* **As well as featuring the Fritz Fryer remix of 'Dearg Doom', it includes 'Motorway Madness', the band's oldest unissued recording, and the Fab Four tribute 'Come Back Beatles'.**

May 9: *The Book Of Invasions* **is officially released in the United States by DJM, having already been snapped up as an import by keen fans.**

May 12: A UK mini-tour begins at the Dundee University Union Ball. In his review of the Dundee gig for *NME,* **Ian Cranna reports:**

'The beauty of Horslips is that they appeal to the head, heart and feet all at the same time. The head because theirs is a work of intelligence and perception, fashioning something thoroughly modern from their heritage; the feet because they have the carefree spirit of the ceilidh and the power to excite of rock; and the heart because there is something likeable about this happy crew playing thrusting, melodic, high calibre music.'

May 18–22: A German tour is followed by a rare break. Devlin and Carr holiday separately in Greece, Lockhart heads for Paris, Fean is spotted at an Eric Clapton concert in Dublin and O'Connor spends his time exploring antiques.

July 25: A remixed version of 'The Power And The Glory' from *The Book Of Invasions* **is released as**

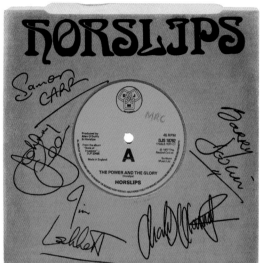

a single in the UK on DJM Records (DJS 10792), with 'Sir Festus Burke' from the *Drive The Cold Winter Away* sessions as its B-side. The single is pressed on green vinyl and presented in an 'autographed' sleeve.

August 9: Horslips play *Jamborora '77* at Mount Mellaray Scout Activity Camp, County Waterford – an event held as part of the celebrations for the centenary of the Boy Scouts of Ireland.

Devlin: I don't recall us doing another gig like it, before or after. Around 10,000 scouts from all over the world converged on Mount Mellaray. It was like *Glastonbury* with woggles. I also remember there were many blonde girl scouts from Scandinavia. Given that this was a camping event, I wouldn't be too surprised if a few cherries were popped that week.

It was refreshing to play such a different kind of gig, and for years afterwards we met mad young people in clubs and arenas around Europe who had their first taste of rock'n'roll at the *Jamborora* in 1977 and gone to hell in a handcart after it. We must have done something right.

In 'Sophisticated Boom-Boom' (Jonathan Cape, 2003), John Kelly's account of growing up in 'seventies Ireland, his alter ego narrator Declan Lydon describes the band's presence:

'With punk raging in London and Elvis Presley about to die in Memphis, our battlefield landscape of tents, flags and smoking fires began to boom with the sound of funked-up, rocked-up reels, jigs, set dances and marches. I faced into the setting sun, tied my neckerchief around my head and opened my arms wide to Barry Devlin's spine-trembling bass as it rumbled like escaping fear through my guts. It was glorious.

'"Daybreak", then into "Trouble (With A Capital T)", then "The Power And The Glory" and I was right at the front, at Johnny Fean's feet, watching his fingers fly, Charles O'Connor's fiddle bow flash through the air, Jim Lockhart hunched over a whole city of keyboards and the skeletal Eamon Carr, scary like one of the living dead, thundering behind the silvery kit – "O'Neill's March" mixing with "Shaft" and turning into "Dearg Doom" and "Toss The Feathers" crashing into "Sword Of Light" and "The High Reel" and "King Of The Fairies" and the sound of a thousand valves opening up in my soul.

"Scouts from all over the world converged — it was like *Glastonbury* with woggles ..."

Jamborora '77 at Mount Mellaray Scout Activity Camp, County Waterford.

'In some places, like Los Angeles or Seattle or Dublin perhaps, teenage boys were ... talking earnestly about Gibsons and Rickenbackers and Strats and Telecasters – but not in my tiny universe, where a tin whistle was as rash as it could be. If you could play a tin whistle even half well, then you could play 'Dearg Doom' ... and that was the coolest thing I could ever imagine.'

August 14: During a month-long European tour, Horslips appear at the *Jazz Bilzen* festival in Belgium, playing to a crowd of 10,000, as they share the bill with Thin Lizzy and Elvis Costello.

September 16: Recording sessions with Alan O'Duffy begin at Dublin's Lombard Studios and will continue until October 13.

October 16–November 12: The success of *The Book Of Invasions* earlier in 1977 prompts Horslips' first full-scale American tour, which includes arena supports with native stars such as Blue Oyster Cult, Molly Hatchet and Black Oak Arkansas, and recorded dates at New York's The Bottom Line. Tracks from the forthcoming *Aliens* album will regularly feature.

Deeny: When I was negotiating the deal with DJM Records, I told Carmen La Rosa that it would be absolutely necessary to provide support for an American tour later in the year to help get this band back on track, and he agreed.

The *Jazz Bilzen* festival in Belgium, August 14 1977.

You can't break America just through touring if you aren't on radio, so you need to achieve a good level of airplay. Through his network of regional promotion reps, Carmen was very successful at getting the radio stations to respond, and 'Warm Sweet Breath Of Love' was popular on FM. You approached America city by city, and had all the promotion lined up in advance. It required a lot of complex forward thinking.

Maguire: We went over to America on Laker Airways, and I did all the driving between gigs, using my father's driving licence because I didn't have one. This wasn't new for me – I had driven Fleetwood Mac's truck at the age of 14, which is about as illegal as you can get on the road. After driving something like 25,000 miles across America on caffeine tablets to keep me awake, I was wrecked by the end of that autumn 1977 tour.

November 4: *Aliens* is Horslips' eighth album release, and the second of a trilogy dealing with themes of exile and immigration – in this case the plight of Irish emigrants in 19th-century America during the potato famine.

Recorded with Alan O'Duffy at Lombard Sound Studios in Dublin, the harder-edged sound of 'Sure The Boy Was Green', 'New York Wakes', 'Speed The Plough' and 'A Lifetime To Pay' (working titles: 'Nothing To Say' and 'The Executive Way') suggests the band have American rock DJs in their sights.

Devlin: We were forever reaching into ourselves to establish roots that we could relate to. Through the tours that promoted *The Book Of Invasions* in the States,

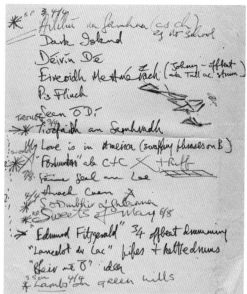

Rehearsing material for *Aliens* in a County Clare cottage; suggestions for tune sources.

we were living the American experience. At that point I think we all agreed that we'd done as much as we could with ancient mythology, and decided to tell a comparatively modern tale that had parallels with our own situation as Irishmen new to this huge continent. *Aliens* was reaching out beyond the cultural roots.

Carr: For us there was a creative and mental leap from the birth of the Irish nation and suddenly this great migration to America brought on by the horrific famine. But when we broached the subject with American record company personnel, they looked at us as if we were completely mad: 'You're doing an album about a potato blight? That shit won't sell!' We had to put up with a lot of this negativity.

I think *Aliens* fell between two stools and it could have been a lot stronger, but part of the problem was that we played down the traditional instrumentation that was such a key part of the band's formula. It felt like a rush job, and we were even recycling old ideas.

'Speed The Plough' was written years before *Aliens* and was originally part of the song cycle for *The Tái,* in an attempt to broaden the story. The narrator is either a footsoldier or MacRoth, or possibly both. Knowing that, it should be easy to spot the connecting threads

with 'Faster Than The Hound' and 'Time To Kill!'.

Devlin: We occasionally played 'Speed The Plough' live from 1973. It always had a cool rhythm and the harmonies added a unique twist. It's mainly Jim's music with Eamon's lyrics. For some reason we had trouble with settling on a tempo. But when we came to record *Aliens,* it suddenly felt right within this new frame, so we locked it down and fell in love with it.

Lockhart: Every album we did had a different feel and approach, with rock and roots, and acoustic and electric all blended together. I think that was still evident on *Aliens* as much as any earlier work, and there are some wonderful songs on it. Our music had always reflected where we were at personally, and America was increasingly where we were at. We were revelling in being a solidly-honed band, and the tightness particularly shows on *Aliens.*

Devlin: In 'The Wrath Of The Rain' we're asking where the sons of those people might be, because we're in America and are probably touring amongst them now. The track might sound Lizzyesque to some people, but we what were actually trying to do was imitate the Steve Miller Band, which goes to show how the best laid plans sometimes work out. Whilst we were being

. . . .

incredibly grandiose, we also had an aversion to it in the sense that we didn't want to be pomp-rockers.

The instrumental 'Exiles' is a fine showcase for Johnny Fean's guitar playing.

Fean: 'Exiles' still stands up so well today. This was another tune that Jimmy brought to the band, and he played it to us at a rehearsal on keyboards and flute. Turning it into a guitar-driven piece felt natural, possibly because 'Fantasia' had worked so well on the previous album. It was such a beautiful, sweet melody, and it gave my new 1960 Gibson Sunburst Les Paul Standard a chance to really shine.

I'd bought the 1960 Sunburst in March 1977, and it was the most heavily featured guitar on *Aliens*. There was a certain tone about it that everyone loved. From that point I used it in the studio until we broke up the band. Around the time that I got the Sunburst, I bought a very similar-looking '70s Sunburst Deluxe as a back-up, but I seldom played it. Our friend Paddy Goodwin now owns that guitar.

Even though he was very much his own man, I think Gary Moore may have taken some notice of what we were doing around the time of *Aliens*, because I picked up on a few things that Lizzy recorded soon after, like 'Róisín Dubh' [1979], which sounded very Horslips-influenced. If that was the case, then it's flattering.

Lockhart: 'Exiles' is based on 'Fill, Fill A Rúin Ó', which means 'Return, return, my dearest'. The B tune is the third line from 'Carrickfergus', a song that's been passed down through the years and recorded by the Clancy Brothers, Van Morrison and Bryan Ferry.

'Sure The Boy Was Green' was built around 'Morrison's Jig', and it took a co-operative effort to prevent it from turning into a clichéd blues shuffle, because it's in

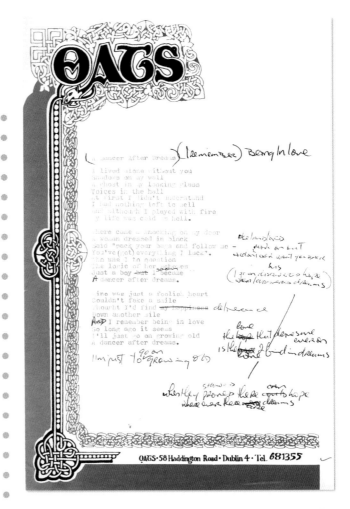

12/8. It was a slightly new approach for us, and one that Lizzy would have found more natural. So Eamon had to manufacture a new way of attacking that on drums, which I thought was pretty clever. He did a whole lot of fairly innovative stuff that I never fully appreciated until much later on.

If 'Second Avenue' sounds a little like the riff from

O'Connor: *Aliens* was originally going to have a gloss black and white cover in a very late 19th century, old Americana style, with coloured badges overlaid. Inside, the inner bag would have been in full colour, with the Celtic swirls on our faces.

I really wanted that strong contrast of black and white on the outside and colour on the inside, which would have been quite unpredictable and cool, but it didn't get the vote. The band thought that as we were paying so much for the printing, we may as well go full colour on the outer sleeve as well.

All of the Celtic motif slides I'd created for *The Book Of Invasions* were reused to project on to the band's faces.

I wanted the guys to look a little run down, possibly a little gypsy-like and anonymous, to fit the theme of newly-arrived immigrants. So I bought a pile of clothes for us to wear for the photo session with Ian Finlay; I crumpled them up, tied them with tape and sprayed them with metallic car spray paint. The boys seemed a bit reticent to wear them, but they looked great.

Jethro Tull's 'Teacher', it's pure coincidence. Maybe it was a subliminal tribute. 'Come Summer' was an attempt to use the tune 'Tiocfaidh An Samhradh' [meaning 'Summer Will Come'], which was also used by Iarla Ó Lionáird recently. We adopted it for the chorus.

The opening riff of 'New York Wakes' is a partial steal from 'The Fox Hunters' Jig', which was in 9/8 and would have been a standard exhibition piece for pipers. Turning it into a riff that sat well in 4/4 time and still had a lot of drive was the trick that we were aiming for.

Originally titled 'A Dancer After Dreams', 'Ghosts' deserves a special mention as the favourite Horslips song of Johnny Fean's wife Maggie, and the author. On the 2009 reunion shows, it will be dedicated to loved ones and notably former Horslips crewman Paul Verner, who passed away in 1991. Sung by Fean, Eamon Carr writes the heartfelt lyric, and the driving tune is the traditional slow air 'An Chúilfhionn'.

Fean: We all knew that 'Ghosts' was pretty special when we started recording it. There was a quality about it that made me think a little more carefully about how I approached the vocals. I'd been listening to the new Jack Bruce album, *How's Tricks*, and was reminded of how great he sang when he slipped into his gentler, falsetto style, so I tried that and it suited the sentimental feel of the melody. I adored Jack's voice, in the way he phrased lyrics and projected with so much power and sensitivity.

Carr: I'm in awe at how hauntingly beautiful and complementary the music is. The same observation applies to a wide range of pieces, including 'Sideways To The Sun', 'The Blind Can't Lead The Blind' and 'Everything Will Be Alright'. It's a tribute to the group ethic upon which Horslips was founded that our

various individual, and often idiosyncratic, voices, which undoubtedly enriched the overall narrative, were not simply accommodated but warmly embraced.

Lockhart: We had different angles of approach for blending in Irish influences. In some cases, we would take an Irish tune and use it as the main riff so that it made it do something unexpected. The riff would generate a chord structure and then you'd superimpose a song on top of it, making sure that the two elements sat together comfortably.

Another approach was to take a tune and use it as a countermelody, as we did in 'Ghosts' and 'Sideways To The Sun'. The tune is set up, and once a chordal framework is set, the tune acts as a counterpoint to the vocal melody, with both starting at different times and forming a complementary relationship where disparate elements illuminate each other. That was always a very satisfying way of writing.

Aliens will be the final Horslips album to feature Alan O'Duffy as producer/engineer.

Devlin: My theory that Alan O'Duffy produced our best albums holds a lot of water with *Aliens*. It was another great piece of work, on which we probably played better than at any other time. In many ways, it's one of my favourite albums for songs.

Lockhart: Alan had a great pair of ears and, although we sometimes felt that his productions lacked the bite that we got from other producers, he was more sensitive to what we were about musically, and was brilliant with layered vocal harmonies. Our natural emphasis was on keeping things basic and rocky, while Alan had a more symphonic vision of our music and was prepared to leave more sonic space between the instruments than some others might have allowed.

"We all knew that 'Ghosts' was pretty special when we started recording it ..."

America '77. Top right: fans George Doyle and sister Maureen backstage with Horslips at Paul's Mall in Boston.

O'Duffy: Lombard was a good [24-track] studio to work in at the time. It later became Westland. Their Helios desk was a joy to mix on, and a bunch of new state-of-the-art processors had recently been installed that helped us achieve some really great guitar sounds for Johnny.

We worked hard and the band were still open to experimentation where it counted – the haunting, reversed vocal reverb on 'Stowaway' being an example. But for the most part the aim was to produce a very punchy, rock sound, and I think we achieved that.

I had no ongoing contract with the band, so it was their decision to switch to another producer again after *Aliens*. It was a fine album on which to part company.

November 10–12: Continuing their American tour, Horslips play three consecutive gigs at Starwood, Los Angeles, as support to Ram Jam, who are currently riding high with their international hit single 'Black Betty'.

Fean: The reaction from audiences on that tour reached a new peak. We played lots of showcase club gigs from the east right across to the west coast, gathering momentum along the way. Most of the people who came to see us seemed to know everything about the band. People were coming to us after gigs with older albums for us to autograph, which we saw as a good sign. It was like they'd been waiting.

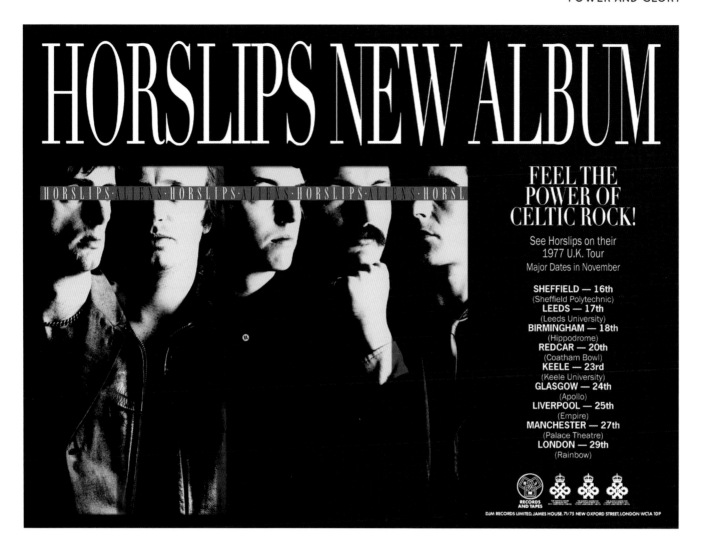

Carr: America was a huge buzz, like one massive theme park in which we were let loose. Everything we heard about touring America in the '60s and '70s was true. We always had a fantastic time there but, still, not everyone understood what our music was all about.

In 1977, there was the big AOR [Adult-Oriented Rock] explosion, with bands like Boston and Foreigner, and albums such as the Eagles' *Hotel California* and Fleetwood Mac's *Rumours* hogged the top of the charts. Then we came along and people had to think a bit harder.

The Irish-American contingent represented only a small portion of the overall American audience, and we would have had to smooth out all the edges and straighten up to become really successful. We had a fiddle and concertina for fuck's sake! We generally went down extremely well, and there was a hardcore fringe element who were big fans, but we didn't have a hope in hell in middle America. They just thought we were weird hippie Paddies.

One experience at a party we attended made it clear how Irish heritage is often misunderstood. An American businessman came up and said, 'Hey guys, why don't you play some of that Irish music for us?' So Charles took out a concertina, Lockhart took out his whistle and Johnny got hold of a banjo, and we all started playing some upbeat traditional tunes.

The guy came over looking really pissed off and started shouting, 'You guys are full of shit, I said play some traditional Irish music!' We said, 'Well, this is about 600 years old!' 'No,' he replied, 'Give us "Toor-A-Loor-A"!'

November 16–29: The *Aliens* UK Tour, supported by Lindisfarne founder Alan Hull's short-lived band Radiator. The tour is one of several promoted for Horslips by the legendary Harvey Goldsmith, later of *Live Aid* fame.

O'Connor: Harvey was a big, outspoken lad who genuinely liked music and got behind our UK tours. We got on well. Robbie McGrath's girlfriend worked for him and that's probably how he became our promoter.

Rather like Denis Desmond in Ireland, Harvey wouldn't put up with any shit. He gave the impression that he was on our side, probably because he liked that we weren't a snotty bunch of upstarts who made diva-like demands.

We were everyday, friendly blokes who would share our drink

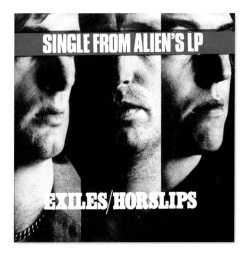

with anyone who came into our dressing room, and he probably found that refreshing.

After years of treading the fine line between obsessive fan and aspiring roadie, Steve Iredale finally joins the Horslips entourage full-time as the *Aliens* tour – one of the band's most successful in the UK – begins in Sheffield.

Iredale: When the summer was over, I had to face the real world and that meant getting a job. To satisfy my parents, and not have them thinking I was throwing away a good education on some stupid teenage whim, I spent three months as a trainee manager at Burgerland in O'Connell Street, with the distinct feeling that this wasn't going to be forever.

One evening, I was in The Bailey when Pat Maguire came in and asked if I'd be interested in looking after the backline as an actual job. I had to break it to my parents that I was running away with the circus, and they were very unhappy about it for a long time, but I knew this was what I wanted to do for a living, and who better to work for than a bunch of musicians who are friendly and caring? So I started taking care of the band's stage equipment, while Pat moved on to sound; Paul Verner did the lights and Maurice Daly was the truck driver. I just walked into something that I'd wanted to do for years.

Horslips broke the mould in the Irish dancehalls by taking the front-of-house control position midway down the hall, whereas the mix had previously been done at the front of the stage. It caused a problem at first, because the way the migration of the audience went, mixing from the middle of the hall became an

obstruction. You wouldn't get away with it now under current health and safety law, because you'd use proper safety barriers. But we ended up walling the console in with flight cases, like Fort Apache.

I had a good relationship with Joe Wynne early on, but the person to whom I owe a lot for taking me under his wing and giving me a lot of support and guidance was Pat Maguire. His attitude to how we worked and moved forward was very inspirational, and I've taken that with me throughout my career. Pat was a genius at problem-solving. He always had a Plan B.

November 24: The instrumental 'Exiles' and 'Speed The Plough' are paired for an Ireland-only single release (MOO 15). It stays on the chart for seven weeks and reaches No. 9. In the UK, 'New York Wakes' / 'Ghosts' (DJM DJS 10820) is set for release, but withdrawn at the last minute.

November 29: The final date of the *Aliens* UK Tour is at London's Rainbow Theatre, with folk singer-songwriter Dave Cartwright stepping in to cover Radiator's absence. The author of this book is in the audience, immersing himself in his first live Horslips experience.

Devlin: We only ever played the Rainbow twice, and both times it was brilliant, with really good reviews. I loved that venue. Unfortunately, there was no rest for the wicked after that November '77 gig. Early the next morning, we flew to Germany to do some television spots in advance of a run of shows over there. We were so exhausted that we could hardly speak, but we somehow managed to stay true to the 'show-must-go-on' spirit.

Tony Stewart writes a positive live review for the *NME*:

'Their show ... was enough to prove the course of their career is no longer haphazard. On stage they've tirelessly experimented with their style, moving from early beginnings as essentially a rock group whose work dripped delightfully with their Irish heritage of jigs and reels to become a blatant rock'n'roll act, and finally reach their present position, which falls comfortably between the two.'

November 30–December 18: Horslips tour Germany to coincide with the German release of *Aliens* on the Polydor label.

December 5: Carr and Lockhart are arrested by German police under suspicion of being members of the Baader-Meinhof terrorist gang.

Lockhart: It was all very strange. We were at our hotel, just getting ready to leave for our next gig in Munich, when the cops showed up and shoved us into their Black Maria. It was clearly a case of mistaken identity, but some bright spark had tipped them off that we were dodgy characters. It took several hours of very frustrating interrogation before they were finally convinced we were innocent rock musicians and not terrorists.

December 23–31: The *Irish Christmas Tour '77* sees house attendance records broken almost everywhere. It concludes with the now-traditional New Year's Eve party at Red Island Holiday Camp in Skerries, where there is a live link to Larry Gogan in the RTÉ radio studio.

CHAPTER 6

THE AMERICAN WAY

 January 13: Horslips' New Year tour of Ireland brings them once again to the Culdaff Arms in Carndonagh. In March 2012, Neil McGrory, the owner of local music pub McGrory's, remembers the Culdaff gigs in an interview with Marianne Ashcroft for ICR FM (now Inishowen Live).

McGrory: They were the only band I can think of who toured the circuit and only played original music. Brendan Faulkner, who ran the Culdaff Arms Ballroom, recognised that Horslips were bringing something unique to the area with their music, their clothes, their roadies, their big PA system and lights, at a time when there was no access to anything like that.

I loved that they never took themselves seriously. When they were doing *The Book Of Invasions* in Culdaff, Charles leaned down to grab his concertina and one of the roadies, probably Pat Maguire, had put a live crab in his case. Charles jumped out of his skin! Stuff like that always endeared you to them. They did great business as professionals, but there was always fun around them.

Horslips gigs were always a great opportunity to meet people. There was a very strong group of fans that followed the band around, almost like an unspoken club. My brother John and I used to help out at the Culdaff

Arms gigs as stagehands, and we also did advance promotion, going around with posters. The gigs were so packed that they had to build a barrier across the front of the stage, and I'd help to look after it before the band came on.

They were so influential to aspiring musicians, and always had time to talk to them after gigs. A lot of musicians came to check out how it was really done. I think the effect that Horslips had on young bands has been underrated.

January 29: The latest Irish tour ends at Fountain Blue in Longford. Two weeks later, on February 14, Horslips fly from Heathrow to snowy New York for another American adventure. Meanwhile, 'Sure The Boy Was Green' / 'Exiles' is released as a DJM single in the USA (DJM DJUS1036).

Carr: At most gigs in Ireland and the UK, you'd get ready in a broom closet, and there was no such thing as a band rider. Sometimes, you even had to demand to be paid. In America, it was remarkably different – you were usually treated with respect. There was an infrastructure, with crews there waiting to help our roadies. We'd arrive and be directed to a proper, clean dressing room with towels and an assortment of food and beers, and we were made to feel really welcome.

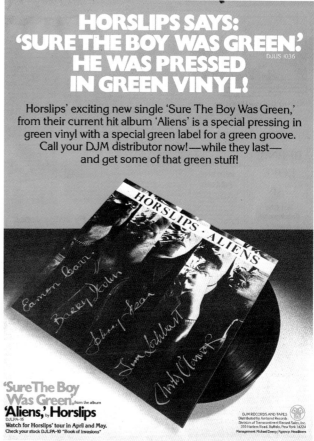

**HORSLIPS SAYS:
'SURE THE BOY WAS GREEN.'
HE WAS PRESSED
IN GREEN VINYL!**
DJUS-1036

Horslips' exciting new single 'Sure The Boy Was Green,'
from their current hit album 'Aliens' is a special pressing in
green vinyl with a special green label for a green groove.
Call your DJM distributor now!—while they last—
and get some of that green stuff!

'Sure The Boy
Was Green,' from the album
'Aliens,' by Horslips
DJLPA-16
Watch for Horslips' tour in April and May.
Check your stock DJLPA-10 "Book of Invasions"

DJM RECORDS AND TAPES
Distributed by Amherst Records
Division of Transcontinent Record Sales, Inc.
355 Harlem Road, Buffalo, New York 14224
Management: Michael Deeny / Agency: Headlines

**The tour extends to May 14, and Steve Iredale
gains his first experience of America.**

Iredale: The band must have had tremendous faith in
me to offer that kind of opportunity within just a few
months of joining them full-time. Straight off the plane
I went into Manhattan, and the next day I was given the
keys of a van and told to go to New Jersey to pick up
new backline. I had to learn very quickly.

Record companies were much more involved with
touring in the '70s, and DJM decided they could save
money by purchasing a minibus for the band and a van
for the crew, so all the equipment went in and we were
self-contained whilst in America. We thought that was
very generous and supportive. The minibus was quite
nice and well kitted out, with a good stereo system and
air-conditioning. But then we saw the crew wagon.

They gave us the most inhumane crew vehicle that's
ever been put on the road. It was like the most basic
UPS parcel van, and it wasn't even painted. It was raw
steel; it had three seats, a crackly AM radio and air con-
ditioning was notably absent. It was like a furnace in
there as we drove across Texas and the Arizona desert in
scorching temperatures of up to 130°F. Because of the
bare steel body, there was nothing to stop this van from
absorbing the heat. And when we went to Canada it was
–30°. It was the most horrible thing you could inflict on

a human being, and we lived in this thing! We booked hotel rooms at every opportunity.

Things we take for granted, like power, were big considerations once you crossed the Atlantic, because of the voltage differences that I'd never had to even think about before. Plus, you drove hundreds of miles between gigs, and got no sleep, but it was a fantastic way to get to know this business.

March 3: Horslips are unable to perform alongside Blue Oyster Cult and the J Geils Band at the Baltimore Civic in Maryland after it is discovered that their equipment is missing.

Maguire: It was a disaster. We arrived early in the morning for the Baltimore gig having driven through the night, so the management told us to get some sleep at the hotel. They called us at 3pm, but when we turned up our truck had disappeared. We freaked. Bob DeJessa had taken over from Joe Wynne by then, and he was trying to make some sense of it.

Although the J Geils Band offered us the use of their backline, we didn't have what we needed and had to abandon the gig. As we drowned our sorrows back at the hotel, a very apologetic Peter Wolf from J Geils called me at 3am. He explained that their lighting guy had been sent to fill their truck with gas, but had taken ours by mistake. I was aghast. The one good thing to come from it was that J Geils were so embarrassed by the cock-up that they helped us to get some extra gigs.

March 10: Aragon Ballroom, Chicago, Illinois – with The Tubes & Pat Travers Band.

O'Connor: The crowd at the Aragon behaved like they'd left their brains at home. Clearly, most of them had only come to see Pat Travers 'widdle' on his guitar, and when we started our set, we were hit with an avalanche of coins and beer cans, just like that scene from 'The Blues Brothers', except there was no chicken wire screen. They didn't give a fuck and it was pretty horrible, but we weren't having any of that. We really played our hearts out and I think at least a portion of the audience respected the fact that we didn't appear too fazed. But The Tubes, bless 'em, they were hated with a vengeance. We felt that maybe this was normal at the Aragon.

March 11: Royal Oak Theater, Detroit, Michigan – 2,500 tickets are sold in 3.5 hours, breaking Bruce Springsteen's previous record for the fastest sell-out at the venue.

March 24: Horslips spend the Easter break on a fishing trip in the Gulf of Mexico.

March 30: Old Opry House, Houston, Texas.

Fean: I always loved the opportunity to check out music shops whenever we were in America, although it was rare that we ever had the time because of travelling. We had a few hours to kill before a gig in Houston and so Charles, Jimmy and I strolled around for a while, and found an interesting second-hand store with a lot of instruments on sale.

One of them was this lovely old Silvertone guitar with a 'lipstick' pick-up [below right] that was a favourite of slide players like Jimmy Page and Rory. I couldn't resist it! It wasn't a guitar that I used on stage, but it would be useful in the studio whenever I was looking to play a slide piece.

April 14–15: At both the Shrine Auditorium, Los Angeles (14), and Winterland, San Francisco (15), The Jam open for Horslips and Be Bop Deluxe.

Carr: Playing the Shrine Auditorium and Bill Graham's Winterland was the stuff of dreams. The Jam played a blinder every night. They were light years away from Horslips' style of music, of course, but that bill added up to a very energetic mix.

HORSLIPS IN AMERICA • SPRING '78

At the end of the tour, Horslips take a week's vacation in the US, and Martin Mulligan leaves to join The Stranglers' crew.

June 7: Eamon Carr watches the fledgling U2 in action at McGonagles in Dublin.

Carr: Paul McGuinness had just become U2's manager and he invited Michael Deeny and I to see his new baby band. Bono was doing his thing even then; he was all over the place as a brash, bold, energetic frontman. Larry was a workhorse drummer with a military feel and Adam Clayton was the inscrutable bass player – part-Entwistle, part-Wyman, but much cooler. The unique feature of the band, however, was The Edge's guitar playing.

I thought they'd be more accepted in America than England at that point. But Larry seemed very young and I wasn't sure that he'd cope with playing two sets a night, back to back. So I advised Paul to put some effort into preparing Larry. The next time I saw U2, I couldn't get over the change. They were steaming! And Larry had gone from being almost like a callow youth to an adult in his playing.

June 22–23: A short Irish tour is followed by two shows at Wembley Empire Pool as 'special guests' of Thin Lizzy on their *Live And Dangerous* tour. Paul McGuinness attends with U2's bass guitarist, Adam Clayton.

Brian Downey (Thin Lizzy): There's a kinship between the members of Thin Lizzy and Horslips that stretches back to the Tara Telephone days. When Horslips formed, I would often see them around Dublin and I already knew Johnny Fean as a great guitarist from the Limerick scene. We lost contact for a while when Lizzy were based in London but we'd occasionally meet.

Wembley was a major breakthrough for us, and doing it with Horslips made it all the more special. Having two top Irish bands together in such a high-profile venue was a bit of an event, and the feedback from the fans was phenomenal. I was aware of the sense of occasion and a bit nervy before we went on, as I'm sure Horslips were. But they really rose to the occasion, played superbly and went down really well. Maybe too well! The reviews that came out afterwards were verging on the ecstatic.

There was a big party backstage. We were reunited with Paul Verner, who had worked with Lizzy in the early days. Obviously the drink flowed. A lot of Guinness and Irish whiskey was consumed over those two nights, and it carried on into the early hours at the Speakeasy.

Lockhart: Playing Wembley with Lizzy had a bit of a full circle feeling to it. We were probably at our peak around then, and although they had gone stratospheric with countless monster hit singles, they remained very grounded as people. Backstage it felt like one big,

"Playing Wembley with Lizzy had a full circle feeling to it ..."

Above: After-show craic with Brian Downey, Noel Bridgeman, Phil Lynott, Joe O'Donnell and Brush Shiels.
Below: Horslips on stage at Wembley Empire Pool (now Arena).

friendly gang with a great, upbeat vibe and none of the competitiveness that you might get with other bands in that situation.

Horslips had been building up a good, loyal audience in London over the previous few years, and it was a rare opportunity for fans of both bands.

Phil didn't have to give us that slot at Wembley. He had nothing to gain from doing that. It was a wonderful gesture on his part to acknowledge us in that way, but that was Phil. When we came off stage on the second night, he said, 'Jaysus man, you really blew us off stage!', which was very generous of him. Then, of course, Lizzy went on and tore the roof off the place.

Devlin: Paul McGuinness had recently taken on the management of U2, and he asked me to have a look at them, just as he'd done with Eamon. When we played Wembley with Lizzy, a very young Adam Clayton came backstage to meet me, and we chatted about bass guitars. Paul asked if I could produce some demos at Keystone Studios in Dublin. I didn't see myself as a producer, but they wanted someone to help them who they could trust and who'd be objective.

I was amazed by their determination, their hard work and almost tunnel-visioned ambition. We did 'Shadows And Tall Trees', 'The Fool', 'Street Missions', and an early version of 'Stories For Boys'. Even though nobody could have predicted they would become the biggest band in the world, their chemistry just sparkled.

Larry Mullen Jr. was just 16, and his dad, Larry Snr arrived at 2am to take him home. I said, 'I still haven't finished the session,' to which he replied, 'Yes, you have!' and took him away.

The Edge: There was no sitting around musing over what we were going to do. It was literally get in there, get the gear set up, get the drum sound and then just go for it. You couldn't want for a better person than Barry to introduce you to the whole concept of the recording studio, because of his easy way with people. The demo was the most true to our live performance recordings that we did at that time, and I think we played a lot better than we would have done if Barry hadn't been there.

Paul McGuinness: Barry showed them how things worked, and explained that if you're in a studio and you are an artist, you're in charge – you're paying the

Right: Steve Iredale models the latest addition to the band's merchandising range while Pat Maguire sets up the mixer.

Right: Steve Iredale models the latest addition to the band's merchandising range while Pat Maguire sets up the mixer.

rent, and the producer is working for you. This completely changed the band's attitude.

June 23: DJM issues 'Speed The Plough' as a single (DJS 10859) in the UK, with a cover of Johnny & The Hurricanes' 1959 hit instrumental 'Red River Rock' (recorded live in February on the US tour) and 'Bridge From Heart To Heart' on the flip side.

Fean: Jimmy wrote the music and lyrics for 'Bridge From Heart To Heart', which echoed 'Exiles' because of its similar use of the tune from 'Carrickfergus'. I've always had a soft spot for it. We recorded it for *Aliens*, because there had been an idea to reprise that tune in the same way that we used 'My Lagan Love' on *The Book Of Invasions*, but at the last moment we decided against it.

June 27–August 13: Irish tour

Iredale: Pat Maguire and I used to meet at the Band Centre on Harcourt Street, which was owned by Fran Quigley, who was Thin Lizzy's original roadie and now owns CAVS, the Dublin-based audio-visual company. The Band Centre was a great resource that helped to keep Horslips on the road by repairing equipment.

We were just about to head off to Limerick to start a tour, when Pat told me he was taking a break and I was now doing the sound. What he meant was I would be setting up the PA, soundchecking and mixing the gig. But I'd never had any experience with sound, and

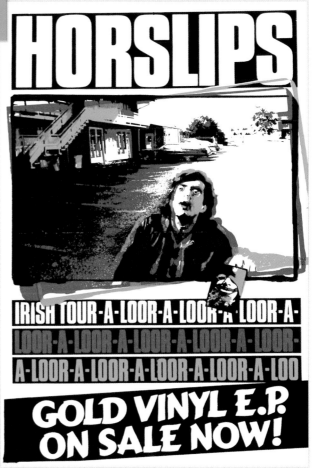

hadn't taken much notice of what a mixing console did. The band were about to play the biggest room in the country, and I was at the start of a huge learning curve. A couple of days later, the *Irish Times* reviewed a gig and complimented the sound – I was overjoyed!

July 7–8: Horslips rehearse 10 new songs for their next album in Glencolmcille, south-west Donegal.

179

The provisional titles are 'Loneliness', 'Summer Comes Along', 'Long, Long Time Ago', 'Tonight', 'Think This Long Weekend Through', 'Takin' The Easy Way Out', 'If It Takes All Night', 'Man Who Built America', 'Go Out And Get It' and 'Take A Little Lovin' (a.k.a. 'Goodbyeee').

July 28: Ireland sees the release of the *Tour-A-Loor-A-Loor-A-Loor-A* EP (MOO 16) in a special gold vinyl and '3D' sleeve, featuring 'Sure The Boy Was Green', 'Red River Rock (live)', 'Trouble (With A Capital T)' and 'Bridge From Heart To Heart'. It will peak at No. 9 on the Irish chart.

O'Connor: The EP was given that title because the routing of our tours was often reminiscent of the song 'How Are Things In Glocca Morra?' in which the towns namechecked are nowhere near each other. Sometimes we had to travel from Dublin to Belfast, Cork to Derry. Man, we burned fuel! One of our Irish tours saw us driving 750 miles for five gigs, because of bad organisation.

Mid-August: Recording sessions for a new album commence at Dublin's Lombard Sound Studios. Within a few weeks, the sessions are aborted and Horslips relocate to Advision Studios in London to complete the project.

October 27: *The Man Who Built America* (MOO 17) is released. The recording marks the involvement of a new producer, Steve Katz, a former songwriting member of Blood, Sweat & Tears, who influences an American stadium rock sound. The album is the third in a themed trilogy of albums and will be Horslips' last for DJM.

Devlin: We felt there was a legitimate reason to continue the migration theme, which is how *The Man Who Built America* came about. It was originally going to be titled 'The Wheels Of The World', after Mickey MacGowan's Irish language book 'Rotha Mór an tSaoil', which means literally 'Big Wheel Of Life'. The title had been hanging in the air since we

included the phrase in 'The Power And The Glory' and we saw it had additional merit.

MacGowan [Mici Mac Gabhann] was a Donegal native who left for America, worked in steel mills and mines, and then took part in the Klondike goldrush. And so his book was a fascinating record of life and wanderings in the late 19th century that completely fitted the theme of migration. 'Green Star Liner' [featuring Lockhart on electric harpsichord and guest uilleann piper Tommy McCarthy] was essentially his story compressed into one song.

Aliens and *The Man Who Built America* were held together in how they looked and felt by the remnants of a trilogy idea, to follow *The Book Of Invasions*. When we finished *Invasions*, we all agreed that this approach worked for us, in that this was what Horslips was always about, and that there were other tales of migrations to deal with.

Michael Deeny: On the back of the great *Book Of Invasions* and *Aliens*, and the increased airplay and press exposure that DJM helped to achieve, Horslips were playing to bigger audiences in the UK and things were looking good. In 1978, DJM switched its American distribution to Mercury, a major part of the Polygram group that coincidentally had Thin Lizzy and were very successful with rock acts. It was through the relationship with Mercury that we became acquainted with Steve Katz, who had been promoted from East Coast Director of their A&R department to Vice-President.

As part of New York's thriving Greenwich Village scene in the mid-'60s, Steve Katz fraternised with some of the blossoming artists of the day, including John Sebastian, before teaming up with Al Kooper in the Blues Project. After the success of Blood, Sweat & Tears, Katz evolved as an in-demand record producer, notably working with Lou Reed on *Rock & Roll Animal* and *Sally Can't Dance*.

Katz: I was intrigued from the start, and Bob Epstein from DJM and I went over to see them play a gig in

Top: Horslips recording *The Man Who Built America* at London's Advision Studios with engineer Dec O'Doherty and now producer Steve Katz (also pictured above). Opposite: A list of potential songs to rehearse for the new album.

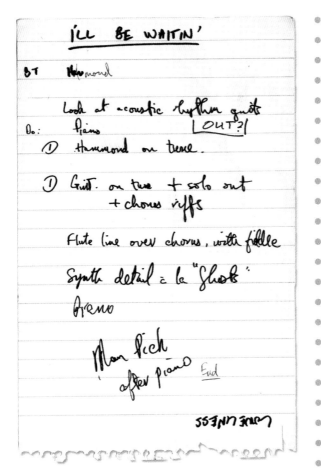

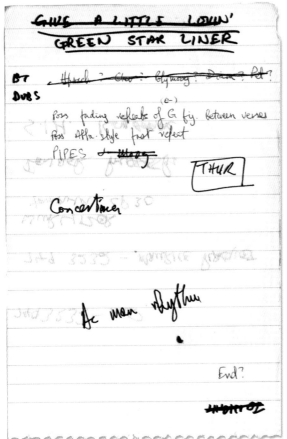

Ireland. They were great, and we hit it off very well. I think they were interested in the fact that I was more a musician than an A&R man, and while I was hanging out with the guys, they asked if I'd be interested in handling their production. They were simply looking for a new character of sound for their next release.

The Man Who Built America was all about opening up the production to appear a little wider and brighter, with extra reverb and echo. We layered a lot of heavier guitar sounds for that album in a bid to be more FM-friendly in the 'contemporary rock' sense.

Devlin: When Steve Katz came in, he heard this new bunch of songs that we had and insisted that we needed to do more work on them before recording. So we put an extra week into honing them. It was a week well spent, because not only did we gain his confidence, we also gained more confidence ourselves. It meant that Steve could get involved in the genesis of new material..

Carr: The recording sessions started at Lombard Studios in Dublin, but there were problems – we heard ghost noises and strange clicks happening on the tape. The studio was stripped down to find the fault and there was talk of an exorcist being brought in, because it really sounded as if the fuckin' place was haunted.

Katz: Oxide was dropping off on the tape head on the Studer machine, so we were losing information every time the tape passed the head. One of the technicians came in and kicked the machine, and still it didn't work!

Carr: We couldn't deal with this any longer, as it was sapping energy and patience, so we moved everything over to Advision Studios in London. The sessions pretty much started again from scratch and Katz got a much bigger sound there. Advision was a good environment, and being in London was very enjoyable.

Declan O'Doherty, a Derry man, was our engineer and a very good pianist [O'Doherty later plays piano on 'The Life You Save' from *Short Stories / Tall Tales*]. Declan was a useful bridge, because he had an ear for the Irish thing and was good on melody.

Fean: I was in favour of a bigger sound, and with tracks

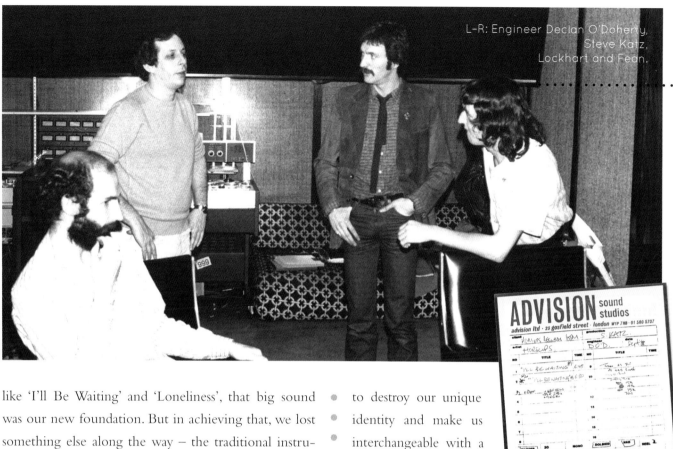

like 'I'll Be Waiting' and 'Loneliness', that big sound was our new foundation. But in achieving that, we lost something else along the way – the traditional instrumentation that was Horslips' original trademark. I think we were so focused on achieving that stadium rock sheen that we overlooked getting the balance of the instrumentation right.

Carr: More than at any other time I felt a style shift. I wasn't happy with the direction of *The Man Who Built America* and it's no one person's fault. I bought into having Steve Katz as the producer. I was there when we were figuring out our drum sound, and I roundly endorsed a third part to the loose trilogy idea. But I envisaged more of a sepia-toned roots approach than embracing stadium rock. There would be electric stuff on it as well as concertina and fiddle, and probably leaning more towards John Mellencamp. We just didn't have that collective vision.

The whole premise of the band had changed, and to me it was summarised in a news piece that was shot for RTÉ during the Advision studio sessions, when Jimmy told the reporter that we were looking 'for the big, fat sound of Boston and Foreigner'. It felt like a great way to destroy our unique identity and make us interchangeable with a lot of run-of-the-mill American AOR bands.

By degrees we were ditching the concertina and mandolin in favour of loud electric guitars and rock'n'roll.

O'Connor: The production does sound American, and that's precisely what we expected from Steve Katz or we'd have asked Alan to stay on. Steve got the most exciting guitar, bass and drum sounds we ever had on an album. It sounds very live, and that was one of the things we agreed had been lacking. As for the traditional elements, I thought they were woven in very nicely and in a credible way, so as not to feel like pastiche. The album is probably a little patchy in places, but the good stuff made up for that in spades.

Devlin: As a soloist, Johnny's one of the most lyrical guitarists who ever put a plectrum to a string. Until 'I'll Be Waiting', my favourite guitar solo was the one Martin Barre played on Jethro Tull's 'We Used To Know' from *Stand Up*, in which he used the wah-wah and kept building it up. Johnny's is prettier and stronger in my

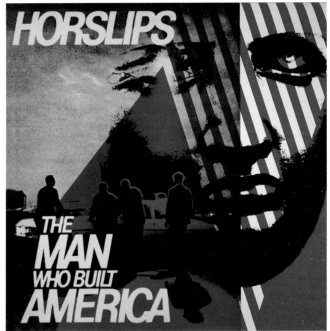

Uh-
huh-
huh

O'Connor: I had to design two different versions of *The Man Who Built America* cover. The first one [above left] was designed for our Irish release. It reprised the Celtic motif from *The Book Of Invasions* to highlight the fact that this was the third in a trio of interwoven, themed albums.

The second design [above right] was for the rest of the world, and it turned out to be the definitive version. Both of them shared the device of the stripes from the US flag. It was a request from DJM Records and there was a bit of hedge-betting going on, but ultimately it confused some people.

The default 'international' version had a grainy picture of a helicopter shining its light on a group of fugitives from a scene in a detective book. There was a crime aspect to it, as opposed to emphasising Barry's idea of the Irish exiles.

I saw a close-up photo of the Statue of Liberty's face and I suddenly realised that it looked amazingly like Elvis Presley. Now what sense that made, I don't know, but somewhere in my

mind I could see that having this heavily posterised image of that face on the cover might lend itself to a wide range of interpretation.

We went to Ardmore Studios in Bray with Ian Finlay for the back cover photo of the band, and made an 'alley' out of Styrofoam with studio lighting back and front. I wanted to give the impression of gangsters sneaking around a back alley. The results were very moody.

Ian did most of our album photography. He was very professional, trustworthy and accommodating, very familiar with the kind of things we liked, and brilliant at taking direction as well as suggesting alternative approaches. It's very rare to find someone like that with whom you can build a relationship, so we were lucky to have Ian.

view and, yes, it's the best solo I've ever heard to this day. He still plays it as wonderfully as ever.

Like 'Sideways To The Sun' and 'Ghosts' before it, 'I'll Be Waiting' was a golden moment for me, because we tapped into something truly melodic and achieved a writing peak. The lyrics were written more or less in one go on a rainy Sunday afternoon in July 1978, in the Great Northern Hotel in Bundoran, not too long before we were due to go into studio.

I had 'Sliabh Na mBan' [a.k.a. 'Dingle Bay'] in my head as a chorus. Ó Riada's use in 'Mise Éire' was a revelation to us, and it had an epic sweep that made me think of adopting it as a motif for twin guitars and strings. That epic sense was partly inspired by a young lady who worked at the hotel and was planning to emigrate.

I was also reading Sholokov's 'And Quiet Flows The Don', and I was greatly taken with Aksinia, the heroine. So I thought of an Irish version of her as the girl who was left behind. So the chorus became 'I'll be waiting'.

Johnny immediately played the 'Sliabh na mBan' riff over the chorus. Now because it's played on guitar it isn't too obvious. I knew the song would work, and his lyrical playing over the solo was as good as I'd hoped, if not better.

We always tried to maintain the number of traditional tunes on each album, and that followed through on *The Man Who Built America*, even though they might not have been as recognisable.

Along with 'Furniture', 'I'll Be Waiting' has become a stand-out live number for the band, one where we can relax and let the music flow and build up. Johnny's

skills also extended to bass when we recorded 'Long Weekend'. I handed the burden of the bassline to him and he did a really nice job.

***Melody Maker*'s Harry Doherty identifies several traditional source tunes spread across the album, including 'Behind The Bush In The Garden' ('Homesick'), 'The Eagle's Whistle' ('Green Star Liner'), 'Gardaí An Rí' ('Long Time Ago') and 'My Love Is In America' ('Long Weekend'). The latter tune is revisited for Horslips' *Roll Back* album. Doherty writes:**

'*The Man Who Built America* is as close to the realisation of Horslips' ideal of presenting traditional Irish forms in a contemporary rock format as the band will ever achieve. The band's writing ... has never been stronger, and the conscious clash of periods and styles that has always marked Horslips' sound is utterly convincing.'

The album's title track will eventually be lifted as a single.

Devlin: It was a sort of sequel to the theme of 'The Wrath Of The Rain', specifically from that line 'I see them today in the streets of their cities, we nod to each other again'. I was following on to see what kind of America they'd built and had been built around them. Hence the golden spike where the Eastward railroad met the Westward. The golden mile was the gold-lined umbilical cord of the space walker with the distant Earth reflected in his visor.

"We tapped into something truly melodic and achieved a writing peak ..."

'You coloured kids on the borderline and all you golden children of the sun' was about white, black and Hispanic in the Watts riots, as was 'in every precinct a golden mile', but more specifically about Robert Kennedy and Martin Luther King. And 'you kill the rich and you con the poor' was a kind of upside-down version of Republican and Democratic politics. It was a go at pretty much everything.

During a demo session with U2, Devlin treats the young Dubliners to a sneak preview of the song, as Bono remembers in *The Return Of The Dancehall Sweethearts*.

Bono: We were all getting ready to play what we were doing and then [Barry] said, looking around as if he was going to produce something illegal, 'Would you like to hear a new Horslips single?' And we all said, 'Yeah, yeah ... we really would!' He put it on. And our little demo sounded so ... sort of, it just sounded like it ... it didn't sound at all. It had no sound. And this extraordinary thing came on. It was 'The Man Who Built America', a song that, years later, I would rip off [for 'The Hands That Built America', from the 2002 Scorcese movie, 'Gangs Of New York']. And nearly win an Oscar. It *did* win a Golden Globe.

October 27–November 26: As the new album is released, Horslips begin a new Irish tour, with support from the Brown Thomas Band.

HORSLIPS. THEY ARE DRAWING FROM THE PAST AND SHAPING ROCK'S FUTURE.

Horslips uses the past as no other rock group ever has before. Even their name is borrowed from a legendary 11th century Celtic warrior.

And their music itself takes small touches of the past and integrates it with a driving contemporary sound. The unique combination produces a music so fresh and inventive, it could well be pointing toward rock's new direction.

So maybe it's prophetic that Horslips took their name from an old legend. They just may be creating a new legend.

HORSLIPS
THE MAN WHO BUILT AMERICA

Produced by Steve Katz

December 31: Red Island, Skerries. This will be Horslips' final appearance at the legendary holiday camp venue, which is soon to be demolished. In the local newspaper, *Skerries News*, Eamon Carr remembers the good times ...

'My first trip to the Head wasn't with the band. It was to visit my schoolmate, Tommy, who had taken a summer job there as all-round gofer and dishwasher.

'The ballroom in Red Island appeared enormous to us. It seemed inconceivable that we'd attract an audience. While the pre-gig soundcheck was fraught, as the crew did battle with particularly tricky acoustics in the room, we enjoyed the most splendid vista afforded by any gig, anywhere.

'Those who were there will recall an enormous window wall at the opposite end to the stage. We watched the light turn the blue sea to a sheet of silver out past the Captain's and all the way to Rockabill. It was magical.'

Fean: I think 1978 was a strong year for Horslips. The charts were full of fantastic rock songs that had grown out of the punk scene and matured. We had done well in America on the back of *Aliens*, and our popularity was at an all-time high.

We didn't all share the same positive feelings about *The Man Who Built America*, but it had a certain confidence about it, and there was no doubt that it had greater market potential than anything we had done before, so 1979 was going to be a important for us in terms of whether we could take everything to the next level.

HORSLIPS GET FUNKY

Lockhart: The Horslips Funky Fun Club was started in Charles' flat in Oaklands Park, Ballsbridge, by Sue Calvert [right]. She used the pseudonym 'Samantha Martins' when writing the quarterly newsletters and sending out membership cards and gig lists.

O'Connor: It was mostly Sue's idea, because our mailbag was getting full of requests for information on what the band were doing, in terms of forthcoming gigs and, if we were going abroad, how long we'd be away. We didn't want anyone to forget about us, so we came up with a way of communicating in a fun and funky way.

Carr: We later moved the admin of the Club to our office in Haddington Road and over the next few years we put together very punky-looking, handmade supplements to go with the newsletters, that were like postcards from whichever tour we were on.

There were some mad ones we did while we were in America and some of the crew got involved, too.

We were just geeking off, like most bands did, and that's what our fanbase loved. It kept them in touch.

On January 12, The Meanies, a conglomerate of Horslips and The Radiators From Space, play a one-off gig at McGonagles, Dublin.

Fean: We played a bit of a random set that included a couple of Horslips songs and our version of 'Red River Rock', plus some Radiators' numbers like 'Television Screen'. Paul Verner [pictured right] from our crew got up to sing a couple. Another number we did was 'Shakin' All Over', and it was a bit of an eye-opener because it went down a storm. From that moment on, we played it as an encore at Horslips gigs. It was lot of fun to do something so off the beaten track.

January 19: *The Man Who Built America* **is released in the UK by DJM (DJF 20546).**

January 29: Horslips film a video in Beckton, east London, with Australian director Russell Mulcahy

to promote the upcoming single release of 'The Man Who Built America'. Mulcahy will become well known for his work with Duran Duran, The Human League and Ultravox, while his video for The Buggles 'Video Killed The Radio Star' will be the first screened on MTV.

Devlin: The idea was to replicate the scaffolding set that we were going to use on stage for the new UK tour. We got out to this godforsaken place at the crack of dawn for this shoot and it was fuckin' freezing! I like that video. It's got a powerful vibe and we look like we're on Benzedrine, with our eyes popping, and Eamon looking a bit scary, as if he's an extra in a Hammer horror.

A clip for 'Loneliness' was filmed at the same time. Johnny had a trampoline that he jumped on and then flew over the camera for one shot. No one liked it. so it was never seen and then it vanished.

January 31–February 19: With support from The Ronnie Paisley Band, Horslips embark on their Harvey Goldsmith-promoted American Tour of the UK. On the eve of the tour, Pat Maguire leaves to start his own sound company, and Barry Mead is hired as tour manager.

Mead: I hadn't long quit as the manager of Chicken Shack when Michael Deeny asked me to attend a meeting in London about Horslips. He said that whilst Joe Wynne was still taking care of their tour management in Ireland, Peter Clarke had recommended me as a new tour manager for a short tour of the UK and then America. It was a job I was only too happy to take on.

The differences between the audiences in the UK and America were quite profound. In England, there was a large contingent of hardcore Irish fans and people who were into folk-rock, and they were often quite boisterous crowds. In America, the audiences were harder to define. They just appeared to love live music, and I expect it was

Highlights from Russell Mulcahy's promo video shoot in east London for 'The Man Who Built America'.

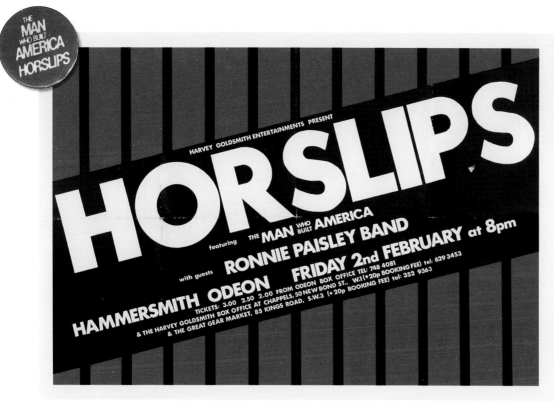

either repeat business for some of the crowds or people who were taking a punt on a band they'd heard about.

I was obviously aware of the political issues coming out of Northern Ireland, but I'd never experienced anything personally. When we played in Manchester, we booked into a small, local hotel. As we arrived, we all heard some very strong Northern Irish accents in the bar. Barry quickly turned to us and quietly said, 'Let's not go through there.'

We felt there might be trouble, but these were different times and it's very difficult for today's generation to understand what that environment was like. Working with Horslips and talking with the guys made me appreciate the realities of this political struggle.

Iredale: The picture of the Statue of Liberty on the album cover was taken when it was being refurbished and so it had scaffolding all around it. Charles had the idea to adopt that theme for a stage set using plastic tube scaffolding instead of steel.

We also had risers of different heights and Eamon in the middle of a semi-circle, and it all looked really good. What I remember most about that tour are the horribly strenuous load-ins and outs, because our artic didn't have a ramp.

February 13: Horslips appear on BBC TV's 'The Old Grey Whistle Test'. Annie Nightingale introduces the freshly-edited video of 'The Man Who Built America'.

February 16: 'The Man Who Built America' and B-side 'Long Weekend' are coupled for a new UK single (DJM DJS 10888) with a yellow vinyl special edition, limited to 10,000 copies.

February 19: The Venue, Victoria, London.

O'Connor: I bought some new stage clothes for the band for that UK tour, to represent the colours on the album cover and, loosely, the brave new world aspect of the record. We didn't intend to look like a pop band although it might have come across as an attempt to be more mainstream. I just thought it was time to break away from the leather we'd been wearing for a while.

Above: Out with the leather, in with an explosion of colour – Horslips dressed for excess on the road in '79.
Below: Starring on TV's 'SBB Ina Shuí'.

February 23: Pre-recorded performances of 'The Man Who Built America' and 'Loneliness' are broadcast on RTÉ's Irish language TV show 'SBB Ina Shuí'. The theme tune of the series (which runs until 1983) is 'Sword Of Light'.

February 24: Supported by the Wailing Cocks, Horslips' final live UK appearance will be for 'BBC Radio 1 In Concert'.

March 8–May 18: North American tour. After rehearsals at Studio Instrument Rentals in Chicago, the tour begins at The Palms, Milwaukee. As the band arrive in the US, press reviews of Horslips' latest album are published …

'Every cut has its own merits; the group is really showing its maturity with this new release.' (*the Chattanooga Times*)

'[*The Man Who Built America*] is the band's most consistently excellent effort yet, with slick arrangements and glistening guitars brightening the instrumental tracks.' (*San Francisco Chronicle*)

'Horslips may finally capture a more mainstream rock audience with this solid outing.' (*Cash Box*)

March 19-20: El Mocambo Club, Toronto (two shows per night).

Iredale: The El Mocambo was a tiny venue, but bands loved to play there, including the Rolling Stones, who recorded their stunning *Love You Live* album there in 1977. We were very aware of this connection, and the prestige that went with it. In fact, it was an honour to be on that stage.

We often played two shows per night on the American tours, with a dinner break in between. It was hard for the band to keep up that pace sometimes, but when the audiences were really up for it, which fortunately was most of the time and was certainly the case at the El Mocambo, it didn't seem such a chore.

April 1: Civic Center, Portland, Maine – supporting Nazareth. Disguised as Phil Lynott, Eamon Carr plays an April Fools' joke on the audience.

Carr: The Civic Center was a big indoor arena. We already knew Nazareth well from earlier gigs. It was the last gig on their American tour, so their roadies were planning a few pranks and I reckoned I'd get away with something. I spiked up my short hair and put on a disguise that included Barry's leather jacket, a few extra scarves and bracelets, and strapped on his Fender bass, holding it high. As I was already wearing tight jeans and brothel creepers, from a distance you might not be sure if you were a bit tipsy.

On a selected Nazareth number, I came out. Only the drummer, Darrell Sweet, and new guitarist Zal Clemenson [formerly of The Sensational Alex Harvey Band] saw me initially. Poor Zal didn't know what the fuck was happening. I waved and the crowd responded. Then I threw a few Philo shapes and they began to go wild. It was hilarious – especially when I went to the edge of the stage and hunkered down with the bass and gave them the old clenched right fist routine. The band thought the cheers were for Manny Charlton's solo!

Their bass player, Pete Agnew, was the one I was worried about, but he got the joke and nearly fell over in fits of laughter. Dan McCafferty eventually spotted me and he laughed, too. Then I beat a hasty retreat. Paul Verner, a close friend of Philip, was involved.

We sprayed 'April Fool' on a big sheet of cardboard. Charles was supposed to bring it on stage, but he hung about the wings. I think Paul and Johnny also came out onstage. It was a mad session, as befitting American tours in the 'seventies.

April 2: Onondaga County War Memorial, Syracuse, New York – with Rush.

Iredale: On this tour we would often play with great bands like Nazareth, UK, Molly Hatchet and Lizzy. The Rush gig in the Spectrum stands out as being notable, because it was the first time I'd seen and heard a Clair Brothers rig, and been up close and personal with a Clair custom mixing desk. This was world-class stuff.

Billboard promotion for *The Man Who Built America* on Sunset Strip, Los Angeles, 1979.

April 5: An Irish-themed reception for 400 people is organised by DJM and Mercury/Phonogram for Horslips at Christopher's in Manhattan. It is hosted by actress Geraldine Fitzgerald, who, a year later, stars as Martha Bach in the Dudley Moore comedy film 'Arthur'. New Hampshire's *Valley News* runs an hilarious, off-the-wall account...

'Six wayward nuns were strolling down 63rd Street in Manhattan when they heard the sounds of a traditional Irish band coming from a restaurant, where a party for the Irish rock band Horslips was being held. "Is that Paddy Noonan on the fiddle?" one nun asked keyboardist Jim Lockhart, who was standing in the doorway. Lockhart invited the nuns in to see for themselves, and they wound up jigging the night away with two hired midgets dressed as leprechauns.'

Lockhart: That's about as close as we'd ever get to matching the decadence of Queen's after-show parties.

During the band's stay in New York, an alternative explanation behind their name begins to enter the news columns. With an air of convincing authority, *News World* journalist Linda Solomon writes:

'Their moniker is certainly strange to untutored American ears. The name "Horslips" belonged to a legendary Irish warrior circa 900AD.' [In their research for *The Táin*, the band had, in fact, discovered a character in the saga named Eirrge Echbél, meaning Eirrge Horsemouth.]

April 6–7: The Bottom Line, New York – supported by Chris Rush. On both nights, Horslips play two shows. Bob Grossweiner of *The Good Times* reviews the final performance ...

'At The Bottom Line, the Americanization of Horslips was realized with a set that should make them more popular in a commercial sense even if they sold out artistically.

'With a black-and-white backdrop spelling out their moniker, the group performed an impressive, eclectic program that utilized their intelligent lyrics without sounding artsy.'

Fean: We were all listening to Scott Muni's radio show whilst driving down Fifth Avenue in a limousine, and Scott played 'Loneliness' back to back with 'Eleanor Rigby'. For me, it just didn't get any better! Earlier, I stopped by Manny's music store and bought a brand new Hamer Explorer guitar that had caught my eye. That was a very memorable day.

O'Connor: Whenever we were in America, we tried to make time to see the sights. Rather than stare at the four walls of a hotel room, we went out to visit exhibitions, art galleries and sites of historical importance. I think we tended to do more of that than most bands, who went over there and got caught up in the rock star thing of incessant partying and self-abuse.

We could party with the best of them but we looked after ourselves because we didn't want to miss out on the American experience.

April 15: Memorial Auditorium, Greenville, South Carolina – with Molly Hatchet and Nantucket.

Iredale: Some gigs with Molly Hatchet could be a bit scary because of the type of audience they often attracted in the southern states. When we ventured into Greenville, we had to have our wits about us, because we'd be playing to crowds of rednecks who didn't necessarily take too kindly to a bunch of Irishmen.

Two years earlier, the Memorial Auditorium was the last gig that Lynyrd Skynyrd played before their fateful plane crash. It was the only gig I remember where, for safety's sake, Horslips began their set with the riff from 'Rocky Mountain Way'.

Quite often, Horslips were very ill-matched with certain headliners. The audiences would come to see their favourite band and, as the support act, we'd be presenting a style of music that was markedly different. But exposure was what counted. Sometimes we'd be the

"We could party with the best of them but we looked after ourselves ..."

great, unexpected surprise of the night and go down an absolute storm; at other times, people would be scratching their heads, wondering what the hell this was all about. You rarely knew in advance how it would go and there was a lot of fun in that.

Mead: America still has massive cultural divisions. I don't think there was particularly an anti-Irish attitude in the South. It was more about the Southerners connecting Irish people with the North where there was a greater Catholic population. To me it didn't seem any more profound than the traditional rivalry between Scotland and England.

Carr: There was always something exciting to do after a gig or if you had a night off, and we would occasionally find ourselves hanging out with people like Pere Ubu or The Flamin' Groovies. On the night we arrived in Atlanta [April 16], Paul Verner and I went to see Cheap Trick. Unfortunately they were a bit too typically AOR for our taste, so we ducked out.

As we were walking through the lobby, two women who we'd noticed earlier because of their distinctive Southern Belle dresses were also leaving, and we got talking. I asked them if they knew of anywhere locally that might be fun to go to. It turned out that one of these 'women' was a transvestite performer who had been nominated for something at an awards night for the gay and transgender scene, and that's where they were heading. Paul and I grinned at each other, and asked if we could tag along. 'Yeah, let's get a taxi,' said one of them, who seemed taken by our 'European' accents.

It was all very glitzy. Our new nominated friend was the closest thing to Keith Richards in a dress, but she was game for a laugh. We were ushered to a table with some sensational looking 'women', and all the men looked like Tom Selleck in their tuxedos. For a couple of Irish fellas this was jaw-dropping stuff, and it took a while for the penny to really drop with Paul. He whispered in my ear, 'Hey Eamon, these girls are all fellas.' It didn't seem to bother him – after all, we were getting nicely drunk with some fantastic people.

Horslips were playing at the Agora in Atlanta the following night and word had got around the city's nightclub scene that 'friends of friends' were doing this gig. Barry, Charles, Johnny and Jim were on stage, and suddenly they noticed that the first few rows were filled with these exotic creatures. The boys couldn't be absolutely sure of what was going on, especially when a bunch of them arrived in the dressing room after the show, and Charles couldn't resist getting his camera out.

May 17: Two days after playing the Whiskey A Go-Go in San Francisco, Horslips appear at Rather Ripped Records' 8th Birthday Party in Berkeley. Michael Branton reports:

'Observers have compared Horslips favourably with Jethro Tull (much to the Irelanders' chagrin). On 'Trouble (With A Capital T)' such comparisons are not invalid. But as Barry Devlin has said, Ian Anderson "is trying to fashion a culture of elves ... that never really existed. We're pinching from a culture that's alive."'

June 2: 'Loneliness' / 'Homesick' are paired for a DJM UK single release in two formats: 7" vinyl with autographed sleeve (DJS 10916) and a 12" green shamrock-shaped disc in a clear wallet (DJT 15001). It is also released in the shamrock format in the United States (DJMS-1105).

RATHER RIPPED RECORDS
8th *Birthday Party*

thurs may 17th
Keystone

2119 University, Berk
Door Opens 7.00
Show Starts 8.00

STARRING
HORSLIPS
REAL KIDS
VERSE
JARS

Minors Welcome

THIS INVITATION GOOD FOR THE
PURCHASE OF 4 TICKETS (AT THE DOOR)

NO INVITATION
NO TICKETS

June 18: Jim Lockhart and Frances Swift are married at University Church on St Stephen's Green in Dublin. Barry Devlin is best man.

June 21: Another long run of concerts begins in Ireland at the Astoria Ballroom, Bundoran.

Devlin: The difference between the venues we played in America and those at home was vast. We'd play the Spectrum in Philadelphia, which had a 13,500 capacity, and return to Ireland for the summer to play venues like the Astoria in Bundoran that were a fraction of the size. But we liked the contrast.

There's a thing called 'teaching English as a foreign language' and we did 'touring Ireland as a foreign country', and it worked. You could either say, 'It's gloomy old Ireland,' or, 'This is really interesting.' Our attitude was that Ireland is a beautiful place to tour. Winters might be a bit grim, but on a nice summer evening you wouldn't change it for the world.

Top right: Hanging with record label staff in San Francisco.

Right: Jim Lockhart and his long-time girlfriend Frances Swift finally tie the knot on June 18.

July 25: National Ballroom, Dublin. O'Connor, Fean, Carr and roadie Paul Verner perform as members of The Defenders, an 'all-star' line-up that includes Billy Morley (Revolver), bassist Gary Eglington, Frankie Morgan (Sacre Bleu), and Steve Rapid & Mark Megaray (The Radiators From Space).

Created in 1977 by Pete Price and Jude Carr, brother of Eamon, *Heat* ceases publication after its allegations against the working practices of Paul McGuinness result in the U2 manager successfully taking out a libel action.

The gig is organised to raise money for *Heat*'s legal costs. Declan Lynch writes:

'Johnny Fean, hair greased back, rammed it all home on 'Shakin' All Over'. Eamonn [sic] Carr played drums like he cared for the first time in 10 years, and what a great drummer he can be. Big and hard, straight and firm, the beat, just the beat. Can you blame him?

'The repertoire was massively funny and eclectically well-chosen, probably by O'Connor. 'Superman', 'High School Confidential', 'Teenage Boogie', 'Who Do You Love' and 'Flea Brain'. I laughed for hours. Paul Verner shone on deadpan doo-wop, and was joined by the ubiquitous swingin' DJ, Uncle Karl.'

October 5–November 10: Irish tour.

October 16: As Horslips play the National Stadium, Dublin, the single 'Guests Of The Nation' / 'When Night Comes' (MOO 20), is released from their forthcoming album. It will peak at No. 8 during a six-week chart run. The A-side features the handclapping contribution of the mysterious Ztak Evets, later revealed to be a certain Mr. S. Katz.

Fean: I wrote 'When Night Comes' at the beginning of 1979, when power pop was very much in vogue and as a band we were rising to that. I was disappointed that it didn't make it on to the album, because I thought it was a good song – one of favourites from the late period. But at least it came out as a B-side, and we also played it live on a few occasions.

October 23: Cork Opera House, televised by RTÉ.

Lockhart: Dave Fanning introduced us that night, and it was his first television appearance. He had just started presenting on the newly-launched RTÉ Radio 2 [renamed RTÉ 2fm in 1988], and as fate would have it, I became the producer of his show in 1995.

In his book, 'The Thing Is...' (Collins, 2010), Dave Fanning refers to the concert:

'My job was straightforward: to introduce the Celtic rock band Horslips. I was in the wings waiting to go on and John McColgan was on stage. John said, "Now, to introduce the next act, please welcome Radio 2's Dave Fanning ..." and then you couldn't hear a word he said, because the audience were all cheering and yelling so much. It was the last thing I expected, and I was flabbergasted. It wasn't exactly The Beatles at Shea Stadium – but it was proper pop star-style screaming.'

October 31: Horslips are the first band to appear on 'Green Rock', a new series of six concert specials transmitted by BBC Northern Ireland and filmed at its television studio in Balmoral, Belfast. Horslips' set includes several numbers from *Short Stories / Tall Tales*. 'Green Rock' is one of the first programmes to be hosted by future 'Blue Peter' presenter, Caron Keating.

November 5: Mercury releases 'Rescue Me' as a double-sided (stereo/mono) promotional single in North America (Mercury 76030).

November 16–December 14: The second North American tour of 1979 begins at the Triangle Theater, Rochester, New York.

November 16: Produced by Steve Katz at Windmill Lane Studios, Dublin, Horslips' swansong studio album, *Short Stories / Tall Tales* is released both on Horslips Records (MOO 19) and on the band's new international label, Polygram's Mercury Records.

Deeny: After *The Man Who Built America* came out, we got the feeling that we needed to increase our support in order to push forward in the States, but there was only so much that DJM could do. So I made an agreement with DJM whereby we moved over to Mercury and gave points on sales to DJM as an override.

The album is recorded amidst significant disagreements over musical direction.

Devlin: The basis for the tension was the dividing line between the US and UK approach. In 1978, America was still largely unmoved by the punk explosion and their charts were still full of dinosaurs. The British thing was sharp, stripped down and exciting, but I thought it was too big a jump for us. However, by the time we recorded *Short Stories*, we had firmly tipped our cap in favour of the British scene. There was almost a Buzzcocks feel to some of our new stuff.

Above: The *Short Stories / Tall Tales* wrap party at Windmill Lane Studios.
L–R: Fean, Iredale, O'Connor, Katz, Carr, Lockhart and Devlin.

Katz: The punk influence didn't come in until *Short Stories*. When I saw them in rehearsal, it was clear that the band had split into two parties. Barry was still firmly waving his folky flag with his writing, while Charles, who one might think was the more traditionally-orientated of them all, was bringing new wave sensibilities into the mix, both musically and in the way he dressed.

It made it very difficult for me, because the challenge was to take these contrasting elements and form a composite unit. Unfortunately I don't think I succeeded, and the result was schizophrenic.

This was a genuine reflection of what was going on. I was leaning towards what Barry was doing, which was

what made me fall in love with the band in the first place. And I felt that the other stuff really wasn't right for Horslips. It certainly wasn't what Mercury thought they'd signed.

Deeny: As ever, there were some good, clever songs, but *Short Stories / Tall Tales* presented everyone with a serious dilemma, because none of the tracks got any airplay. Consequently, Mercury got quite upset. If we had started with Mercury at the time of *The Book Of Invasions*, I think the situation would have been a whole lot happier for everyone involved.

Devlin: *The Unfortunate Cup Of Tea!* and *Short Stories / Tall Tales* both marked ends of chapters, creatively speaking. The difference being that whilst the 'low' of the 1975 album provoked us into trying harder, *Short Stories* represented a more terminal dip, because there was no unifying purpose afterwards.

O'Connor: It was rare to not have a good pool of ideas for songs to choose from when approaching a new album, so when the writing didn't come easy, it really felt like a chore. On *Short Stories*, the well was drying up. We didn't have much material, but I chipped in with a few things that unfortunately weren't very loved. Even though the band were never too enthusiastic about playing it live, I still like 'Law On The Run', the cartoon song I wrote about the 'Hotel Inexpensive', and it seriously rocked when we did it on TV at Cork Opera House.

Devlin: We were originally looking for a unifying theme of Irish writers. Jim and I wrote a song that never made it on to the album called 'The Trusting And The Maimed', which was inspired by a Flannery O'Brien short story and based around a traditional tune. I think the others felt that it was a bit doom-laden, since it was another story of death and decapitation from the Horslips boys, but it probably just wasn't good enough.

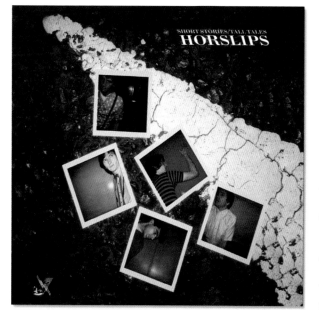

'Rescue Me', however, was in a completely different league and very much in the vein of 'Blackbird'. The melody of the chorus was written around the concertina tune 'The Downfall Of Paris'. I wrote it to be played on guitar with a pick, but if you play it chorded, it sounds Far Eastern, which was intentional because it was about the Vietnamese boat people, who were at that time undergoing a much more cruel version of the enforced emigration the Irish had undergone a century and more earlier. Harassed by pirates, robbed, raped and murdered, theirs was one of the cruellest exoduses ever … and all this following a long period of devastating war.

Philip Chevron, a member of The Radiators From Space, visits Windmill Lane on the day 'Rescue Me' is recorded, and hangs out in the control room as Devlin works on his vocal track.

Chevron: Affecting and vulnerable, it's the best thing [Barry] ever did, gathering up a lifetime of formative elements – The Beatles, the folk clubs, Paul Simon and Irish tunes – in one place. And the unexpected and anachronistic 'arable land' is inspired, as befits a sometimes man of letters.

Katz: There are things I really like about the album. In retrospect, I think that if Horslips had held on to their traditional roots and taken them in a different direction, they would eventually have achieved the popularity in the US that they were aiming for, and maybe even exceeded it.

If they'd stuck with the traditional-meets-rock style, Mercury wouldn't have been the right label for them, long-term, because it was too hungry for hits. Warners would have been much better; in fact, it may have been the best company all along.

Devlin: *Happy To Meet* and *The Táin* came out of nowhere in terms of audience expectation. We didn't know what people wanted to hear; we only knew what we wanted to do. When you've done your first few albums, if the audience are with you, you've then got to keep delivering, and that's a very tough challenge. You begin to conform to your own idea of what the audience wants to hear from you, and confusion creeps in. You start questioning who or what you actually are.

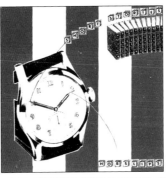

O'Connor: The boys always trusted me to do the design work. I often did stuff while we were on tour and it was rewarding if they liked it. I'm proud of most of the album sleeves, although a few weren't as impressive as they might have been. *Short Stories / Tall Tales* would be one of them, and it's my least favourite design of them all.

There were two attempts at the cover. The band didn't like the first version [above right], which still is my favourite of the two by a long way. The rough that I made looked a little like the homemade style of the albums that came out of the Stiff or Chiswick stables.

For the purposes of the design I interpreted 'Tall Tales' as being lies and 'Short Stories' as an Agatha Christie crime thriller reference, even though that wasn't the intention behind the music. So I organised a photo session with the aim of showing people breaking and entering a building, and doing other simi- larly illegal acts. For instance, we had Jimmy appearing to rob items in a darkened room. It was all a bit 'undercover', which is why I added little insets to the cover like a gun. Musically, it was spasmodic and that original design was a better fit.

My lasting impression of the one that did come out, with the Polaroid snaps on the car bonnet, was that it was very boring by comparison. The pictures were quite good, but I thought that the overall artwork [by O'Lochlainn Design Associates] was bland.

For the most part, every album we made until *Short Stories* was a progression on the previous one in some way. I'd love to claim there was intelligence at work, but I'm not entirely convinced, other than we were keen not to repeat ourselves. Ultimately, *Short Stories* feels like an unfinished body of music to me.

Whilst I'd written 'Rescue Me' about the Vietnamese boat people, I later realised that, subconsciously, it was also about myself and the way I felt towards the band at that point. We were falling apart.

Carr: Charles was saying, 'I'm writing songs.' And we probably all were. This was the album where everybody brought in their stuff and it ended up like four or five solo records, like the *White Album*. The songs are mostly good, but the recording experience was fractious and fairly unhappy.

There was always the spectre hanging over it that if, by chance, one of these tracks exploded on radio, what sort of a band would we then have? Would it be Charles O'Connor's Horslips, Barry Devlin's Horslips, Jim Lock- hart's Horslips? This hadn't happened until around that period, and it was a situation that I don't think could have been sustained. It started on a subtle level with *Aliens* and manifested itself fully on *Short Stories*.

Lockhart: In our last two years, we were listening to stuff like the The Clash, Elvis Costello and ska-reggae, but we had set ourselves up to be a particular kind of band that was light years away from all of that. Our first album had been fearless, adventurous and there were no boundaries to our creativity. Now, several years down the line, we found ourselves in a situation where we could no longer be as daring.

Devlin: It's an album that I would still defend because it contains Jimmy's song 'The Life You Save' – a beautifully understated number that uses 'Róisín Dubh' incredibly well. It was a very good performance, with a tasty piano part by Declan O'Doherty.

Despite mixed feelings within the band, some reviewers are positive. After attending a playback at Windmill Lane Studios, Karl Tsigdinos of *Hot Press* writes:

'I'll venture a supportive affirmation that this is a 'new' Horslips and that they've made the first Horslips album I'm eager to play. It is, after all, a modern album. From what may at last be a modern Horslips.'

November 22: Following The Defenders' gig for *Heat* magazine in July, the line-up release a Christmas single, 'Happy Surfin' Santa' / 'Xmas Up On Venus', on Guided

Missile Records (ABM 1001) – a small, independent label owned by Jude Carr and Karl Tsigdinos.

December 14: Horslips end their 22-date American tour at Park West in Chicago. Typical of the rest of the tour, their set list at Park West is: The Power And The Glory / Summer's Most Wanted Girl / Guests Of The Nation / Amazing Offer / Law On The Run / Trouble (With A Capital T) / Sword Of Light / Unapproved Road / Warm Sweet Breath Of Love / Sure The Boy Was Green / Speed The Plough / The Man Who Built America / Ricochet Man / Soap Opera / New York Wakes / Loneliness / Dearg Doom / Shakin' All Over.

The Chicago *Daily Herald* comments:

'On the last night of their latest American jaunt, Horslips gave an unforgettable performance. Chicago loves these boys ... here's hoping they will return soon.'

Barry Mead: The time I spent on the road with Horslips was very valuable to me. Apart from Michael Deeny, for whom I had the greatest respect, all of the band members were very smart guys, who taught me a lot just by the way they handled themselves. They weren't so much a band I was trying to lead as much as keep up with.

I joined them again towards the end of 1979 for their second American tour of the year, and by the time we were reaching the end of it, I was witnessing tension. This was often something I experienced with bands that had been together for a long while.

My role was to ensure that from the first date through to the last, the tour was fulfilled to the best of everyone's ability, so any friction I detected got cemented over in my mind. Frankly, it's not something I would have wanted to get involved with, but it did seem to me that they might be on the verge of breaking up.

December 31: Horslips are back home to say farewell to 1979 at Beechmount Hotel, Navan. Supported by Pulse, formed by brothers Pat,

John and Tommy McManus as an early incarnation of Mama's Boys, Horslips start their year as they will end it – playing at Belfast's Ulster Hall on January 8. This is the opening show of a new Irish tour that will include dates at the Opera House, Cork, the Silver Slipper Ballroom in Strandhill and the National Stadium, Dublin.

April 5–May 1: Second Irish tour of 1980.

April 29–30 / May 1: Whitla Hall, Queen's University, Belfast. Producer Steve Katz organises for the last two of three consecutive sold-out

shows to be recorded by the Manor Mobile for a forthcoming live album.

Paul Muldoon's contribution to the book 'The Show I'll Never Forget: 50 Writers Relive Their Most Memorable Concertgoing Experience' (editor Séan Manning, Da Capo Press, 2007) is a chapter concerning Horslips' Whitla Hall performance on April 30. He describes the opening of the show:

'There was a howling that came close to Pandemonium in its strictest sense. Any moment there'd be a great disclosure. Some revelation was at hand. We'd see if Horslips were indeed "gods or real folk". Yes … one by one they came on stage, each with a following spot. Just as we expected … gods.'

May 3–12: Mixing the Whitla Hall live tapes with Steve Katz (right).

Katz: We tended to work overnight and for about a week we hardly saw the light of day because we would mix for about 12 hours at a time, and sleep during the day. They slightly varied the set for each of those gigs at the Whitla Hall, which meant I had a lot of numbers to mix, and we were all determined this would be a much better live album than their 1976 effort, so a lot of work went into it.

July 18: The simultaneous release of Horslips' second live album, *The Belfast Gigs* (MOO 20), and the live single 'Shakin' All Over' – a cover of the 1960 No.

1 by Johnny Kidd & The Pirates resurrected at The Meanies' one-off gig in January 1978. 'Sword Of Light', also recorded at Whitla Hall, is the B-side.

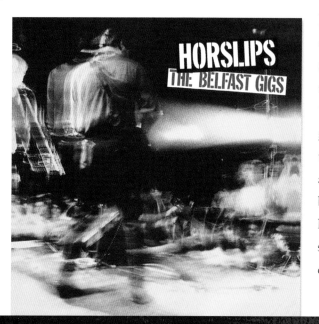

Lockhart: As a live album, I thought it did a great job of preserving a moment in time. There were reels and reels of multitrack tapes from *The Belfast Gigs* that didn't get used. We were planning to issue two volumes of that album, probably a year apart, but by the time we would have looked at putting together the second volume, the tapes had disappeared from our office.

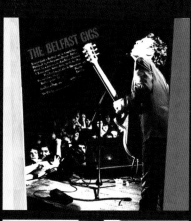

O'Connor: For *The Belfast Gigs*, Ian Finlay's assistant Susan Byrne was employed to photograph the band on stage at the Whitla Hall, with the emphasis on action rather than nice, well-composed portraits. She was right there on the stage with us, and because she was a girl we allowed her closer access than a bloke!

It was Sue's first proper gig shoot, and that can be scary in such a boisterous environment. Perhaps her inexperience showed in the grainy, sometimes slightly blurred results, but that was precisely the flavour we were looking for.

We knew that we wanted this live album to capture the intensity of our performance, so we went all out to make the package enhance that feeling, right down to the stencil font that mimicked our flight cases.

[Pictured left are O'Connor's rough artwork guides for the front and rear of the album sleeve.]

Billy Moore worked to my brief on the final art, and what makes it for me is the audience at the front and the little faces looking up at the band. I look at that cover and the unbridled excitement of it all comes flooding back.

A Volume Two of *The Belfast Gigs* was lined up for release in 1981 but abandoned. In advance, however, I'd already put together the artwork for it, which simply had Eamon's out of focus bass drum on the front looking like it was shaking, like a motion blur.

I thought those recordings were really well done, and I take my hat off to Steve Katz who organised the mobile side of things so smoothly. The results were definitely a huge improvement over the roughness of the previous *Horslips Live*.

Deeny: Belfast audiences were always fantastic to play for, and that was why the band chose to record their final album there, probably knowing by then that this would be their last release.

Katz: It was effectively the farewell party. They were ready to unleash all their frustrations on stage and have a great time, and I think that really comes over on the record. They really nailed that one.

July–October: Touring throughout Ireland continues throughout the summer and early autumn, leading to a fateful, inevitable night.

October 8: At Belfast's Ulster Hall – almost 10 years to the day when Spud Murphy unwittingly named the band – Horslips play the last show of their original lifespan.

As if any further poetry were needed, their final song is 'The Last Time', the song written and made famous by the band whose mobile studio gave birth to their début album. After 12 genre-defining albums and more than 1,000 gigs, the band part company by mutual consent.

Devlin: We had known for three or four months that we would be going our separate ways, and didn't tell anybody. Nothing was announced about Ulster Hall being our last show and there was never any suggestion that we would bow out on a big farewell tour.

The band congregated backstage afterwards, shook hands and said, 'See you in the next life', only it was a lot more emotional than that.

At the end of 'Sword Of Light', Charles broke his fiddle over one of the monitors and threw it into the crowd. As it arced we heard a very deflated 'wooooh' sound from the audience. It was very symbolic of what was happening within the band. Some people claim to have seen the 'fiddle-tossing incident' at an earlier gig, but we've all compared notes and it was definitely that night.

O'Connor: Throwing my fiddle out was semi-premeditated, because the idea had crossed my mind before we went on stage – not that I had loads of spare fiddles to waste. I suppose it was a subliminal way of saying, 'Right, that's your lot, we're done.'

Devlin: There was a long pause backstage before going back out to play 'The Last Time', and I remember having a lump in my throat when we announced that final number. Part of me wanted that song to last forever.

Iredale: I recorded a cassette of the final gig through the mixing desk and gave each of the guys a copy some time later. It was done cheaply but the quality was surprisingly good, not least due to the band's fantastic performance. It's Horslips at their ballsiest best, and I'm glad I had the forethought to capture that night for posterity.

Devlin: It felt like someone had kicked me in the guts, because I knew the reality of this as soon as we came off stage. I was deeply upset and remember sitting on the staircase at the top of the venue in a sorry state. The last 10 years were flashing around in my head like a set of movie highlights, and it was all coming to a close right there.

The good news is we had nine blissful years followed by one year when it hurt. Talking to lots of bands subsequently, I've discovered that most of their lives were spent in the period that we didn't like, so we were blessed.

We'd always believed that we could be the biggest band in the world, and then it suddenly dawned on us that it might not happen after all. One of my biggest regrets is that we never truly cracked America. And the possibility of playing to diminishing numbers of the same faces was something we feared.

Iredale: I saw Barry at the end of that last gig and he was in a bad way. I felt gutted for him, the others and myself, because we were all leaving behind a life. But the period leading up to that night had not been pleasant. The laughs that we used to have had become fewer. They started to not bother with soundchecks, and the brotherly love just didn't seem to be as apparent as it once was.

When we left the Ulster Hall, Barry drove us home and hardly a word was spoken. I think everyone was in various states of shock and disbelief.

Devlin: The break-up was truly traumatic for all of us, like the end of a marriage. But did we hate each other by the end? No, categorically no. Were we scathing about each other's musical tastes? Occasionally, yes, but we never lost respect for each other as people and musicians. There was nothing vengeful about it.

Few bands can claim to have pioneered something. Although the press coined the phrase 'Celtic Rock', thank you very much, it's now a recognised musical genre and there are bands all over the world doing it. But we were the first. Ultimately, I didn't feel that our best work was ahead of us any more, so it seemed a good time to cut and run.

Melody Maker journalist Mark Plummer, who later reinvents himself as the novelist Brixton Key, is left frustrated by the split, having not seen Horslips rise to the mainstream international star status he had once predicted.

Plummer: It constantly surprised me that Horslips didn't become the truly massive band that they deserved to be. 'Dearg Doom' is a great anthem, and they had tons of fantastic songs, but what they really needed was a huge international No. 1 and that would have sealed it. I don't know why that never came, because they were such gifted musicians and writers, and their live shows

were legendary. But that's the roll of the record industry dice for you. I know so many great artists who didn't even make it to where Horslips got to.

O'Connor: We were a long way from being millionaires, although by the late 'seventies we thought we should have been. We didn't take the money and run like some other people in the Irish music industry have done; we paid our roadies, paid our overheads, and put the rest aside as development money.

When I look now at our touring schedules, I really don't know how we got through it. The last American tour had been particularly tiring and we came back to Ireland in shreds. Throughout the whole of our profes-

"The good news is we had nine blissful years followed by one when it hurt ..."

sional career, we very rarely managed to take time off. We often gave up our Christmas Eves and New Year's Eves, but we still weren't rich.

Creatively, I think *The Táin* was an early peak, in as much as it was our musical constitution signed, sealed and delivered in the most credible form. After that, I think it went a little askew here and there. Trying to find a direction when you already had one was a mistake. *The Táin* was the direction, and it could have been capitalised on more.

I look back at those 10 years with absolute wonder, because this band came together by accident, and we learned so much about ourselves, about each other and

about life. Most bands these days don't last half as long. Above all, we were a solid unit who stuck to our principles. I'm very proud of what we did.

Fean: I joined Horslips just before my 21st birthday and grew up as a member of the band. They gave me a life I could never have dreamed of as that skinny little kid. Even though the last year had been very frustrating, I hadn't given up hope entirely. I think that if we had managed to reconcile the conflicting musical policies and decided to stay together, I would have been happy

to continue, and perhaps we'd have achieved a lot more recognition in both the USA and Britain.

Twelve albums came out of the eight years we were together as the definitive line-up, and that is a staggering amount of output that you couldn't hope to achieve today.

Carr: In my mind, the unsaid words were, 'Let's just wind this down, step away from it and see how we feel at some stage later.' We probably should have agreed to take a long holiday, followed by a serious discussion about how to deal with the future, but we were all too wasted.

One of the things that defined 1980 for me was that it was 'the year of meetings'. We had meetings about everything you can imagine, and the amount of actions receiving unanimous approval was dwindling.

The break-up period was horrible, and it almost got to the point where we might have needed counselling. It was the cause of so much psychic grief, and if we had known that was going to happen we wouldn't have put the band together in the first place.

Goals had shifted among the band members and it became very niggly. I was beginning to not recognise my band anymore. But I always felt that there was another big album in us, another *Táin* or *Book Of Invasions*, and perhaps that is why I didn't leave earlier even though I'd been tempted to do just that. We all abandoned ship together and I think that was a relief in the end, but it also took me a long time to get over it.

Lockhart: The punk scene did a pretty effective job of cleansing the album charts of conceptual rockers and only a few, like Genesis, survived after 1980, because they were willing to change. I've no great regrets that we couldn't reinvent ourselves, because I dread to think how it might have sounded.

The evidence of the two directions that might have fully emerged is there on *Short Stories*. One is a stripped down, new wave approach; the other is an extension of where we were at on *The Man Who Built America* – a more spacious production, but still including traditional cameos. Trying to make all this fit into the post-punk landscape whilst retaining some shred of our identity was always going to be futile, and fans weren't going to accept it.

There's every chance we would have written enough material between us for a further album, but the things that we were really good at doing were no longer sale-able. We were still mates, but we had resigned ourselves to the reality that this was as far as we could go.

Deeny: Right from the start, I believed that Horslips could become a big act and I think Paul McGuinness agreed, because in 1972 he wrote an article for *Rolling Stone*, saying that this was a band that could play Madison Square Garden. I was probably being a little too optimistic back then, because their originality prevented them from fitting neatly into the conventional mould that record companies can really get behind to propel them into the mainstream.

I thought it was to their credit that they called it a day when they did, and didn't choose to carry on regardless. I always considered them to be smart guys, and they proved me right in their decision, as tough as it may have been.

They remain a very important band in many ways. Horslips brought exciting rock music to young people in rural Ireland whose only exposure to live music up to that point was by seeing showbands wearing blazers who only played covers of hits. So by persuading ballroom operators to let us play at their venues and make a success of it, we opened up a completely new national circuit for rock bands.

Horslips also demonstrated that musicians could achieve artistic control. They made a massive con-tribution to the future of Irish popular music and helped to cultivate careers for Irish musicians. It can be claimed that they were trailblazers for U2 because, like Horslips, they have always been in charge of their material and image.

Iredale: I arrived back home knowing that Horslips now ceased to exist. That still reigns as one of the emptiest feelings I've ever had. It was a tremendous loss.

The industry has changed so much since then and my journey from being a fan of Horslips to eventually working with them was a time in my life that I cherish. I can't possibly express how excited I was. Every day I woke up feeling so thankful that I had this job, because I couldn't ask for more.

I really had been the luckiest teenager in the world.

'I appreciate what Horslips did for the Irish rock industry. They did an awful lot to keep the industry alive.

'What I loved was their management, their sell. They showed groups how to do it professionally.

'They spent a lot of money getting the best equipment possible ... they hired lights ... and did everything to project their music, which I feel they had integrity in doing.

'Horslips worked hard at their craft ... and a lot of people learned from it.'

Philip Lynott

(from an interview with Smiley Bolger)

CHAPTER 7

ZEN AND THE ART OF REINVENTION

The period that will come to be known as the 'longest tea break in rock'n'roll' gets underway, as the individual members of Horslips set off on new creative journeys.

Some relish the chance to re-shape their lives and embrace new musical opportunities. For others, slowing down and adjusting to an existence no longer regimented by touring and recording schedules is not so easy.

Before 1980 comes to a shattering end with the tragic murder of John Lennon, Eamon Carr and Johnny Fean (right) form a new band ...

ZEN ALLIGATORS: Back To Basics

Fean: Eamon and I lived quite close to each other in Leahy's Terrace, Sandymount, and around November 1980, we dreamed up the idea of forming a new band called The Alligators. By the time we got the first [three-

piece] line-up sorted out, all the material was ready to rehearse. It wasn't at all the case that we were thinking of a new band while Horslips were still going, but our involvement in The Defenders' benefit gig probably had an influence on how things might shape up. We were impressed with Gary Eglington's bass playing at that gig and thought he'd be someone we could work with.

Carr: After the turmoil of the last few months with Horslips, I just wanted to play a little bit of rock'n'roll and the idea of playing with Johnny in a sort of a scaled-down band appealed to me enormously. There certainly was never a world-domination plan with the Zen Alligators, which is what we eventually called ourselves. Our transition meant downsizing to avoid the emotional bends. We went into a cottage for a month after the Horslips split and just played, worked up a set and prepared ourselves to play gigs.

Fean: The idea was to get back to our R&B roots

Zen Alligators: Gary Eglington, Johnny Fean, Philip Fay and Eamon Carr.

and play fairly simple rock and soul music, effectively distancing ourselves from our Horslips past. About three months later, we added Philip Fay [ex-The Soul Survivors & Vultures] on rhythm guitar to make it a four-piece.

From our first appearance at the National Ballroom in Dublin in 1981, we did a lot of live work. We played absolutely everywhere and were seen live on RTÉ's 'Campus Rock' series.

Some people were disappointed that we didn't dig out a few oldies but it was too soon after the spilt and best left alone. Our only concession was to play 'Shakin' All Over'.

Carr: The gigs were very enjoyable and Johnny's guitar playing went from strength to strength during that phase. The predominant audience we had were kids who were into Mod and R&B. We mostly played our own songs, mixed with a few covers by Al Green and similar artists.

Vocally, I think Johnny reached a peak between 1979 and 1982, and I think that's certainly evident on the singles that the Alligators released. Our first proper single was 'Who Can That Someone Be?' which did quite well and charted.

Steve Iredale: As soon as they were ready, I went out with the Zen Alligators as their road manager, and we

CHARLES O'CONNOR: Dirty Work

The multi-instrumentalist begins a new life and a new love affair on the streets of London.

O'Connor: It took a year or more to sink in that Horslips had really thrown in the towel. When you're used to the pace of a fast-moving treadmill and then suddenly the brakes are slammed on, it's a very strange feeling and I was devastated. Who was I now?

One day I might feel relieved that I didn't have to get up and jump in the back of a bus; the next I'd be terribly depressed, almost as if I was in mourning. I had no idea how to exist outside of that bubble. I'd also broken up with Sue, my long-term girlfriend, and I was about to leave for London.

Something very strange happened when I was on the way to London. I stopped off at a motorway café and saw U2 sitting in a corner, looking like they were planning their future. It felt like there had been a spiritual handing-over of the baton. They were starting out on their journey to world domination.

The last thing I wanted to do was play music, but I was staying in London with Robbie McGrath and one thing led to another. Eventually, in 1982, Robbie persuaded me to form a band with him and Chris Page, a bass player from Southend-on-Sea, and we called it Dirty Work.

I wrote and sang all the songs, which were quite unusual. I also played guitar while Robbie played drums. Our look and sound was veering towards the New Romantic style, but I think it was all doomed to fail, because after a year we still hadn't played any gigs and weren't very serious about it.

While I was in London. I got together with Numi [Solomons]. Through friends, we'd met at the end of 1979 and after our existing relationships broke up we started to see each other. We ended up living together at Murray Head's flat in South Kensington for two years, before finding a place in Bethnal Green.

took the Horslips PA system with us. I was with them for about a year when I got a call one night from Tim Nicholson, U2's tour manager. He said that Barry had been talking with Paul McGuinness and recommended that we have a chat about me getting involved with U2.

My first job was to go to Heuston Station in Dublin to pick up Joe O'Herlihy, their sound engineer. I'll never forget Joe's words: 'This is not your normal band.' These words would echo many times over the next 20 years on the road with them.

Touring around Ireland with a different band wasn't appealing to me but the prospect of getting back to America and Europe was. The greatest thing to emerge from touring with U2 was meeting the woman whom I'd later marry, Sue [a.k.a. 'Duchess'], and work with on numerous major tours, as well as Horslips' 2009 arena shows.

Fean: Towards the end of the Zen Alligators, we were finding it hard to get decent bookings although not through any fault of our own. Live music began to play second fiddle to discos. DJs were becoming increasingly favoured by venue operators and promoters, and because they were half the price, it badly impacted on good working bands.

Above: O'Connor with Robbie McGrath and Chris Page as Dirty Work.

For years, I'd been very keen on photography. I was lethal with a Minox camera and did some work for some adult magazines, which was kind of interesting and very lucrative. I also got back into design and worked on some projects with Geoff Halpin, who was then with Hipgnosis. It was like rediscovering all the stuff I'd learned at college. I designed some packaging and record sleeves for Murray Head, then after a while I was itching to play music again.

Very occasionally, I'd make a guest appearance on someone's record. Phil Chevron asked me to do a session for a band called The Mighty Clouds Of Dust in 1983. Later on, I recorded some fiddle on Lal Waterson & Oliver Knight's album, *Once In A Blue Moon*. Lal was such a talented, distinctive singer, with a family that was steeped in folk music tradition. It was so sad to hear that she died very soon after we worked together.

THE HOST: Season Of The Witch

Three-fifths of Horslips team up to collaborate on a project with a dark theme.

Fean: In the summer of 1983, while the Zen Alligators were still trying to make a living, Eamon and I were starting another project with Charles, as The Host. Working again with Charles was a big boost for us; we were joined by Chris Page on bass, and Peter 'Sid' Keenan on keyboards. Our aim was to record an album called *Tryal*, based on the dark story of Bridget Cleary, who was burned as a witch by her husband in Tipperary in 1895.

Carr: This was a bizarre tale that we never really considered in Horslips. I'd only ever read folklorish accounts until a friend of mine gave me an academic paper on the subject, which was fascinating because all the facts were there. I automatically thought there was

Above: O'Connor, Fean and Carr mixing The Host's *Tryal* album. Below: The final touring version of The Host: Brian O'Briain (Uilleann pipes), Brian Narty (bass), Fean, Carr, John Ryan (keyboards) and Paul Murphy (guitar, violin).

a screenplay waiting to be written, and that it begged a good soundtrack. An equally good album was just one step away from it. It was obvious that we needed Charles on board. There was a good freshness and spontaneity about this project.

O'Connor: It came out of the blue. Eamon told me

about this really interesting story that might just be a movie, and that maybe we should just go ahead and work on a soundtrack album. It was quite a thrilling prospect to be handed such a framework. So I went over to see Eamon and Johnny, and we approached some people about getting the project financed. The creative juices flooded back.

We gave ourselves the name The Host, and agreed that the album would be called *Tryal*. Eamon had the narrative nailed down, so it was a case of teaming up on the general songwriting.

I think the album came together really quickly with Robbie McGrath as the producer. He had been working in studios and had some good ideas. It was exciting to work again with music that had thematic substance. In some ways it felt like a natural progression from what we had done on albums like *The Book Of Invasions*,

Right: John, Tommy and Pat McManus, a.k.a. Mama's Boys.

and with Robbie there with us it was almost a reunion.

Fean: Although *Tryal* now sounds entrenched in 'eighties production values, the music turned out to be very inventive. Charles wasn't very enamoured with the prospect of coming over to do a full Irish tour and the movie idea didn't work out either, although we got a decent album out of it.

Carr: Johnny and I worked on the opening music and incidental passages for an interesting play for UTV and Harlech TV called 'The Hidden Curriculum', by Graham Reid. Off the back of that, a tour was offered to The Host. With Charles now out of the picture, we roped in Paul Murphy who played guitar and fiddle; John Ryan, formerly of Granny's Intentions, on keyboards; and a young uilleann piper, Brian O'Briain.

Everybody in that particular variation of The Host really sparkled. Johnny and Brian made a great partnership. Then, just as it was settling into place, Brian left to join In Tua Nua. The Host then fell apart, and I was pretty upset because I thought it would develop.

BARRY DEVLIN: Star Codes & Silver Screens

Initially returning to the advertising world and guesting as a record producer, Barry Devlin makes his only solo album before chancing upon a new career as a director and screenwriter.

Devlin: After we broke up I was so traumatised that I started to get everything wrong, and my life was a bit of a mess for a while. Some days I would drive near Sandymount, where Johnny and Eamon lived, and just park up with the engine running, imagining I was there

to pick them up for a gig. That's how much I missed the band.

I tried to keep myself as busy as possible by working with the McManus brothers, Mama's Boys. Pat, John and Tommy used to come to our gigs in Bundoran and they eventually formed their own group, called Pulse. Their sister Molly [now Molly Kavanagh] suggested we check them out, so I went over and saw them rehearsing at home. I thought their hard rock sound had enormous potential, and so we gave them some support slots.

Our roadie/driver Joe Wynne took on their management, while Steve Iredale recorded a live 'bootleg' for them. When they changed their name to Mama's Boys, I was asked to produce a couple of singles and their first two albums, *Plug It In* and *Turn It Up*. Both albums were done quickly and I was very pleased to help them.

They were all superb musicians and very nice lads; in fact, all the McManuses are lovely, but they've not been immune to tragedy. It was devastating when they lost their other sister, Valerie, in a car crash and then in 1994, Tommy succumbed to leukaemia, after being in remission for a long time.

Alongside my work in advertising, I produced a few other acts in that early 'eighties period including The Crack [featuring Stephen Travers], Alma Carroll and Neuro, an arty new wave band from Waterford. They were all people who I either knew personally or through

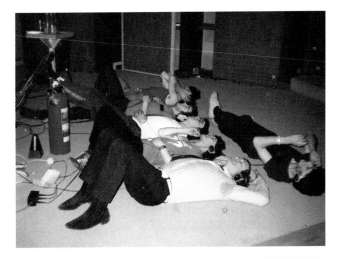

Left: Devlin, the producer, working flat out in the studio with new wave band Neuro; the astrology-themed *Breaking Star Codes*.

about certain issues was to change the locks on our doors, and so I had to find my own dwelling place. Her ploy concentrated my mind, and within four weeks I was hoping that she'd let me come back because I was so miserable without her. Thankfully she did, and about a year later, on October 9 1982, we finally got married and had three amazing children, Paul, Jack and Kate.

I went back into copywriting for advertising, working part-time at Saatchi's Dublin office, and continued to do that on and off for Aer Lingus and Volkswagen until 1990, taking three months off here and there to work on other projects. I enjoyed this pattern, and later on, when I was with Peter Owens Advertising, I was paid a retainer as a freelancer. It was a good way of keeping a roof on the house until other things showed up.

In 1983, Devlin returns as an artist and records the only solo album of his career to date.

Devlin: *Breaking Star Codes* was recorded at Windmill Lane Studios, and came out in the spring of 1983 on WEA Ireland, although I'd been working on the songs for it ever since Horslips finished. It was an attempt to rekindle my music career, but it felt slightly alien because I didn't have a band and I wasn't gigging.

The songs were about people I'd met on the road who believed in astrology, and based around real situations I had encountered. It was originally inspired by conversations we'd had in places like New York bars, where someone would say, 'I really love your accent ... are you a Sagittarian?'

I was slightly poking fun at the idea that all this meant anything, because I don't actually believe in astrology,

friends, and sometimes people would come to me because they'd been Horslips fans.

I had proposed to Caroline [Erskine] at the end of 1980s but things weren't going too well and she wanted to be sure that I intended for our relationship to continue. One of the stumbling blocks had been that she had her own brilliant career as a journalist and broadcaster, and with me being away all the time with Horslips, she'd had the space and time to develop it. When the band broke up I was twiddling my thumbs at home, and it led to some problems between us. She believed I wanted to get married for the wrong reasons.

Caroline's way of helping me to make my mind up

Right: Bass players united – Devlin with Adam Clayton backstage in Fort Lauderdale at the start of U2's *Elevation* tour on March 24 2001.

but I could see that it was a good subject for a concept album. Having Roger Dean, the king of prog-rock art, do the sleeve was pretty exciting.

We had some good players on *Breaking Star Codes*. Jim played on a few tracks and we had Paul McAteer on drums, Tommy Moore on bass and Mark Costigan of Stepaside on guitar, plus several other session guys.

The track 'December 21' features Jim Lockhart doing an American voiceover. It's one of a couple of songs that I'm really proud of. I love that line, *'I'm touching 34 though I can still touch my toes'*, because I was 34 then and must have felt old. I'm nearly twice that age now.

It was meant to be a video album, in the sense that there'd be a different video for each number. RTÉ filmed it all, and it was broadcast as a one-hour show about three times, but like a lot of RTÉ's programmes it got wiped. I couldn't really see myself as a solo artist, because I'm naturally shy and nervous, but with video fast becoming the popular music medium, I hoped to develop something interesting without having to tour. However, that pretty much marked the end of my career as an artist for the time being, apart from a few jingles and some music that I co-wrote with Jim.

Just as I thought my very ad-hoc production activities were coming to an end, I scored a No. 1 with a comedy single I recorded, 'Thank You Very Much, Mr Eastwood' by Dermot 'Father Ted' Morgan, which was his tribute to boxer Barry McGuigan, who famously used 'Sword Of Light' as his walk-on theme. Jim and I had worked as musical directors on 'The Live Mike', a variety show on RTÉ 1, and Dermot was one of the regular character actors, so that's how we got to know the great man.

Meanwhile, advertising was taking me around the world. For Bulmers, I went out to LA to shoot a pastiche commercial of ZZ Top's 'Gimme All Your Lovin'' video, with the girls and everything, but with the iconic

red 'Eliminator' car replaced by a Bulmers delivery van. It was work, but I use that word guardedly.

It was my connection with U2 that really got me started in the TV, film and video world. I ended up doing pop videos completely by accident, because I was working on a documentary with U2 about the making of *The Unforgettable Fire*. Pretty soon I found myself doing a variety of things for the band, like the videos for 'Pride (In The Name Of Love)', 'A Sort Of Homecoming' and 'Bad', and the European tour in 1985-6. I had a touching faith in my own capacity to put things together in an unscripted fashion.

I came back into the picture in 1987 to make the 'Outside It's America' documentary around the time of *The Joshua Tree*, and the promos for 'I Still Haven't Found What I'm Looking For' and 'Where The Streets Have No Name', when we held up the traffic and caused chaos in Los Angeles. I continue to have a lot of affection for U2 because of the work I did with them over that time and later on with things like 'A Year In Pop', which I wrote and Dennis Hopper narrated, covering the band's *PopMart* tour. It was a fascinating gig to be on, and they're still a great bunch of lads.

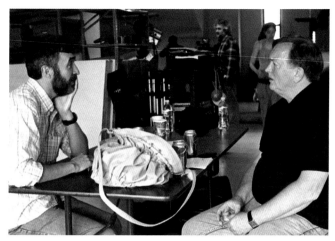 

Above: Devlin with 'A Kiss For Jed' star Mark O'Halloran and, lurking in the background, co-writer Maurice Linnane.

The bug for directing pop videos stayed with me for a while, and I made things like the 'Shipyard Town' video for Gerry Rafferty, Clannad's 'Harry's Game' and promos for Hothouse Flowers, River City People and Silent Running, amongst others, but from around 1988, I started to direct and write scripts for the BBC and RTÉ.

'Lapsed Catholics' [RTÉ, 1987] was a spoof drama about a 1970s Irish rock band who reunite for a one-off charity gig, and if this sounds familiar, it was never intentional. The story looks at the usual kinds of absurd band tensions that come to the surface with musicians, and I suspect that I may have been trying to exorcise some old frustrations.

The film included two songs that I wrote as cod prog-rock numbers: 'First Steps In Irish' and 'Open A Good Book'. If you could imagine Genesis and Yes at their most indulgent after taking an awful lot of acid, then that's what they sounded like.

'All Things Bright And Beautiful' (1994) was semi-autobiographical. It was based on the events that took place after the Virgin Mary appeared in my parish in 1953, when I was an alter boy. After I wrote and directed 'All Things Bright And Beautiful', I got a few offers to direct. However, I wanted to spend more time with my family, particularly as Jack was still a very young boy. I then began to concentrate on being purely a writer.

I worked on some episodes of 'The Darling Buds Of May' and 'Ballykissangel'; I did 'A Man Of No Importance' with Albert Finney, 'Perfect Scoundrels' with Peter Bowles and Bryan Murray, 'Messaggi Quasi Segreti', an Irish-Italian story, and several other projects, including a BBC mini-series, 'Runway One'.

It was fun to make 'Soul Survivors' (1995), another BBC mini-series, which starred Ian McShane as a Liverpool DJ who loved a band called The Tallahassees and went out to America to reunite them. I got the chance to work with Isaac Hayes and Antonio 'Huggy Bear' Fargas, who both played members of the band. Having listened to Isaac's *Black Moses* so many times on the way to gigs, thanks to Eamon, I was in awe of the great man.

'A Kiss For Jed' is a film that I wrote with Maurice Linnane, and after being shown at a number of film festivals, it got its general cinema release in May 2012. That's the latest of my films to hit the screen, but I'm constantly making TV pilots for all different things that may or may not extend beyond one episode.

Devlin has also been working as a 'script doctor' on 'Hound: The Legend Of Cúchulainn', a CGI/ live action epic based on 'The Táin', as well as continuing the development of 'The Virgin Of Las Vegas', a film co-produced by Bono and starring Liam Neeson as an Irish showband singer.

JIM LOCKHART: Radio Days

Shortly after the break-up of Horslips, Lockhart's career takes a detour as he cultivates an interest in broadcasting.

Lockhart: When you gather the kind of momentum and camaraderie that Horslips did over a 10-year period and then slam the brakes on, you're bound to feel a jolt, and I really felt it. Whilst the others had a trade to fall back on if needed, I had joined the band from a purely academic background and had been quite successful in avoiding gainful employment. Unfortunately, I was too ahead of my time with my environmental research to make a career of it, although it would be very useful today.

The end of Horslips was part of a rapid period of change for me. I was newly married; my mother was having a very tough time after my father died, and finding a new career direction fed into all of this. Meanwhile, there was still some unfinished business.

In the spring of '81, Eamon and I found ourselves [pictured below right] at the launch of K-Tel's compilation, *The Horslips Collection*. Jim Slye did a deal with K-Tel on our behalf, and it served a good purpose because we had never put out a proper 'best of' album until then. Promoting that was a bit like going to your own wake, but it was a way of keeping things afloat.

Music continued to dominate my life, albeit in a different way. My 'career rehabilitation' began in a round about way fairly soon after the break-up, when I started writing and producing music for advertising and jingles. I already knew that world to some extent, and Frannie worked as a producer in some ad agencies, so I had connections in place to find that work, and earned a reputation for being a good writer and arranger.

I always liked the recording environment and doing arrangements, and I soon found myself working again at familiar studios like Windmill Lane and Lombard. I was no longer interested in gigging for gigging's sake. I did it when it was important and interesting to me, but it was good to be free of it and focus on rebuilding a life.

Frannie went back to work after Ciara was born in 1982 [Ian and Jess followed in 1984 and 1990 respectively], and I spent about a year as a house-husband. Around that time, I had keyboards and recording gear permanently set up at home so that I could quickly make demos of any new idea.

I began writing for string quartets and, in a few cases, a full orchestra. I felt a need to get a better handle on certain elements of this, so I enrolled at the College of Music in Dublin and studied orchestration for a couple of years under a guy called Barra Boydell. I've been able to constantly draw from that knowledge ever since.

Larry Masterson was a friend of mine from way back. He married Áine O'Connor and also drove the band around when we rehearsed at Galerie Langlois. In later years, he became a producer at RTÉ, and suggested to Barry and I that we work together as musical directors for some of the TV programmes he produced, including 'The Live Mike' and 'Kenny Live'. As a result of that, I started to get another stream of work, doing incidental music and signature tunes for TV dramas and films. Whenever it was possible, I would sit in on the editing, which fascinated me immensely.

John Lynch, whom I met through Larry, was about to produce a new rural-based soap opera for RTÉ called 'Glenroe'. He asked me to write the theme music. A lovely traditional melody came to mind called 'Eireoidh Mé Amárach' (I Will Rise Tomorrow) that I'd learnt in Irish College and considered using on *The Man Who Built America*.

Three options for the theme music were presented to John, but it was the one based on 'Eireoidh Mé Amárach' that got the thumbs up. The arrangement is jointly credited to Barry and myself, which was how we did things at the time. A re-recording went out as a single on CBS and was a hit, but it was an even bigger hit four years later when it was the B-side of 'The By-Road To Glenroe' by Mick Lally, which I also produced. That was No. 1 for five weeks.

Then I had another No. 1 when I produced 'Watch Your House For Ireland', the Irish football squad's single for the 1994 World Cup, which had Christy Dignam from Aslan on vocals, Davy Spillane [pipes], Anto Drennan [guitar] and Paul McAteer on drums, with the football team singing along.

My radio career began in 1985. After hovering around television for a while, I began to prefer the idea of being a radio producer at RTÉ. With TV, you need a big production team, but you can pretty much make a good radio programme on your own and the results are a lot more direct.

I did a number of different programmes when I started in radio, but my main gig was a late night show with Mark Cagney. It was a bit of a rock'n'roll existence for a few years, because a group of us at Radio 2 – as it was before it was renamed 2FM – were like a band when we went on the road to do outside broadcasts. Dave Fanning, Gerry Ryan [who died in 2010], Ian Wilson, Mark and I would do a night or a weekend of shows on location, and shack up in a hotel, creating mayhem.

Ian Wilson was Dave Fanning's producer for many years, and has been very responsible for the direction of modern Irish music. He was the man behind the screen, a sort of unseen Irish John Peel – Ian's championing of so many new bands was so influential in developing that whole rock scene.

I produced some very good live concerts for RTÉ 2FM with Ian that were released, including one that Van Morrison bought back from us, shows by Deacon Blue

Lockhart's 'Theme From Glenroe' was a hit single in 1986, and reached No.1 when re-issued in 1990. Four years later, he produced another No. 1 – for Ireland's World Cup squad.

Below: The radio man at RTÉ.

Opposite page: Van Morrison, one of many major artists to have live recordings produced by Lockhart.

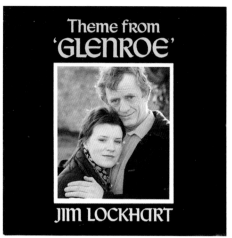

and The Divine Comedy, and also The Stone Roses gig at the 1995 *Feile* festival in Cork. Four of the tracks we recorded at that gig came out on their 'Crimson Tonight' live EP. I'm constantly reminded how cool that was, especially in the light of their reunion.

Those producer credits are something I'm almost surprised to look back over – we had tons of serious people come through for live sessions. I produced the first Cranberries session when they came in, and similarly The Corrs, The Frank & Walters and The Frames. My studio experience with Horslips proved very valuable; I already had experience of how a mixing desk worked and I enjoyed pushing the envelope with RTÉ's multitrack facilities.

I also continued to write and record in my own right. One of the more challenging and enjoyable projects was the score for Robert Quinn and Ciarán Ó Cofaigh's 2008 feature film, 'Cré na Cille'. I got Johnny in to play slide, and it picked up an IFTA nomination that year.

I used to accompany Dave on interviews with people like Paul McCartney and U2, and looked after the sound while he did the chat. In 2001, we went out to Miami to meet them at the start of their *Elevation* tour, when The Corrs were supporting. It was like one big family.

When things started to kick off again with Horslips, I had to do a bit of a dance in terms of meeting my responsibilities with RTÉ, and walk in two separate pairs of shoes. I've always religiously kept the whole Horslips

thing outside of regular work, but they all know what's going on and give me some friendly slagging!

I always fancied myself as more of a backroom facilitator, so I preferred the idea of producing rather than presenting. But over the last couple of years, when there were gaps in the Radio 1 schedule to fill, I started to present. I thought I'd be bricking it, but it felt completely natural and I instantly loved doing it. To discover something like that after skirting around it for so many years – and get a lot of positive feedback – is quite a buzz.

In early 2013, Lockhart officially retired from RTÉ, but continues to work on a freelance basis for the station.

Carr with Irish footballer Paul McGrath (far left), collecting awards for sales of their hit collaboration 'Ooh Aah Paul McGrath'. Below: Miscellaneous Eamon Carr productions.

EAMON CARR: The Producer

Carr: My passion was trashy garage music and I started to encourage and mentor a couple of young bands. In 1984, I put out a compilation called *Hip City Boogaloo* on my own label, Hotwire, through EMI. One of the bands on it was Light A Big Fire, and Robbie Foy and I started working with them. Their profile developed to the point where a TV producer picked them, along with Aslan, to represent Ireland as part of a pan-European music programme.

Craig Leon, the producer of Blondie, Suicide and The Ramones, saw it and contacted me through Robbie. He came over, saw the band and got right behind us. We did a mini-album, *Gunpowders*, through

Warners, licensed to Static, and then signed the band to Siren for their album *Surveillance*, in the mid-'eighties.

John Porter was recording the band's next album in 1988 when internal arguments lead to the band imploding. It was a sad waste of enormous potential.

Nevertheless, I was still very busy with Hotwire Records, producing bands like The Golden Horde with 'Illuminatus!' author Robert Anton Wilson, Stars Of Heaven, Bar Karma Beckons – whose line-up included my brother Jude – and the London outfit The Sting-Rays.

I've always enjoyed making new musical discoveries, and my period as a producer and record label owner gave me a lot of satisfaction and good times. But towards the end of the 'eighties, other activities began to take over my life.

UNDER PRESSURE: Revisiting A Classic Riff

In 1990, Horslips' most enduring anthem is back in the news as the Irish Republic prepares for World Cup fever. Produced by U2's Larry Mullen Jr. and based around the 'Dearg Doom'/'O'Neill's Cavalry' guitar riff (recreated in the Fean style by Anto Drennan), 'Put 'Em Under Pressure' is recorded at Windmill Lane Studios. It is released on the Son label during the summer as the official song of the Republic of Ireland soccer team's *Italia '90* FIFA World Cup campaign.

Carr: I like the interface between technology and acoustic music, so when I heard it I was delighted. It's probably the best football single ever made. When Larry's idea came along it was right up my street. 'Put 'Em Under Pressure' was Jack Charlton's phrase and they sampled his voice for the track. I thought that was genius and, for a few months, Horslips were able to bask in a bit of retro glory.

JOHNNY FEAN: London Calling

March 1985 sees Johnny Fean and Eamon Carr taking part in the recording of the single 'Show Some Concern' by The Concerned – an amalgam of Irish artists gathered in aid of African famine relief. The single reigns at No. 1 in Ireland for three weeks, until being deposed by USA For Africa's 'We Are The World'.

Fean: Being on a No. 1 single was a great feeling and it was all for a good cause. I've appeared on a few charity recordings over the years. At Steve Travers' request

I was part of the Miami Showband single 'Joy To The World', to benefit the children of war-torn Africa. And then Barry, Jim and I worked on a version of 'Trouble' to aid the Irish Youth Foundation.

I often played on other people's records. When Barry McCabe was recording his *Beyond The Tears* album, he asked me to play some guitar solos. Chisel was another band I did some stuff for. They were a Dublin-based ballad group, and Eamon, who was producing, asked me to contribute some acoustic guitar.

Eamon and I worked on numerous things. One of the less serious projects was 'A Hundred Thousand Welcomes For Boy George', which went out under the name of The Saints & The Scholars in 1984. For a laugh, Eamon co-founded The Boy George Welcoming Committee, to welcome the Culture Club star to his Irish ancestral homeland. Lots of people were on that record, including The Golden Horde, and I wrote it with Eamon, as well as playing some tenor banjo.

The guitarist relocates to London in April 1986 and begins to reinvent his music career.

Fean: After The Host, the last thing I did before moving to Wandsworth in south London with my wife Maggie was an acoustic album, *The Last Bandits In The World*, with Nikki Sudden and Simon Carmody. Once in London, I basically started all over again from scratch, doing a few bits of session work and forming a new line-up as The Johnny Fean Band.

It had been seven years since Horslips last played in London, so I automatically assumed that no one would remember me. But people were always coming up to me at gigs, saying they had great memories of Horslips and asking if I'd play some of our songs.

A project kicked off around 1989 called Spirit Of Horslips, which was prompted by a promoter. He had a band that knew all the Horslips songs and I was asked to front it for a tour of Ireland. It went down well, but it felt strange to be doing this stuff without my old band mates. That tour came and went, and I headed back home to London to start a band called Treat.

I met up with Steve Travers [pictured right] around 1996, and we began to play together as The Psychopats, with Dave Lennox on keyboards. Dave was from Dún Laoghaire, and had played with some big names like Ginger Baker and Al Green. But the economics of running a full band became difficult to manage, and after a few years with The Psychopats, I downscaled to a duo with Steve and a drum machine, calling ourselves Fean & Travers.

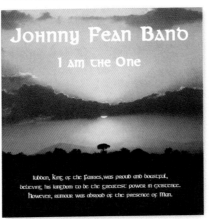

I stayed in London until 2001, when Maggie and I returned to Ireland. Steve also moved back and we decided to revive The Johnny Fean Band with drummer Mick Rowley, playing at venues around Ireland for the first time in a long while.

Steve and I had been writing with the intention of producing an album of Celtic-inspired material, based on an old Irish tale of a fairy king who ruled in a 'Gulliver's Travels' type of kingdom. Our first song was 'I Am The One', a powerful rock number with a strong guitar riff ['The Road To Lisdoonvarna'] that brought Celtic Rock into the modern era.

After gigging for a few weeks, we had the finances to record the song at Spector Studios in Cork City, and release it on CD. I got cold feet about doing a concept album after a while, so we never pursued it further, but I was very happy with the single.

As well as playing regularly with a bunch of musicians down at Shannon Knights, a venue near to where I live, I continue to gig with Steve and our current drummer, Blendi Krasniqi. The great thing about Steve is that he has been able to style a bass counterpart to my Celtic guitar style by adopting using bodhrán rhythms in the way his plays and it forms a really tight, rhythmic and melodic wall of sound.

EAMON CARR:
The Journalist

Carr: I never imagined a time when most of my income would be generated from journalism, but sometime in the 1980s, I started to get asked to write the occasional column or opinion piece.

I'd been doing some radio work, contributing reviews and commenting on cultural news and events. The editor of *In Dublin*, the Irish equivalent of *Time Out*, asked if I'd write a feature on my years with Horslips. I thought I'd try my hand, and it got a good response. It was recycled about 10 years later, when a new editor took over and found it in the archives. Getting paid twice for one article was like getting airplay royalties.

Second time around, I won an award for it, and it prompted a few commissions from *Magill* magazine, and some book and theatre reviews for newspapers, as well as a column for *Hot Press,* which gave me a vehicle for introducing hip-hop to Irish readers, because I wrote a lot about people like Schooly D, Public Enemy, Run DMC, Afrika Bambaataa and The Beastie Boys' 'Cooky Puss'.

Above: Carr interviewing Taoiseach Albert Reynolds, and meeting radio guest Dolly Parton.

This work expanded fairly quickly and it began to take over my life. The *Irish Independent* newspaper group heard what I'd been doing and offered me a regular music page, which was something of a rarity amongst Irish papers at the time, and pretty soon my workload increased.

In 1988, the idea of a weekly celebrity interview in the Q & A style of Andy Warhol's *Interview* magazine was proposed by my editor. The series ran for a long time. The first one I did was with Jack Charlton, then the manager of the Republic of Ireland football team. Jack was astonishing. It was probably one of the most explosive interviews he'd ever given in his life.

I was on a roll, interviewing all sorts of fascinating people, from Malcolm McLaren and Charlie Watts to Rudolf Nureyev, the most impressive person I ever interviewed. Sinéad O'Connor was the toughest of all of them. Politicians were always the most slippery.

I wound up covering wider news, like the funerals of Princess Diana in London and Mother Teresa in Calcutta. In Kosovo there was shelling in the distance and a fucking small earthquake. Suddenly this gig had become very real.

I now work for Independent News and Media, exclusively on the *Herald*, and concentrate largely on on sport and music. Press deadlines keep you grounded! As well as writing, I've been in and out of broadcasting with FM104, Century Radio and 92.1 Choice FM, where I hosted 'Carr's Cocktail Shack' and interviewed stars like the divine Dolly Parton.

CURIOS & COLLECTABLES: Life in Whitby

O'Connor: Numi and I recognised very early on that we were kindred spirits and, although we've never married, we've stayed together since the early 'eighties and our wonderful daughter Aphra was born in October 1991.

We moved to Whitby in 1988 and started trading in unusual 20th-century collectables. Our current shop, The Stonehouse Emporium, specialises in everything from vintage copies of *Vogue* and furniture, to ceramics and musical instruments. I've been interested in this stuff for as long as I can remember, and Numi was dealing in antiques in Portobello Road as a teenager, so it was inevitable that we'd run a business together some day.

O'Connor's two albums with Paul Whittaker; the Stonehouse Emporium in Whitby; taking a stroll along the banks of the River Esk behind the family home.

I was first introduced to Paul Whittaker during my London period, when he was the MD of Murray Head's band and producer of some of his records. I played on one, *Innocence*, and we later went out on three tours of France that were riotous affairs because Murray is such a theatrical bloke. Numi and I persuaded Paul to move to Whitby, and we started to do more together.

In 1994, I recorded an instrumental album with Paul called *Angel On The Mantlepiece*, and it was released on a German label, Koch, the following year.

Paul and I co-produced, and played pretty much everything, after converting my drawing room into a studio environment. It was very enjoyable to do. We blended folk and classical styles, with maybe a touch of jazz and Cajun, and gave it a modern feel. One track, 'Bottom Buttons', was used on the soundtrack of the film 'A Day At The Beach'.

Some years later, we recorded some more music, that was inspired by the HM Bark Endeavour, Captain James Cook's famous Whitby-built ship. We released a five-track CD, titled *Breaking Waves*. Aphra sang on one of the tracks, 'Ice Blink', and we also had a guest appearance by the brilliant Martin Simpson, who played acoustic guitar and banjola.

'Transit Of Venus', a song featured on *Breaking Waves*, also appears on a third album that I've done with Paul, called *The Shell*. It's been finished since around 2007, but I've not organised a release yet. I'll get round to it one day because, ultimately, I'm still primarily a musician, who just happens to also sell collectables, at least when I'm not gardening or managing the fishing along our private stretch of the River Esk.

Miracles
<u>do</u>
happen

CHAPTER 8

ROLLING BACK

March 1: On the steps of the High Court in Belfast, a long-running legal action steered by Horslips' new business manager Shay Hennessy against the Outlet Recording Company ends when the five band members accept a 'substantial' financial settlement and regain the rights to their entire catalogue, after many years of unofficial, unapproved and poor-quality releases by the Bel-

fast company. The band are represented by Donnell Deeny QC, brother of former manager Michael. Spanning 15 years, the events that lead to the settlement begin with a chance discovery.

Lockhart: After we broke up in 1980, we were able to close our account with Michael Deeny in a fairly straightforward manner, but it was more complicated

Opposite: Celebrating in March 1999 after successfully reclaiming the Horslips back catalogue.
Back row, L-R: Shay Hennessy, Barry Devlin, Robert Martin, Jim Lockhart, Michael Deeny, Donnell Deeny,
Johnny Fean. Front row: Eamon Carr, Charles O'Connor, John Coyle.
Below: Examples of Outlet's CD reissues.

· ·

with Jim Slye. It was certainly never intended that he should sell the band's master tapes or copyrights. Unfortunately that's what happened, but it took a long time to come to that conclusion

Devlin: For two years after we finished, we didn't even want to look at where we'd been. We were too concerned with reconstructing our lives. The thing I most regret about the break-up was that we took our collective eye off the ball, and allowed a window to exist whereby our catalogue became totally abused. We'd been so hubristic about the way our product was presented, and suddenly we were like every other band whose copyrights had been misappropriated, like the Small Faces who had so famously been ripped off.

Hennessy: It was in 1983, whilst working on The Host's album *Tryal*, that Eamon and I started to talk about Horslips again, and I was curious as to the whereabouts of their album masters. We did some investigation, and could only deduce that the tapes had all disappeared. Most of the band members had little interest in what had happened to them by that stage, but I kind of took it upon myself to dig deeper into this mystery.

There didn't seem to be a lack of product on the market but there were several unanswered questions, such as who was paying the royalties; who was getting paid and why; and what was happening with copyright issues, because the band weren't seeing any money.

Lockhart: Within two or three years of our break-up, we started to notice the existence of unofficial versions

of our albums. They looked like bootlegs, which they were, effectively.

Fean: You would see these shoddy old covers of your albums. It was so insulting.

Carr: The audio was as bad as the artwork. There were strange edits and misspelt titles all over the place. It was a huge embarrassment. We were being grossly misrepresented in every way.

Hennessy: Jim and Barry came on board the mission and went to one solicitor, while Eamon and I were seeing another. Whilst we weren't working in unison to start with, very soon we were all working from the same hymn sheet, and looking for some serious answers.

The masters appeared to be with Stoic, so we took an action against them. Their initial attitude was that they'd had four or five good years with the albums, and weren't particularly bothered about losing the rights. They were just at the point of handing everything back to us when they went into liquidation. The liquidator decided that these were valuable assets of the company and they weren't going to give them up without a fight, because they had a buyer who was willing to part with £30,000.

My argument was that the tapes were of no value whatsoever to Stoic or their buyer, because Horslips owned the copyright and any further releases would be in breach of that copyright. After a while, the liquidator gave in, and I bought the tapes for £500. We quickly realised, however, that we had only dealt with part of the problem.

Lockhart: It was discovered that the albums had filtered into the North via the Outlet Recording Company label in Belfast, run by William McBurney, an old-time business guy.

Hennessy: We took the view that Outlet had been supplied the product from Spartan. What we didn't realise until around 1987 was that Outlet had somehow managed to buy the rights to the masters for the rest of the world from Jim Slye, without the knowledge or approval of the band.

After a lot of searching, we finally found documentary evidence of this sale, and it was a severe blow to find that someone who had been trusted by Horslips had been so disrespectful.

We contacted the London firm of solicitors, Clintons, whose David Landsman initiated proceedings against Outlet. Because there was a fragmentation within the band, it wasn't always easy to get a unified agreement on some important issues, but fundamentally we were all driven by the same sense of justice, and we managed to get into court in Belfast in 1992 to ask for an injunction. But instead of this being awarded, we were given a right to trial, and Outlet were obliged to keep a full account of everything they were doing with the Horslips catalogue.

The journey from initial investigation to eventual settlement took nearly 15 years, and all sorts of craziness went on, but there would be long periods when the whole thing went to sleep. When we got Donnell Deeny [Michael Deeny's brother and an eminent senior counsel] involved, along with a young solicitor called Robert Martin, things started to accelerate. Robert had been appointed by Clintons as their agent in Northern Ireland, and he had a very keen interest in the band.

Lockhart: Also representing us as junior counsel was John Coyle, who was a massive Horslips fan and used to go to our gigs in Derry. I'm sure John invested a lot of his energy into batting for a moral victory. Between all of us – and notably thanks to encouragement from the likes of U2 and Gilbert O'Sullivan, who had previously gone through a legal battle of his own – we kept the momentum going and, after much perseverance, we finally got the case to court in Belfast in 1999.

Fean: At no point since the end of 1980 had all five of us been together in one place, and there we were, on the steps of the court. The stories and the jokes flowed as if no time had passed.

Hennessy: We never actually got to have a full hearing, but there was a fascinating tug-of-war match that was put before the Master of the High Court, and Outlet caved in during one of the recesses. So we ended up negotiating a settlement that included a substantial sum of money to compensate for lost income, and the master tapes held by Outlet were returned. It was a successful outcome to a long, drawn-out battle.

Those tapes were the quarter-inch production masters, containing the final mixes used to create the album pressings. The multitrack masters appear to have vanished forever, which is a huge pity because it made any future remixes impossible.

Carr: The only legitimate CDs that had been released before this time were on K-Tel, a reputable label. In 1997, we authorised a CD reissue of K-Tel's 1981 compliation, *The Horslips Collection*, which we'd originally agreed to because we'd never managed to put out a 'best of' during the band's lifetime. We also allowed K-Tel to release some of our material as part of their *Celtic Collections* CD series. Shay agreed an advance, and the royalties contributed to our legal fund.

Lockhart: That long, drawn-out legal process made it impossible for me to listen to any of our recordings for years, and none of us could do any promotion on behalf

"The journey from initial investigation to settlement took nearly 15 years ..."

Above: Abbey Road Studios engineer Peter Mew (left) digitally remastered all 12 of Horslips' original albums in 2000.

of the Horslips name, for fear of contributing to sales of the unauthorised albums that were circulating. If we had in any way given the impression that we were supporting them, it might have endangered our mission to win back control. So publicly, for a long period, we all had to remain silent about our old band, and it was often very frustrating.

The settlement was a great day for the band, and for musicians in general, and we all went out to celebrate afterwards.

June 1: The domain name HorslipsRecords. com is registered. The band's official website is soon launched, spearheaded by O'Connor and ultinately administered by Noel Ferris.

 April: Horslips digitally remaster their original albums with engineer Peter Mew at London's Abbey Road Studios and, over the next five years, they will release their first official CDs on the Edsel label, part of the Demon Music Group.

Hennessy: Having been vindicated in court, the guys went through the tape library, engaged with each album, and prepared a viable plan to remaster each item in the entire catalogue and get it all back into the marketplace. We cut a five-year deal with Demon in the UK to reissue the catalogue on CD, with a new set of generic cover designs by Charles. The CDs sold well.

The five members and I had made an earlier agreement, whereby I would handle their publishing if the court action went in our favour. There was some fragmentation between the Irish and international deals. Horslips had a policy of keeping as much of their work within Ireland as they could, including their publishing rights, which they had assigned to Emma Music, so we spoke to Emma and picked up the publishing rights for Ireland, and then started to investigate where everything else was.

There has been an ongoing challenge in terms of dealing with RCA and DJM for the rest of the world. DJM had been taken over by Universal, who now controlled the publishing for the 1976-1978 songs. Similarly, RCA was now owned by BMG, and they were looking after all of the pre-DJM rights. Both of those deals had been signed in perpetuity, which was unfortunate for us.

RCA were refusing to move at all until Clintons came back on board to make sure everything reverted back to us. Those songs are now controlled through my company, Crashed Music.

The DJM catalogue has been more difficult, and there are still 32 songs that Universal refuse to let go. Fortunately, we can release everything out of Ireland without breaching copyright.

Lockhart: When the production masters were returned to us, we noticed that they sometimes varied quite wildly in quality, because of the different Dolby noise reduction settings from the range of machines they'd been recorded on. So when we had them all cleaned up and digitally remastered in 2000, we chose Abbey Road Studios, because we knew they would have the widest range of tape machines available to handle this quality variation, and Peter Mew had such a brilliant track record as senior mastering engineer.

Carr: Hearing the remasters was the first time in about 18 years that I'd sat down and listened to any Horslips album, and it was such a surprise. The subtleties I'd forgotten about were brought out by the remastering.

O'Connor: We had to distance ourselves as much as possible from the previous unofficial releases, and that meant giving our CDs a different look. This was the point at which I started to work with Chris Ellis on our CD designs. He had a studio in Whitby, and we shared the design passion. The idea was to give the collection a 'library' theme of different coloured, textured backgrounds, featuring the original covers as insets.

Spring: Attempts to write new material together at Charles O'Connor's home in Whitby,

North Yorkshire, are abandoned after approximately 40 minutes' worth of material is recorded.

Lockhart: We did a couple of sessions in Charles' home studio after remastering the albums. It seemed like a good idea to get together and play some music, with the exception of Eamon, who couldn't make it.

Devlin: It was relatively tenuous, and the exercise was more about trying to develop an approach to writing in a second life, rather than it being the beginning of a project. Some of our doodles sounded promising, but I don't think a single track came to fruition.

O'Connor: Having the lads come to visit me for a change was great. It had been more than 20 years since we had been in a creative situation, and I think we might have done more if we hadn't spent so much time laughing about the old days!

Lockhart: We worked up some nice ideas with some sample loops, dug out some untested traditional tunes, and also revisited a few oldies from a different angle. One of those rehashes proved to be the foundation for the *Roll Back* version of 'Trouble (With A Capital T)', which came out of the blue when Johnny picked up his guitar and started to play a bottleneck slide riff.

May 7: A double CD, *The Best Of Horslips* – the band's first 'in-house' compilation to span their career – is released by Edsel/ Demon (MEDCD700). A special edition four-track CD and limited edition vinyl 12" are also released, containing three dance remixes of 'Dearg Doom' (by producers Metisse, Ufeari & Ear2Ear), along with Horslips' original 1973 version.

Lockhart: After 'Dearg Doom' had a revival because of the World Cup single, 'Put 'Em Under Pressure', it was thought that we should reclaim it as our own, as it was probably our most famous song. But a straight re-release was viewed as a boring idea.

Carr: It was suggested that a remix would be a better idea, but we no longer had the original multitrack tape. That's when the idea arose of getting a DJ producer to do a dance version.

I knew a Dublin club DJ called Goldy, who worked with another guy as Ufeari. Goldy asked if he could have a crack at doing a mix. At the same time, Jim knew Skully, a Cork-based producer, through recording his previous band, The Chapterhouse, and we gave him the opportunity to come up with something. He also worked with a partner, as the electronic duo Metisse.

Paul Murphy, who'd played fiddle with The Host, had a Pro Tools studio behind Shay's office. He and Barry Grace worked under the name of Ear2Ear, and remixing was part of their skills set. So we also gave them a shot. The exercise was all about seeing how they'd reinterpret 'Dearg Doom' for the modern dance market, and the results were really interesting.

December 17: U2's familiar-sounding 'The Hands That Built America' is released as a single from the soundtrack of Martin Scorcese's film 'Gangs Of New York'.

Devlin: Bono was worried that I'd be put out by the close similarity to the title of the Horslips song. He had some cheek! No really, we were extremely flattered.

Bono (as told to Maurice Linnane): You can rob your friends! Someday you can have your arm around them and you're telling them, 'Barry, does this offend you?' 'Not at all, Bono. No, no, no!'

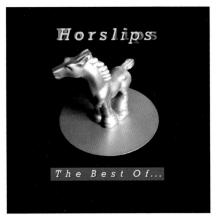

Includes mixes by Metisse..ufeari and Ear2Ear

March 20: After a fallow 2003, Horslips reunite to make a surprise live appearance at the opening of the *History Of Horslips* exhibition, organised by Jim Nelis, Paul Callaghan and Stephen Ferris at the Orchard Gallery in Derry. It proves to be the catalyst for all future band activities and events. The exhibition is open to the public from March 22 until April 2.

Devlin: It was interesting to see what we had actually been, and getting up on the stage was something I didn't think would ever happen. And we had the wonderful Steve Iredale and Pat Maguire back. This was the first time my kids had seen Horslips play. I think they loved it, and as a band, it reminded us of why we got together in the first place.

Lockhart: Suddenly, there was activity where there hadn't been for a long time, and Maurice Linnane's mission to make the definitive film history of the band was also adding to the excitement.

Parallel to this, I had introduced Jim Nelis and Paul Callaghan to each other. For a few years beforehand, Jim would surface every now and then, and tell me he'd found some concert posters and got them framed. Some of the stuff he was amassing was incredible.

Nelis: The exhibition was conceived in 1999, when Jim informed Paul Callaghan of my existence in Derry,

the history of

HORSLIPS

an exhibition

The reunited Horslips with exhibition organisers Paul Callaghan, Jim Nelis and Stephen Ferris in 2004.

and my vast poster collection. I was working at the Rialto Theatre and Paul rang me.

We decided there and then to showcase our memorabilia by staging an exhibition, but it wasn't until January 2002 that it was rubber stamped by the band, in Jim's house at my wife's 40th birthday party. Jim invited us. Eamon was also present and I'll never forget Barry's words: 'No problem, Nelis; if we would ever give anyone permission, it would be you and Callaghan.'

I assured them that this would be an exhibition they would be very proud of. My only concern was that it would only be complete if all members would turn up to the opening in Derry, and that was guaranteed. Jim and Barry came up to Derry to look at two galleries as potential venues. I reminded them that they played above the Orchard in St Columb's Hall, and the choice was made.

Callaghan: It was like Jim and I had been living in a parallel universe because we had so much in common, not least being Horslips fans since our early teens. I kept every souvenir and record release from those years, many of them extremely rare. So when

we began to look at each other's collections, we were taken aback by their vastness.

Nelis: In August 2002, Johnny and Steve Travers introduced me to Stephen Ferris. We were all die-hard fans, who believed that Horslips deserved some form of commemoration.

Ferris: Jim Nelis designed the entire exhibition with the exception of the photography, which was Paul's specialty. Jim was able to apply the discipline of displaying framed posters that he learned in theatre, and used all his contacts to print and supply all the marketing for the opening.

As well as collecting posters himself, Paul's background as a professional photographer meant that he had something in common with Charles, and a keen eye for choosing the right images to display. I remember Jim and I doing a 16-hour all-nighter in which we scanned all the press clippings for the montage, which was then assembled at random as one of the main attractions of the exhibition.

Callaghan: Charles has a very large archive of prints, negatives and transparencies, so I made a few trips to

Above: Rehearsing for the surprise live acoustic set (opposite) at the opening of the Derry exhibition.
Below: The displays included many rare items from the band's career. Right: Russian flexidisc bootlegs.

see him, and bought a good quality negative scanner to make high resolution scans of many of those images.

Ferris: To strengthen what were already sizeable collections, we were using eBay and Gemm.com to plug the gaps, as well as getting some help from Tim Maher in England, Dorie Jennings in the USA and Brendan McLoughlin in Dublin. The band had also given us all stuff.

Instead of attracting corporate sponsorship, we had a lot of very helpful people, including Paddy Goodwin, Keith Johnston and Pascal McKeown, and some local companies like Lermagh, Framed To Perfection and MK Audio, who all gave valuable assistance. Our currency was goodwill, and affection for the band we had

cared about for so long was in abundance.

It was the same with the exhibits. People would come along with posters, tickets and badges, and the rarest items included Barry's shamrock bass and Charles' *Happy To Meet* jacket. I thought Johnny's battery-powered, brown leather Pignose amp was a beauty. What amazed me most was the bizarre set of Russian flexidisc bootlegs that Jim bought online. Of all the things you might hope to find in a Horslips exhibition, these were the most unlikely. I was amazed when they actually played.

Lockhart: As soon as Jim, Paul and Stephen confirmed the opening date, it became very obvious that people might expect us to get up and play something.

Nelis: One day I rang Jim. Barry came on the phone and said, 'Hey, Nelis, do you hear that in the background?' I said, 'Yeah, I can hear music, what is it?' Barry replied, 'It's us rehearsing for your gig.' I nearly burst into tears on the spot. I had only asked that the band would turn up – this was an unimaginable surprise.

Lockhart: Apart from the brief sessions at Charles' place a few years earlier, we hadn't played a note together, so we had to put some practice in, and over a few weekends sharpened up a little acoustic set in my living room. There was some apprehension, for sure, but it was interesting to hear how voices had matured.

Ferris: Paul drove Jim and I to Jim Lockhart's house. The band were there with Shay Hennessy, and we were

the first to see and hear all of them play 'Furniture' live for the first time in over two decades. It was a very special moment. There was a warm atmosphere in the room and you could feel that everyone was happy to be there.

Nelis: When the band went out there to play that reunion set, the emotion was overwhelming for everyone. It was the best thing that ever happened.

O'Connor: I had played everywhere in front of tons of people, but I was nervous about that day. Looking down from the stage, all those people were singing along with 'Furniture' and we couldn't hear what we were doing, but it didn't matter a jot. It was pure magic.

Lockhart: Nervous? I was shitting myself, but it turned out to be a complete blast. Johnny was the only

Above: Selections from Maurice Linnane's photo diary of the summer 2004 Grouse Lodge recording sessions that produced the *Roll Back* album.

one who was actually playing exactly what he should play, but that's Johnny being the consummate musician that he is.

Fean: The three lads put together an incredible display. It made me realise that there had been a lot of unfinished business. This opportunity to play a bit and spend some time with fans was very healing.

Iredale: I wouldn't have missed Derry for the world. I'd been advancing a Metallica tour in Europe but I swore that whatever happened I would return especially for it.

The bus journey up there and back made me feel like I was 18 again. I had seen all the guys on and off, with the exception of Charles who I hadn't touched base with for over 20 years. It was like nothing had changed in some respects. But now we were all settled with wives or partners, and some of us had children at secondary school or university. This was Horslips in the second life.

Callaghan: The success of Derry encouraged us to take the exhibition to other parts of Ireland, which we did over the next few years. We completed our task and gave the band a greater sense of their musical and social legacy. I was proud that we represented the passion of thousands of people who were now in their middle age and never stopped being huge fans.

December 3: Recorded during the summer at the Grouse Lodge residential studio in rural County Westmeath, the acoustic *Roll Back* album (MOO23) is released. Featuring rearranged classics, the album is packaged with a bonus disc – *Music From An Exhibition* (MOO24) – including tracks and video clips from the Orchard Gallery.

Devlin: We were looking for the kind of studio we had been used to in the early days, like The Manor or Rockfield. Grouse Lodge is actually a very fine, state-of-the-art studio. It's an agreeable Queen Anne complex where the accommodation is in the stables, with four-poster beds; there's 24-hour catering and balconies overlooking babbling brooks. It was perfect.

The Manic Street Preachers had been in for eight weeks just before us. We had six weeks of bliss, and it was great to see how Johnny, Charles and Jim had matured as musicians, like cunning old men.

Roll Back was a very honest approach to arrangement and recording, and I'm very pleased with what we did to those old songs. We didn't allow ourselves the privilege of 3/4 waltz time in the old days, so it was quite joyful to play around with it for the reworking of 'The Wrath Of The Rain' and 'The Man Who Built America'.

What I wanted to do was sing 'Wrath' in 3/4 with just an acoustic guitar, but then it turned into a full band effort when Jim brought in the tune 'The Lambs On The Green Hills', which is usually played on concertina but he was playing it on organ. He did a really smart job of sliding it into the song arrangement, and it turned the piece around.

Lockhart: I was thinking of the way we imported 'Fhir a' Bháta' into 'The Blind Can't Lead The Blind' [*Dancehall Sweethearts*] as a counterpoint. It was always an interesting aspect of our music, so it was a case of trying it out for this one. There was a huge buzz in the control room when we listened to a playback.

Carr: The boys wouldn't have seen me behind a drum kit for 20 years, so to go in and lay it down pretty tightly was very reassuring, and I chose to use the blue Premier kit, previously owned by Brian Downey, that I'd played on the 'Fonn' TV series and our earliest singles. Playing this kit on *Roll Back*, 33 years on from the 'Fonn' shows, was like coming home.

Devlin: This was by far the longest we ever spent on an album, because our schedules were so tight in the old days. People talk about the long time-lapses between Kate Bush releases, but there were 24 years between *The Belfast Gigs* and *Roll Back*.

The album allowed some members of the band to express themselves musically in ways that might not have been possible in the old days, because of how those songs had been arranged in their original formats.

Carr: Everybody's done their 'unplugged' album, and so we were justified in taking that particular direction. It was interesting to revisit old songs and do them differently. After so long apart, it felt unbelievable that we were doing this.

In his final interview, former producer Fritz Fryer expresses how delighted he was to hear *Roll Back*.

Fryer: I always thought Horslips had more left in

"*Roll Back* was a very honest approach to arrangement and recording ..."

THE DOCUMENTARY

Maurice Linnane: In the late nineties, a documentary series, 'From A Whisper To A Scream: The Living History Of Irish Rock' was shown on RTÉ. To me it was a one-sided, over-simplified account of how great Seán Ó Riada was and how shite the showbands were ... but we did have Van, Rory, Philo and U2. The mortal sin at the centre of it all, however, was that Horslips seemed to be disparagingly shoved to one side as if we should be embarrassed by their very existence.

They missed the point in such a huge way that I wanted to make a documentary that told the story of what Horslips meant to me and to the many people I was sure felt the same way. But when I sent my treatment in to RTÉ, the response was a resounding 'no' based mainly on the fact that Horslips hadn't been 'current' for 20 years. Everything went on hold.

Meanwhile, Dreamchaser, the production company I co-owned, collapsed in 2003 and I had a career to rebuild. I revisited the Horslips documentary at the same time that Barry told me about an exhibition that was going to happen in Derry. Apparently, the band would be making their first public appearance since 1980. A bell went off in my head. I remembered RTÉ's objections and thought that we might just have a solution.

Barry insisted that the band would just be there but not play. I said, 'So you'll be in a room with a couple of hundred of your most die-hard fans, and when they ask you to play a song, you'll tell them you can't? Is that the plan?' He thought about this for a few seconds and then mumbled, 'Oh, fuck.'

Expecting a performance, I sent a new treatment to RTÉ. Ahead of a response, I went to James Morris, the CEO of Windmill Lane, and asked if he would give me his film crews to shoot in Derry. He graciously told me not to worry about the money, so I got on with organising the Derry shoot whilst filming the rehearsals and interviewing the band.

When RTÉ turned me down again I suddenly needed to find a way to fund the rest of the project. Lewis Kovac knew a lot about licensing and things outside my experience, and I saw him as a potential executive producer.

I also called Denis Desmond, the concert promoter, and explained that the band were coming to the end of the licensing agreement for their catalogue. If he backed the documentary there could be the option to put out a soundtrack on his label. Denis was engaged by all of this and, of course, started to think prematurely about concerts. After the success of Derry, however, Denis was thinking of a proper studio album. The band had been discussing the same thing. An overall budget was set aside and Denis believed the band would eventually consent to live work.

Tracking down the stills and memorabilia was heavily reliant on the band members and crew raiding their personal archives. Surprises included Robbie McGrath's previously unseen Super 8mm film of the band on tour, and numerous rare items donated by Charles and Steve Iredale. We added these bits and pieces to an invaluable archive of TV shows from RTÉ, the BBC and 'Musikladen' in Germany. But the big kahuna was the Derry exhibition which was the reason for them to stand on a stage again as a band and the key to absolutely everything that followed.

As we reached the end of post-production, RTÉ came back and said they would be interested in featuring it as part of their 'Arts Lives' series. Denis and Lewis did a deal with RTÉ on licensing an edited version for broadcast – eventually – on March 1 2005, followed by the DVD in November, which was more of an escape than a release.

I'm very happy with *The Return Of The Dancehall Sweethearts*. It showed how a band deeply affected a generation way above and beyond just musically. And that was precisely the story I wanted to tell.

them. *Roll Back* is the sound of five people having the time of their lives – the five people I remember. I love how they re-arranged some of those old numbers and injected so much love, creativity and enthusiasm into them. It's much more mature and it comes over as a superbly entertaining album ... which is what Horslips were always about.

January 1: Lora Lee Templeton's ComeBackHorslips.com website is launched.

Templeton: After *Roll Back*, there was so much excitement among the fans that it seemed like anything was possible for the band. I realised that just about every great band had at least one or two 'unofficial' sites orbiting the main one, so I got to work. It would be a place where fans could share music and photos, and give me an opportunity to geek out on the wealth of history, literature and inspiration to be found in Horslips' lyrics. The site's still going strong!

January 21: Horslips perform 'The Man Who Built America' live on RTÉ's 'The Late Late Show' – their first live televised performance since their reunion – and chat with presenter Pat Kenny.

February 16: 'Mystery Train' show on RTÉ Radio 1. The band are interviewed by host John Kelly about their earliest musical memories and influences. An acoustic-flavoured 'Dearg Doom' is aired.

Right: Maurice Linnane and his invaluable documentary film on DVD.

March 1: RTÉ broadcasts the début screening of *The Return Of The Dancehall Sweethearts*, the first ever full-length documentary on Horslips, written and directed by Maurice Linnane.

Lockhart: Barry, Eamon and I first saw the finished version of Maurice's film at a private viewing at the cinema in Denzille Lane, and it was an incredible experience.

Carr: Maurice was anxious for us to see it as soon as we could, because he needed to send it off to RTÉ. I could tell he was slightly nervous about what our reaction might be. We weren't really sure what to expect, but I was delighted with the way Maurice contextualised our story with other events in the 'seventies.

Topping and tailing it with scenes from the exhibition was a smart move, and his choice of talking heads was well thought-out. It took my breath away, to be honest.

Devlin: I live close to Maurice, and had seen some of the rough edits early on. He wanted to find a voiceover artist to do the narration, but I persuaded him to do it himself, as it often works if the writer is also the narrator. We were blown away by how sweet and poignant it was, and also the very vivid social history of the Ireland we lived through.

241

April 28: Formed by keyboard player Michael Rafferty, Horslips tribute act 'Horslypse' plays its first gig at the CBS Grammar School in Omagh, with Barry Devlin in attendance. Also featuring Ryan O'Sullivan (guitar), John Kelly (vocals), Conor McAloon (lead guitar), Daniel McCormack (bass), Damien Maguire (drums & percussion), Michael Kielty (flute), Patrick Bogues (violin) and Niall Moore (banjo and trumpet – related to Ray Moore, who played the trumpet fanfare on Horslips' 'Daybreak'), the band's set includes a complete performance of *The Book Of Invasions*.

Devlin: It was strange but also very gratifying to watch this bunch of youngsters doing such a brilliant job of being us. They're not just fans, they're good musicians who have spent a lot of time on shaping up the authenticity of what they do. Not even the real Horslips ever did the entire *Book Of Invasions*.

August 20: *The Boy Is Back In Town*, a concert tribute to Phil Lynott, plays to a sold-out audience at The Point, Dublin. Organised by the Róisín Dubh Trust with Gary Moore taking the lead role, Johnny Fean is invited to perform alongside Brush Shiels and Thin Lizzy's Brian Downey, Brian Robertson, Eric Bell and Scott Gorham, and wows the crowd with 'Dearg Doom'. The

Below: Highlights from 'Other Voices'.

concert takes place one day after the unveiling of Lynott's lifesize bronze statue in Harry Street.

October 6: The *History Of Horslips* exhibition opens at the Droichead Arts Centre, Drogheda, and runs until October 18. Both Horslips and Horslypse perform at the opening.

November 4: An extended version of *The Return Of The Dancehall Sweethearts* documentary is officially released on DVD (MOO26), with a bonus disc of vintage clips, promo videos and additional content.

December: A live performance for RTÉ's 'Other Voices' (below) is recorded in Dingle, and will be broadcast on February 15 2006. Horslips' set – 'Dearg Doom', 'The Man Who Built America', 'Shakin' All Over' and 'Trouble (With A Capital T)' – is their first 'full-on electric' performance since October 1980.

Pat Maguire: We rehearsed for the show over a couple of days in a pub in Ballyferriter Village, just outside Dingle. The regulars realised that the guys making noise

out the back were actually Horslips. On the second day we told the manager that if any of them wanted to come in and have a listen it would be fine. The punters couldn't believe their luck.

Devlin: It was a good idea of Pat's to bring the punters in. It was the first time we'd played with electric instruments in front of any kind of an audience since we got back together. I was genuinely terrified, and I blundered my way through the set, so this helped me to get my act together for the TV shoot.

Lockhart: Dingle was also the first time we worked with Liam McCarthy, a fabulous lighting designer. We had no hesitation asking Liam to come onboard with us when we did our arena shows in 2009. He had previously toured with The Corrs, and did a stunning job of creating a beautiful environment for 'Other Voices', which is set on a small stage in the 200-year-old St James' Church. Maurice Linnane directed the show, so we were in very safe hands.

Fean: 'Other Voices' is a very interesting TV show. Our set was short, but all the big numbers were present, and I could finally plug in and make the place rock.

February 7: The *History of Horslips* exhibition begins its residence at the Waterfront in Belfast. Originally planned for a month, the residence is extended until March 30 when the venue's officials are impressed with the quality of the exhibits and the attendance figures.

Halfway through the run, on February 25, a reception is held for Horslips, attended by all of the members with the exception of O'Connor, who has prior commitments.

March 25: Recorded at RTÉ Studios, the 'Ardán Horslips Special' on TG4 is billed as a celebration of the band's contribution to Irish music. Horslips play a set of nine songs: 'Trouble (With A Capital T)', 'Mad Pat', 'Ghosts', 'The Man Who Built America', 'Flower Amang Them All', 'Furniture', 'I'll Be Waiting', 'Dearg Doom' and 'Shakin' All Over'. Ian Lockhart, Jim's son, joins in on keyboards for the encore.

Devlin: The best version of 'I'll Be Waiting' we ever did was on 'Ardán'.

Lockhart: We were joined at the end of the show by others on the bill, including Liam Ó Maonlaí from Hothouse Flowers, Eoin Duignan on pipes and Aonghus McAnally, while [presenter] John Kelly joined in on harmonica. Kíla were filmed playing 'King Of The Fairies', which was a very flattering tribute.

October 9: Barry McCabe's new album, *Beyond The Tears*, is released. It includes guest appearances from Johnny Fean on three tracks. Other guests include Pat McManus (Mama's Boys).

November 4: Members of Horslips join friends and fans at The Wellington in Baggot Street, Dublin, to celebrate the 30th anniversary of *The Book Of Invasions*.

Lockhart: This was the first of a number of similar get-togethers [organised by Niall Goode and Brendan McLoughlin] that were based around album anniversaries. As well as being great fun, they bridged the gap between our first reunion performance at the exhibition launch and our eventual step back into full-scale gigs. Those parties certainly kept the flame burning.

March 17: Johnny Fean is honoured with the presentation of a framed portrait to the management of the Fadó Irish Pub in Denver, Colorado, at their annual St Patrick's Day celebration. The presentation is the initiative of photographer Sean Hennessy, Lora Lee Templeton and Damien McCarron of Colorado band The Indulgers.

January 30: Under license from the band, Strange Days Records (through Universal) releases the entire 1972–1980 Horslips album catalogue on CD in Japan, sporting miniaturised versions of the original sleeves.

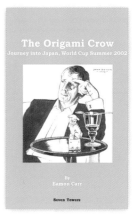

May 30: The Horslips exhibition opens at the Solas Art Gallery, Ballinamore. On the same night, The Johnny Fean Band play live at the nearby Commercial Hotel, with Devlin and Lockhart guesting. The exhibition is re-staged at the Balor Theatre, Ballybofey on July 13–19.

September 5: Henry McCullough's album *Poor Man's Moon* is released, including seven songs co-written with Eamon Carr.

September 17: Johnny Fean makes a guest appearance with The Miami Showband & Friends at a special concert at the Opera House, Belfast, to launch a new tour featuring the Miami's original surviving members. Fean also guests on 'Joy To The World', a Miami cover of the Three Dog Night classic, recorded to aid the Children In Crossfire charity.

October 8: Eamon Carr's book of poems and haiku, 'The Origami Crow, Journey Into Japan, World Cup Summer 2002', is launched in Dublin.

Top: Rehearsing for 'Ardán'.
Bottom: Performing on the show.
Above: Strange Days' Japanese 'mini' albums;
Eamon Carr's 'The Origami Crow'.

CHAPTER 9

THE ROCK REMAINS

May 22: The Troublemakers (below), featuring Johnny Fean, Jim Lockhart, Barry Devlin, 10cc's Kevin Godley and members of Kíla, Republic Of Loose and The Blizzards, perform a version of 'Trouble (With A Capital T)' live on 'The Late Late Show'. A studio recording, produced by Lance Hogan at Windmill Lane, is released as a download to aid the Irish Youth Foundation, while a documentary on the project is aired on 'The Raw Sessions' on RTÉ 2 on June 9.

Lockhart: It was a hugely enjoyable day in the studio with great ideas and great performances coming from every direction. There's a real buzz about getting to work with people you're a fan of, and I'm particularly a fan of the Republic of Loose.

Fean: It's always great to hear a different version of one of our songs and, even better, to get to work with other people on those versions. It was the start of a new mainstream awareness of Horslips.

July 2: Promoter Denis Desmond of MCD announces that Horslips' first major live concerts since 1980 will take place in December in Belfast and Dublin. Guest drummer Ray Fean (born September 6 1962), brother of Johnny, will deputise for Eamon Carr, who remains otherwise fully involved.

Lockhart: Denis bankrolled the production of the DVD and *Roll Back*, and being a concert promoter, he obviously wanted to see us go out and play some gigs. It was a regular topic of conversation for a few years, and the discussions we first had revolved around a similar model to the one adopted by Planxty in 2003, when they reformed for a small, one-off show and then

did some larger, additional shows over the following two years. I think Denis was hoping that if we did something along those lines, we'd get a taste for it and it could lead anywhere.

O'Connor: We thought it was time to stick our toe in the water, so we quietly booked a week at The Village, the club venue in Wexford Street, Dublin, and went in with Eamon to rediscover arrangements and learn how to be a proper band again. The sessions were recorded, and we took CDs home so that we could review them and sharpen up.

Carr: We did a week and gathered a pool of 30 numbers. Around half of them were as tight as we'd ever played them. By the time we'd finished at The Village, we'd nailed a set of sorts, and we could definitely have hopped in a van and done a bunch of gigs. Putting on a real show, however, is an entirely different discipline.

Devlin: Shay Hennessy told us we should play the O2, and we thought he was mad. The thought of playing to 14,000 people was insane. But Denis said exactly the same thing, and also wanted us to play the Odyssey, and he was ready to put his money where his mouth was. That's when we started to take the idea seriously.

O'Connor: The maddest thing ever happened when we mentioned to Denis that we might be ready to do something. Almost immediately, Pat Maguire brought in the evening paper and there it was, a full page ad: 'They're Back!' Denis wasn't hanging around! That was a bit scary, but there wasn't any turning back.

Fean: For a week or two after the announcement there was a bit of limbo, as we asked ourselves whether or not this could actually happen on a big stage. Despite all the pep talk, there was still some doubt.

Lockhart: The main argument we had against playing a big show for a while was that if you go out and screw up, you're not only doing yourself a disservice, you're also messing with the fans' memories, and they are precious. That was a consideration, because there was every chance we might screw it up.

Devlin: Our imagination hadn't run beyond maybe three nights at Vicar Street. The last time we'd played in Dublin was at the National Stadium, to an audience of 2,500, and in Ireland you couldn't play anywhere bigger then. We'd done supports for bands in 15,000 capacity venues in the States, but headlining carries a lot more responsibility.

O'Connor: Live performance in the 21st century is totally different to how it was in the 'seventies. The expectations of the audience in terms of what constitutes a viable show are much more sophisticated. So we knew we had a lot to deal with.

Devlin: Things had been building for a few years and it was just the right time. Some of us were more enthusiastic than others, but Eamon wasn't really keen at all. We agreed that if any of us didn't want to do it, it wouldn't happen, which is why we always refused Denis' offers. The next time he asked, however, Eamon came out with a leftfield solution that was incredibly selfless and broadminded.

Carr: I felt very conflicted about my decision not to play drums on the two big arena gigs. In order for the band to prepare for that level of performance I would have to do the full rehearsals, drum every day and be suitably in shape. It was going to take a lot of work, energy and especially time – a luxury I couldn't afford due to my regular work commitments. But I also didn't want to deny the boys that opportunity, so I suggested bringing in Ray Fean, a wonderfully gifted and respected drummer, as my deputy.

Being Johnny's kid brother, the guys all knew Ray as part of the family and he's grown up hearing all these songs. Fortunately, everyone thought it was a

"Shay told us we should play the O2 and we thought he was mad ..."

Horslips, 2009 style, with Ray Fean (below)

great idea, and he agreed to do it, while I remained very involved in the promotion.

Lockhart: It hadn't occurred to us to ask Ray, but we were obviously aware of how good he is. Ray took himself off to a studio near where he lives, put CDs of some of our old live recordings through his head-phones and started playing along. Before we could blink, he was ahead of the game.

Ray Fean: Johnny was my hero when I was a kid. I remember Christmas 1972, when he came through the back door with a box of albums under his arm. He pulled the first one out and gave it to me. It was *Happy To Meet, Sorry To Part*, and I was instantly awestruck. I'd already started playing drums by then and devel-oped some musical understanding, so I realised just what a huge deal this was, despite only being 10 years old. It just got better from there, and I looked forward to every new album.

So all these years later, to be playing with my big brother made me feel very proud, and it was amazing to play with such a brilliant guitarist. The others always treated me like a younger brother as well, so there was this lovely, warm vibe going on. It was a dream come true, a massive honour.

Fean: What's amazing is that in all this time, Ray and I rarely had the chance to play together, because we've been so busy with our own careers. Maybe just three times over 20 years, which is crazy. So it was fantastic to turn around in rehearsal – and at the gigs – and see our Ray behind the kit.

Above: Eamon Carr is behind the kit as Horslips perform at a party to celebrate the 30th anniversary of *Short Stories / Tall Tales*, on September 19 2009. Opposite: Rehearsing at Beechpark Studio.

August 14: *The Táin* (MOOCCD005), *The Book Of Invasions* (MOOCCD012) and *The Man Who Built America* (MOOCCD017) are officially reissued on CD for the second time. This time featuring bonus tracks, they are released by Celtic Airs and – influenced by the Japanese reissues – presented as 'digipak' miniature reproductions of the original album designs.

Shay Hennessy: When our deal with the Demon Music Group expired in 2006, we placed Horslips' product with Irish Music Licensing and started work on these new reissues. The bonus tracks are mostly live recordings from various sources that had never been officially released before, although a few had been circulating in lesser quality on bootlegs. All of the albums are fantastic miniature reproductions – Charles and Chris Ellis did a brilliant job with the artwork – and we released them in stages over a three-year period.

October 10: Horslips, with Ray Fean, begin six weeks of intensive rehearsals at Beechpark Studio in Rathcoole.

Lockhart: After the rehearsals with Eamon, we moved out to Beechpark with Ray, and by the end it was sounding pretty solid. Everybody came away very

pleased. Doing *The Book Of Invasions* suite and remembering the way we used to play it, with the segued songs, was quite a challenge after so long. We also worked up a few numbers that we'd never played live before, and that was rewarding.

Working in the old days, Alan O'Duffy taught us so much about musical arrangement, and it was lovely to see him backstage after the Dublin show. He'd tell us to make sure everything had a purpose, rather than just giving yourself something to do. It's got to have a meaningful role in the overall piece and earn its keep. We remembered this as we approached the rehearsals, because it gave us better recall of our individual parts.

Devlin: We did a pretty good job of remembering what we once were, using modern aids like iPods. We wanted to be better than we were when we split up. It's surprising how much you forget your own parts. Gradually, muscle memory returned and my hands and fingers began to do what they used to do. One day, we got critical mass and we suddenly were that band again. We started to grin like apes!

It was assumed that all of the idiosyncrasies we remembered of each other would have mellowed, but they were baked on us like ceramics! If Charles was that much more 'Charles', then I certainly had to be that much more 'Devlin', and you forgive everything. What emerged was how much we loved this, and

what a pleasure it was to be together in a room again and still be in one piece to do it.

O'Connor: Beechpark was a bit of a stretch for me, because I had to leave my home in North Yorkshire for long periods, living in hotels. Pat Maguire arrived on the scene like the 30 years hadn't happened. He'd taken all my instruments over to Dublin, and set them up for me. It was a tender moment ... a little like seeing our old Transit van with the fist on it again.

Lockhart: There was a version of 'Furniture' that we did around the start of the Beechpark sessions that probably rates amongst the most moving of all my Horslips experiences.

It was about 10.30am, a ridiculous time for rock'n'roll, and when it got to the middle, Johnny unleashed this incredibly lyrical, powerful guitar solo – probably the greatest I've ever heard him play. I actually felt privileged to be in the same room, let alone be in the same band.

Fean: Sometime in the last week of rehearsals we played through the full set list like a gig, and confidence was fully restored. We all knew we could pull this off comfortably to the extent that anyone who didn't know the history might assume we'd never stopped.

Ray Fean: I learned so much about Horslips during those rehearsals. I didn't make a conscious effort to stick to the parts that Eamon so cleverly invented. In fact, the band were telling me to do my own thing, but you can't in reality. Eamon was much more than the drummer; he was very involved in the structures of those songs, and shaped his drumming accordingly. It ain't broke, so I wasn't gonna be fixing it!

November 13: The release of a second double CD compilation, *Treasury: The Very Best Of Horslips* (MOOCCD027), featuring a special acoustic version of 'Dearg Doom', recorded for John Kelly's 'Mystery Train' show on RTÉ Radio 1 in 2005.

November 20: Horslips perform 'Dearg Doom' live on 'The Late Late Show'.

November 26–27: Warm-up performances at McHugh's Live Bar in Drogheda (opposite, bottom) Barry Devlin turns 63.

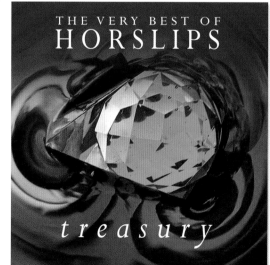

O'Connor: The first gig at McHugh's was amazing. We opened it up to the regulars on our website's Fantasia guestbook, and people flew in from Australia, the States, the UK and parts of Europe, just to be there. I had no idea that something so low-key would be so popular. McHugh's is a tiny venue, and we had something like 250 people in front of us. It was as intimate as it gets, and the adrenaline was really pumping. We could have played anything that night – everyone was so into it. It was a mutual celebration.

December 2: Horslips sign copies of the new *Treasury* compilation at the HMV store in Donegall Arcade, Belfast.

December 3: Odyssey Arena, Belfast, supported by Sharon Corr.

Fean: Belfast was chosen for the first show because that's where we left off in October 1980. We'd grafted so hard that we felt ready to take that leap. It was beyond all expectation.

Lockhart: Support, solidarity and deep affection came at us in huge waves. It was extraordinary. When Eamon came into the dressing room at the Odyssey, he said that he'd never been at a gig where the band were moderately relaxed and the audience were bricking it with nerves.

Carr: I stayed away from the McHugh's warm-ups because I didn't want to be a distraction. As a result,

the first 10 minutes at Belfast were probably among the weirdest in my life. I wasn't prepared for what I was about to see.

Liam McCarthy designed a retro light show for the first part of the set, and it was like stepping back in time. 'King Of The Fairies' cranked up, the bass drum hit four to the floor, and suddenly I was having this out-of-body experience.

I felt a lump in my throat as I recalled arranging and recording that number with the boys in '74. There was a very odd sense of looking at my life unfold in front of me.

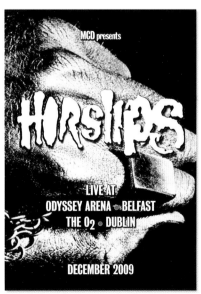

I looked around and saw a number of the audience in tears. Maybe there was something going on that was beyond rock'n'roll; maybe something indicative of what they went through in Belfast during the '70s. Perhaps their lost youth had tapped them on the shoulder. Whatever it was, the emotion was dripping.

In order to survive this two-and-a-half-hour marathon, I made myself busy with John Willis at the mixing desk, and became a kind of remote show director for the band, their eyes and ears out front. Once preoccupied, I was fine and I enjoyed it. Dublin was even better and I was doing what a lot of musicians never do: watch your own band do a gig!

O'Connor: None of our kids were born when we were together first time around, so it was wonderful for them to see what their Dad used to do. My daughter Aphra was very overcome.

Devlin: It was the great support network of the crew that actually made the show happen. Sue ['Duchess'] Iredale had worked on getting every minor detail put to bed and handling things at the sharp end for Shay. And whenever her hubby, Steve Iredale, was off the road, they'd work as a unit. She's an extraordinary professional, who provided a comfort zone for us.

Fean: Pat Maguire looked after the day-to-day stuff like our Guardian Angel. Then there was Liam McCarthy [lighting designer], John Willis [sound engineer], and Gerry Brady [stage monitor engineer], plus Maurice Linnane, who did the intro visuals. It was a big team effort, and we're so grateful for their continued support.

December 4: Each containing three bonus tracks, *Dancehall Sweethearts* (MOOCCD007) and *Aliens* (MOOCCD014) are the next CDs to be reissued by Celtic Airs as part of the digipak series.

December 5: The O2, Dublin – supported by Something Happens. The show is voted 'The Most Outstanding Horslips Gig Ever' by fans on Facebook and the official online forum, Fantasia, in March 2012.

Steve Matthews, the mandolin player with Cambridge folk-rock band Hedgepig, is one of the many 'second generation' Horslips fans present at the O2 to see the band live for the first time.

"There was a very odd sense of looking at my life unfold in front of me ..."

254

Above: Soundcheck at the Odyssey Arena, Belfast; December 3 2009.

Matthews: I nearly collapsed with excitement when I saw an ad for their comeback gigs. When the band arrived on stage, a massive surge went up my spine. They were on fire, far exceeding my wildest expectations. The sound was phenomenal. I felt so privileged to be a part of this.

Devlin: Dublin was special. Unforgettable. Those concerts in 2009 were as much about people reclaiming their youth as they were about us performing on stage. It was all about rekindling the glory days but, unlike the '70s, we were doing it in a time of relative peace.

Fean: Our fans are such a powerful, motivating force. The old regulars had been willing us to get back together, and it was wonderful to make it happen

for them. It was a real pleasure to see so many young people who seem to look upon us as a new band, without any sense of our history.

O'Connor: There were some faces in the crowd I recognised. It was like, 'I know you ...' but they were now 50-something. I suppose they were looking at me thinking, 'He's let himself go ... hasn't he got ugly?' We were watching the crowd as much as they were watching us.

Lockhart: I loved revisiting the whole *Book Of Invasions* sequence. People are a lot more willing to listen to longer pieces these days, and it got a tremendous response.

Devlin: 'Charolais' was an interesting choice. It was

The O2, Dublin; December 5 2009.

"Our fans are such a powerful, motivating force. It was wonderful to make it happen for them ..."

a number we stopped playing in 1974 and we weren't sure about including, because as a rock'n'roll song it makes no sense whatsoever. It's one of those songs that was always terrifyingly close to going wrong, but it's also a great showcase for Johnny and Jim. I'm sure it was a pleasant surprise for some of the audience.

Fean: I've done 'Sword Of Light' with my own bands over the years, but playing it with Horslips again in a full-scale gig was a huge buzz. 'Rescue Me' was also a lovely intimate moment with the acoustic guitar.

O'Connor: I enjoy singing, so my favourite numbers would be the ones on which I sang lead, like 'Flirting In The Shadows'. That song had a lot of breathing space in it, unlike others that were full of instrumental action.

Ray Fean: 'The Power And The Glory' really stood out. It's a great song to get into, and I do some backing vocals on it, too. I loved every minute.

Carr: Johnny's solo on 'I'll Be Waiting' made that one my favourite. No other guitarist could've played so exquisitely. In fact, it was very noticeable how all of them had seriously improved as musicians.

The occasion does not pass without a special on-stage appearance from Carr …

Lockhart: Eamon might not have played, but we felt his presence. It was a complete surprise when he came on stage dressed as Santa, handing out gifts of huge framed disc displays. All the crew knew, but not us. It was a lovely gesture, and everyone loved him for that.

Fean: I walked away from the O2 with a very different understanding of what Horslips meant to people. I've never witnessed such a reaction from an audience. It was totally overwhelming, as if Horslips were needed.

For thousands of people, these were the most important gigs that ever happened. They brought a lot of joy and tears, and even a sense of relief. These are very fine men who cared for their fans back in the day more than any band I knew, and they were getting all that love back.

Newspapers and music websites are unanimously jubilant.

'The striking feature of the gig is how the intervening years have not withered the power of Horslips' back catalogue. This is a band that has paid its dues.' (Sean Flynn, *The Irish Times*)

'At a triumphant gig in the O2 we were reminded of why they are held in such high esteem. The O2 has probably never rocked so much before this. It goes to show how much we pay for gigs these days and how little we get back. These guys reminded people how it was done and played for over two and a half hours.' (Kieran Frost, *State.ie*)

Brian Downey (Thin Lizzy): I was so pleased for them that the O2 was jam-packed. It was a fantastic performance. The only downside for me was that Eamon didn't play drums, even just for one number. Ray Fean is a great player and he really shone that night, and I suppose it was indicative of how selfless Eamon is that he didn't want to hog Ray's spotlight. But he was missed.

That show reinforced my belief that Horslips were a seminal band. It's undeniable. There wasn't another band in Ireland doing that kind of music and I was immediately aware of their originality and ambition to break the mould.

They had so much confidence in their own music and how they looked that they brushed aside any criticism and just got on with it. I applauded them for that, and I know they are held in great regard by a lot of my musician friends. Whatever it was they had, they still have it. The O2 show was emphatic proof.

At the start of 2010, Horslips' confidence is reignited in the aftermath of two triumphant concerts and a wealth of positive reviews.

Fans speculate on the impact this acclaim will have on the band's future live plans. Away from the public gaze, Horslips contemplate one or two festival appearances, and perhaps even a brief overseas visit. But only one date is firmly inked: a headline appearance as part of the *Live At The Marquee* concert series in Cork on Saturday 26 June.

As soon as tickets go on sale, fans snap them up hungrily, reportedly eclipsing the demand for Paul Weller's headline show of the series on the 27th. But on June 9, all plans are put on hold when Jim Lockhart suffers a heart attack.

Lockhart: I'd obviously been overdoing things, because I hit a speed bump on the great road of life and it was a timely warning. I was well looked after; the docs gave me a plugs-and-points overhaul, and told me to do nothing for a couple of months. I was getting my meals brought to me and knocking back handfuls of pills, so it was just like the old days!

It was sad and unfortunate that we had to pull Cork, but there was no way the docs were going to allow me to be so active so soon. I immediately started a major rehab programme that was packed with gym workouts, and have continued to be much kinder to myself because of this wake-up call. I'm now in the best shape I've been in for years.

Devlin: We were all deeply shocked. It's a blessing that Jim was so close to a hospital when he suddenly felt very ill.

O'Connor: After the momentum that had built up, we were on pause, feeling a little lost at sea after Jim's setback. It was fantastic to see him recover, but none of us wanted to rush him into anything or give him any undue stress. He had to spend a few months recuperating.

June 11: *The Unfortunate Cup Of Tea!* **(MOOCCD008),** *Horslips Live* **(MOOCCD010) and** *The Belfast Gigs* **(MOOCCD020) are re-issued by Celtic Airs.**

September 10: Horslips announce their forthcoming tour live on air, on RTÉ 2FM's 'Ryan Tubridy Show'.

September 13: Sharon Corr's solo album, *Dream Of You,* **is released on Rhino Records. The digital edition includes the bonus track 'Jenny's Chickens', featuring Jim Lockhart on flute.**

September 23: Horslips (minus O'Connor) are filmed performing low-key acoustic versions of 'Green Star Liner', 'Rescue Me' and 'Trouble (With A Capital T)' in the Duke of York pub in Belfast for the BBC2 Northern Ireland TV show 'Blas Ceoil' (centre). The Irish language show is broadcast on October 14 and aired on BBC Radio Ulster the following evening.

November 7: *Horslips – The Essential Recordings* **is a 10-track sampler CD of catalogue highlights given away free to readers of the** *Irish Mail On Sunday* **newspaper.**

November 19: Recorded at the previous year's show, double CD *Live At The O2* **(MOOCCD028) is the band's third official live release. A new DVD,** *The Road To The O2,* **is simultaneously released.**

Although recorded by producer and engineer Daire Winston, the owner of Horslips' chosen rehearsal venue, Beechpark Studio in Rathcoole, releasing a live album of the jubilant Dublin show is not originally intended. Neither is a DVD, until the band are convinced there is sufficient live footage from the O2 to justify a separate documentary, focusing on the journey from the initial ideas for a full-scale reunion show to the performance itself.

Hennessy: I desperately wanted to film the O2 gig, but the guys didn't want to pile pressure on top of what was already a big challenge. The video team who were sending live camera images to the side screens had not been instructed to record. I knew this was an opportunity not to be missed, so, without the knowledge of the band, I discreetly asked them to back up the camera feeds to tape.

Devlin: It was shrewd of Shay to organise this, because we had been very much against the idea. We're glad he didn't listen to us!

Hennessy: We wouldn't have had the core of what made *The Road To The O2* a justifiable DVD without the few intact pieces of concert film. That box of tapes remained unopened in my office for weeks until I revealed what I'd done at a meeting with Barry, Jim and Eamon, and we decided that a DVD might be possible.

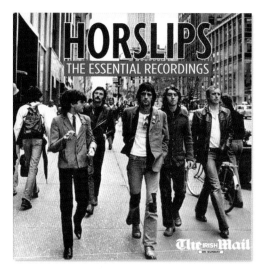

The Road To The O2 is directed by Rossa Ó Sioradáin, who quizzes the band members, collectively and individually, during a set of interviews filmed specifically for the DVD.

Hennessy: The idea of wrapping documentary-style interviews around the footage came about through those discussions with Rossa, and a plan was formed very quickly. I thought it was great to simply get all the guys together and have them discuss the journey.

Devlin: Rossa is a great director. He'd been a driving force behind the Horslips-themed edition of the TG4 TV show 'Ardán', and Jim and I worked with him in the States on his documentary series for TG4 called 'Rotha Mór an tSaoil'. We really bonded, and it felt right to have him do this DVD.

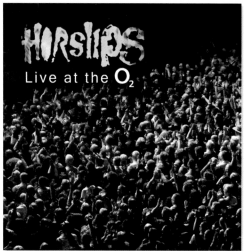

Fean: Considering it's not a concert DVD in the usual sense, I think it served as an excellent alternative souvenir for everyone who went to the gigs.

Daire Winston uses his computer-based Pro Tools HD system to digitally record the entire O2 show on 56 individual channels – a far cry from the days of Happy To Meet, Sorry To Part.

O'Connor: We got my friend Paul Whittaker to sit in on the mixing sessions and help Daire. They both have great ears, and shared the roles of listener and technician.

Winston: It was great to work with Paul, who is a great guitar player as well as a sound engineer; his help was invaluable from a musical perspective. I don't remember the last time I had so much fun in the studio.

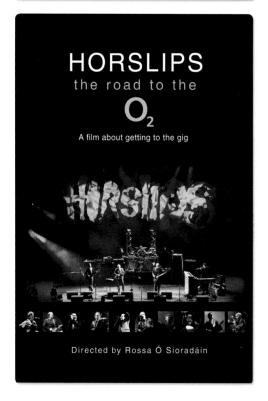

Carr: Live albums are difficult, because there are so many ways to mix them. Some are far too live for their own good, while others can sound sanitised. Being a band member who wasn't on stage, but heard what the music sounded like to the audience, I was able to bring that experience into the studio.

Daire and Paul did a very good job. There's more warmth and subtlety about this compared to our two previous live albums, and certainly better overall sound quality. I think most people were pleased.

Lockhart: The O2 show was very well recorded. I found it hard to believe that both a CD and a DVD came out simultaneously, because it all happened so unusually fast. It was only late summer that we even started talking about it.

November 20: Ahead of their winter mini-tour, Horslips return to Beechpark Studio for four days of rehearsals. On the first evening, the band

are interviewed by Brendan O'Connor on RTÉ 1's 'The Saturday Night Show' and play 'Trouble (With A Capital T)' live on the programme.

Fean: We met Joe Elliott from Def Leppard when we did Ryan Tubridy's radio show on RTÉ 2FM in September, and he's an old fan of the band. He saw us in Sheffield on *The Book Of Invasions* tour, and also at the O2 in 2009. He reminded us how important it is at this level to freshen up the set for a new tour.

Lockhart: You've got to shake the tree in order to keep things fresh. If I were a punter I wouldn't want to see the same show a year later. In hindsight, the previous year's set was too long and some songs hadn't matured quite as well as others, so that gave us the opportunity to replace them with things like 'The Blind Can't Lead The Blind' and 'Nighttown Boy'.

We then had the excuse to bring in some backing singers [Shelly Buckspan, Tanya Twyford and Jenny Sullivan-Wood] and horns [Richie Buckley from Van Morrison's band, Ronan Dooney and Barry McBrian] for authenticity. We also had Anto Byrne, a friend of Ray's, who came on to play a bagpipes intro to 'More Than You Can Chew', just to add a little extra flavour.

Carr: Although we featured female backing vocals on some of our albums, we never considered touring with extra singers in the way that the Stones and Humble Pie did. We probably didn't have enough songs to justify it, but Barry wanted to push the boat out a little and hire people for the 2010 shows, to make a significant difference. I wasn't wholly supportive of the idea to use the horns and the backing singers because I think the dynamic of a five-piece is what Horslips is all about, but they provided an interesting dimension and my scepticism was ill-founded in the end.

Above: DVD director Rossa Ó Sioradáin (front centre) during the filming of 'Rotha Mór an tSaoil'; Daire Winston mixing the *Live At The O2* album.

"We were a much tighter band this time ..."

DUBLIN DEC 4

King of The Fairies
Mad Pat
Blindman
Power & The Glory
High Reel
Maeves Court -
Charolais
Daybreak
Drive the Cold Winter Away
Ride to Hell
Sideways to the Sun
Dusk
Sword of Light
The Blind Cant Lead the Blind
More Than You Can Chew
Nightime Boy
Furniture
Speed the Plough
Sure The Boy was Green
Man Who Built America
••••••••••••encore
Trouble
Dearg Doom

Shakin' All Over

November 21: The band play an in-store session at the Celtic Note record shop in Dublin, and sign copies of their new CD and DVD.

November 27: Horslips kick off their short *2010 Winter Tour* at Irish National Exhibition Centre (INEC), Killarney, supported by Paddy Goodwin's Holy Ghosts.

November 28: Royal Theatre, Castlebar, supported by Risky Business.

December 1: The Waterfront, Belfast, supported by The Alan Kelly Quartet.

December 4: The afternoon sees Lora Lee Templeton host the Horslips History Walk, guiding visiting fans around numerous Dublin sites that have a connection with the band. In the evening, the band complete the tour at Dublin's O2, with support once again from The Alan Kelly Quartet.

Lockhart: We were a much tighter band this time and the performances had a smoother feel. And, frankly, I was relieved that I was back to a point where I could get back on a stage in front of an audience after such a scary summer. It was more relaxed this time. We could all enjoy the music without that 'gobsmacked' effect.

Devlin: I think 2009 was more about a gathering of people in the way that the next winter never could be. It was like, 'God, they're back and we're all going to see them again,' and very much like the intended resolve of that Pulp song, 'Let's all meet up in the year 2000.' Next time around, we were in better shape and old friendships were now continuing in parallel with the band.

HORSLIPS 2010 TOUR INSTRUMENTATION

BARRY DEVLIN
Ampeg Dan Armstrong bass, 1974 Fender Jazz bass, Ampeg 200 watt valve amplifier and Ampeg 8 x 10" speaker cabinet.

JIM LOCKHART
Hammond B3 organ with two Leslie speakers; Roland Fantom X7 keyboard, Nord Stage 88EX keyboard, Yamaha flute and Goldie whistle (D).

JOHNNY FEAN
1959 Gibson Les Paul Junior, Epiphone Wilshire reissue, Atkin acoustic guitar, Fender 40W VM Deluxe combo and Line 6 60W Flextone combo.

CHARLES O'CONNOR
Danville electric mandolin, Gibson Florentine F2 mandolin, French violin, Wheatstone 48-key Tenor Treble concertina, Aola concertina and 1954 Martin 000-18 acoustic guitar.

RAY FEAN
Pearl Reference Series drum kit in a custom 'Shimmer of Oz' green finish, featuring two 22" x 20" kick drums with 'Táin fist' front skins, plus Zildjian cymbals and a Roland TD-10 percussion sound module.

January 18: *Celtic Connections,* Old Fruitmarket, Glasgow (above) – Horslips' first gig on the British mainland since 1979. Reviewer Darius Drewe Shimon colourfully describes the performance as 'the sonic equivalent of a semi-on rising to a full-blown erection and exploding in one's black worsted grundies'. He adds:

'I've seen some legends in my time … and in terms of visceral, sweat-dripping rock excitement, coupled with genuine progressive musical inspiration, Horslips are the equal of all of them. All that remains now is for them to come to London and remind the rest of us.'

March 11: *Drive The Cold Winter Away* **(MOOCCD009),** *Tracks From The Vaults* **(MOOCCD013) and** *Short Stories / Tall Tales* **(MOOCCD019) are the penultimate CD re-releases from the digipak collection.**

March 17: Waterfront Hall, Belfast. Organised by BBC Radio Ulster and Belfast City Council, a special St Patrick's Day concert features Horslips and the 69-piece Ulster Orchestra performing extracts from *The Táin* and *The Book Of Invasions*, masterfully arranged and conducted by Brian Byrne. With Paul Casey guesting as support act, the concert is the result of an invitation by the broadcaster's then executive producer of music, Declan McGovern.

Broadcast live on BBC Radio Ulster, with fans from all over the world listening online, this is the first time the band has performed with an orchestra. The concert ends with a short set of 'greatest hits'. Paul McAteer is the band's guest drummer, in Ray Fean's absence.

Devlin: I had been to see Paul Brady perform at the Waterfront with the Ulster Orchestra a year earlier, and was knocked out by how beautiful it sounded. Speaking with Declan McGovern after the show, I couldn't stop myself saying how much I'd love Horslips to do a similar kind of show, and he was more than happy to run with the idea.

Fean: Most musicians would love the opportunity of playing their songs with the accompaniment of an orchestra, and this was something very special for me. To

play and have this huge sound coming from behind me was an indescribable feeling. It made me look at our material through fresh eyes. 'Sideways To The Sun' sounds so sweet and the way that Brian Byrne arranged the introduction of 'The Power And The Glory' was stunning. It's an experience that I would recommend to all musicians.

Lockhart: We didn't really know what it would be like until the one day that we rehearsed with them and then sound-checked on the afternoon of the show. Our communication had been by e-mail or phone until then. We did discuss a few aspects of different songs and how certain

motifs might be worth accentuating or expanding, but it didn't really prepare us for how this would manifest, and it was an amazing feeling.

O'Connor: As a teenager, Brian had played 'Trouble' in a function band with his father, so I expect he had great fun writing the arrangement for that. It was interesting to hear some of the traditional elements of our songs come through orchestrally.

Lockhart: Some of the songs sent tingles up my spine. 'Ghosts' was heartbreakingly beautiful, and the way Brian interpreted the intro to *The Táin* for the orchestra was extraordinary. Standing there on stage, we felt humbled that we were supported by such an incredible array of talent.

March 20: Croke Park, Dublin (left). Horslips perform 'King Of The Fairies' and 'Dearg Doom' live during the interval of the GAA match between Dublin and Mayo.

O'Connor: It counts as one of our most unusual gigs, because we were on a tiny stage in the middle of a big playing field, with no physical connection with the audience because they were so far away.

Devlin: I had always wanted to play Croke Park, in whatever form that might take, and we finally did it. Unfortunately, there were problems with the sound. Our guys asked us to wait to go on until they'd got the house PA system sorted out, and the time lapse meant we were reduced to just two numbers, but, hey, we were following in the footsteps of Jedward, so it was an honour!

March 27: The first episode of Rossa Ó Sio-radáin's four-part documentary series 'Rotha Mór an tSaoil' is televised on Irish language channel, TG4. Filmed in the USA during 2010, the series explores the stories found in Micí Mac Gabhann's posthumously published memoir 'Rotha Mór an tSaoil' (The Big Wheel Of Life), which had influenced some of the band's late '70s work.

From the steel mills of Bethlehem to the gold fields of the Klondike, Devlin and Lockhart (right) perform some of the songs inspired by Mac Gabhann's journey, and meet descendants of the Irish workers from Mac Gabhann's 19th-century life. Part of the series is shot in Denver during the previous May, when the Horslips duo meet and play live with Colorado band The Indulgers at the Fadó pub.

Larry Kirwan of Black 47 meets up with Devlin and Lockhart during their visit. In his online blog, he writes:

'Ambitious as ever, Jim and Barry are using the book as an analogy for Horslips' own musical travels – and travails – from Ireland to a fabled America. What a blast then to introduce them to Bainbridge Avenue in the Bronx, the dead center of Irish-American music in the latter decades of the 20th century.

'I hear echoes of Horslips in so much of today's Irish-American music ... and one recent summer's evening I was lucky enough to be given a chance to add infinitesimally to the Horslips legend when Jim and Barry joined Black 47 onstage for a frenetic version of their classic "Wrath Of The Rain".'

April 5: IML, in partnership with RTÉ, releases CD and DVD versions of *Ar Stáitse* (meaning 'On Stage'), a compilation of live tracks by various artists from RTÉ's concert archives. Horslips' 'Furniture', and their cover of Steppenwolf's 'Never Too Late' – from the 'Music Makers' TV broadcast of the band's February 1973 National Stadium concert – are included.

April 24: Philip King's 'Spin' series for TG4 focuses on classic Irish albums. For the fifth episode, King covers the story behind *Happy To Meet, Sorry To Part,* and interviews Horslips about the recording and its effect on Irish music culture.

June 19: *London Feis,* Finsbury Park (overleaf). The day after Bob Dylan's headliner, Horslips play a late afternoon set among a bill that also includes Van Morrison, Thin Lizzy, Clannad, Jimmy Cliff, Hothouse Flowers, Paul Brady, Eddi Reader, Mary Coughlan and Teddy Thompson.

Devlin: It was an opportunity to play in London at long last, and to see a lot of people wearing Horslips

T-shirts at a gig that was not exclusively ours was a thrill. Word had obviously got around that we were still alive and, perhaps, even kicking.

Lockhart: Sharing the bill with Lizzy, Van the Man, Clannad and Paul Brady, it was like we'd stepped back in time. Van was having great fun. When he was doing 'The Star Of The County Down' he was rocking. We had some craic that day.

Devlin: I had my family with me, and Kate, my daughter, ran a life-saving service, bringing booze from backstage out to her pals in the guest area!

O'Connor: We had a really great day in London at the *Feis*. The food, the weather, the people and the gig itself were all wonderful.

It appeared that we made a few fans that day and many old friends were also there, including Michael Deeny, Peter 'Supermick' Clarke and Mick McDonagh, who nearly signed us to Transatlantic back in 1971.

July 31: *Galway Race Week Carnival*. Horslips play live in the Big Top, wrapping up a week described as 'the greatest midsummer festival on the Irish calendar, a week long lollapalooza of fun, music, drinking, carry on and craic – a Mardi Gras of Irish madness.'

August 4: The *17th Guinness Irish Festival*, Les Iles, Sion, Switzerland – Horslips share the bill with Breton act Tri Yann and Sultans Of Swing.

August 11: Horslips play the final concert of the *Bulmers Live* series at Leopardstown Racecourse.

Lockhart: From a purely musical perspective, the Leopardstown show was the best we played all summer. Everything fell together really well; we'd had a great day at the races and then gave a very solid performance to round off the evening.

Devlin: I asked my wife, Caroline, to put €10 on a horse called Astrology, because of the link with my *Breaking Star Codes* album. It came in at 12-1, so I was jumping around doing high fives, but Caroline didn't look happy. She revealed that on the way down she'd placed the bet on a horse called Mannheim instead. It came last. Our lawyer friend Paddy Goodwin said that I would be excused for murder, as no Irish court would convict me for such a crime passionelle.

August 13: *Fairport's Cropredy Convention*, Oxfordshire. Horslips are special guests at the 2011 edition of the ever-popular festival, sharing a bill that includes UB40, Seasick Steve (with Led Zeppelin's John Paul Jones), Hayseed Dixie, The Coral, Badly Drawn Boy, The Blockheads, Richard Digance and the hosts, Fairport Convention.

Dave Pegg (Fairport Convention): It only took 40 years for Horslips to play on the same bill as us again [since *Sligo Sounds '71*], which is a mere blip in the history of time itself, and well worth the wait. They played a storming set, one that our audience will remember for a long, long time, and it was a joy to see the guys having so much fun.

Simon Nicol (Fairport Convention): Horslips were without a doubt one of the most popular bands that we've booked since our festival began more than 30 years

FairLips United FC, with 'super sub striker' Bob Harris.

Above: *Arthur's Day,* with Eamon Carr back behind the kit. Below: The intimate Cloth Ear gig. Opposite: Ulster Hall.

ago. The very long queue at the signing tent served as good evidence of that. People were still lining up for autographs when we started our finale set! That in itself probably set a record.

Pat Maguire: One of the guys running the CD tent told me he had never seen a band do a signing session for two hours and 40 minutes, and still be smiling at the end.

O'Connor: The thing about playing in a band is that you might have three members thinking it was a great show while the other two will tell you it was a bit crap. The only time you can be sure it was brilliant is when everyone agrees it was. That happened at *Cropredy,* which I think was one of our greatest-ever gigs and for all sorts

of reasons. It's never about having the audience in the palm of your hand, because that doesn't really happen; the audience decides when you're that good and they let you know. They certainly let us know at *Cropredy,* and got the hump when we didn't come back for an encore.

I think we'd have played for longer, given the chance, but it was impossible. Poor old Badly Drawn Boy had to go on after us, because Fairport needed a low-maintenance solo act to bridge the gap while their gear was being set up for their headline set.

We got off stage and I just wanted to get pissed, I was so thrilled. It was great to meet up with the Fairport guys and Bob Harris. The whole *Cropredy* vibe was just wonderful.

September 22: *Arthur's Day,* **Belfast. Eamon Carr receives a frenzied reception as he sits behind the drums for his first major concert performances with the band since 1980. Horslips precede their headlining slot at the Ulster Hall with a surprise 'pop-up' gig at nearby pub The Cloth Ear, where they play 'King Of The Fairies', 'The Power And The Glory', 'Mad Pat', 'Speed The Plough', 'Sword Of Light', 'The Man Who Built America', 'I'll Be Waiting', 'Trouble' and 'Dearg Doom'.**

Devlin: *Arthur's Day* was the true reunion of all five of us playing in the venue where we did our last gig in 1980. The arena gigs of 2009 and 2010 were huge milestones, but going back to the Ulster Hall was our big full circle moment. That was very special for us.

Carr: It worked for me, because it didn't require me to spend a lot of time in rehearsal – just a couple of hours a day or two in a studio in Stoneybatter before the gig, and that was enough to get back into the swing of it. It was only a short set and you tend to just lock into that stuff. If you do that nearly every night for about 10 years as I did, you physically remember what to do.

A few times in the set, I'd hit an accent and Johnny turned around with a big grin on his face. We had a ball.

Pure instinct kicked in and it was hot, sweaty stuff! And then I looked more closely at the room which felt familiar. I never expected to play on that stage again.

Fean: Playing at the Cloth Ear with the audience right on top of us was one of my favourite moments of the last few years.

Lockhart: Something happens when the five of us play together that you can't replicate. The gigs with Ray have been fantastic, but there's a wonderful chemistry with Eamon that instantly takes us back to our essence of Horslips. It was wonderful to look over and see our old friend banging away.

O'Connor: I think the pub gig was better than the Ulster Hall. It was more impromptu and everyone had a good laugh. At one point I honestly thought my fiddle bow was going to shoot up someone's nose, it was that much of a squash at the pub. I loved every minute, and the party back at the hotel after the gig was just as great.

November 19: Friends, family and Horslips members celebrate Johnny Fean's 60th birthday with a surprise party and all-night jam session at Carrygerry House in Shannon. Guests include Johnny's former Jeremiah Henry bandmates Guido DiVito and Jack Costelloe.

"Something happens when the five of us play together that you can't replicate ..."

November 25: *Live With The Ulster Orchestra* (MOO 30) is released on CD. The album is dedicated to Maureen Powell, the late sister of Charles O'Connor.

Shay Hennessy: The album was recorded by Davy Neill and mixed by Richard McCullough of RTÉ, while Charles and Chris Ellis worked on the package art in good time to meet the deadline. A couple of songs were filmed by BBC Northern Ireland, but other than that there is no broadcast-quality footage, which is such a pity because of the nature of the event. It could so easily have made for another great DVD.

Devlin: With our old albums we didn't have a budget available to hire an orchestra [with the notable exception of 'High Volume Love' on *The Unfortunate Cup Of Tea!*], so I'm thrilled to bits with the live album. I'm so glad that we all survived long enough to see it happen.

In his review of the album for RTÉ's website, Paddy Kehoe writes:

'Fans of "I'll Be Waiting" will hear an orchestra play along with the tune as if they had been working with Horslips from the time it was first performed.'

 February 23: Horslips record four songs – 'Furniture', 'Flower Amang Them All', 'Trouble (With A Capital T)' and 'Dearg Doom' – and an interview at RTÉ's Donnybrook studios for Miriam O'Callaghan's 'Miriam Meets' Sunday show on RTÉ Radio 1. Fans rate the performance as being among the band's best.

Lockhart: Damian Chennells engineered and mixed the session, and the results he achieved in the short time available were very impressive. Colm Flynn filmed us during the session and so we came away with a nice little package that seemed to please a lot of people.

Carr: I used the kit that Myles Lally plays in his band Risky Business. Damian is a really fast but precise worker, as good radio engineers are. I can't think of another time when my drum sound has been sorted so quickly. They were fine performances. I think it's a great sounding document of Horslips in the present tense.

February 24: *Happy To Meet, Sorry To Part* is re-released in digipak CD format, packaged as a faithful miniature reproduction of the original concertina-shaped sleeve and booklet. This edition completes the digipak collection of the original 12-album catalogue.

March 2: The press launch of the *2012 Rory Gallagher International Tribute Festival* is held at the Mansion House in Dublin, attended by Lockhart, Devlin, Mama's Boys legend Pat McManus and Boxtie frontman, Johnny Gallagher.

Lockhart (at the press conference): Donegal is a spiritual home for Horslips, so returning after many years and doing it for Rory in Ballyshannon is going to be classic.

Above: In session for RTÉ Radio 1's 'Miriam Meets' show.
Below: Johnny Gallagher, Devlin, Lockhart and Pat McManus at the 'RoryFest' launch.

March 5: 'The Lady Wrestler', Horslips' long-lost, unreleased song from 1971, is covered by The Radiators From Space on their album *Sound City Beat*. Eamon Carr makes a guest appearance on a cover of Thin Lizzy's 'Dublin', giving a sensitive reading of Phil Lynott's lyrics.

March 17: On the 40th anniversary of Horslips' début single release, Barry Devlin, Jim Lockhart and Johnny Fean perform as guests of Paddy Goodwin & The Holy Ghosts at a St Patrick's Night gig at McHugh's in Drogheda. Guitarist Henry McCullough also guests with the ensemble.

March 23: Devlin, Lockhart and Fean star once again with Paddy Goodwin & The Holy Ghosts at McGrory's in Culdaff – a gig opened by The Teraways, who give a rare performance of 'Come Back Beatles'. The following day sees a screening of *The Return Of The Dancehall Sweethearts* at the venue.

Fean: To be back in Culdaff was a bit of a nostalgia trip for me. It was Paddy Goodwin's suggestion that we play at McGrory's, and he was absolutely right. It's a venue that was made for live music, with a first-class sound system and very friendly acoustics. We had a great night and the crowd were really up for it!

April 26: Barry Devlin and Jim Lockhart, and Hothouse Flowers' Liam Ó Maonlaí and Fiachna Ó Braonáin perform 'Don't Go' and 'Dimming Of The Day' together on RTÉ Radio 1's John Murray Show, broadcast live from the CHQ building at Dublin's IFSC.

Above: Horslips appeared with Sharon Corr, Liam Neeson and other major stars on the 50th anniversary broadcast of 'The Late Late Show'. Below: Performing at 'Roryfest' with deputy drummer Sean Devitt.

The performance is part of the launch of the 'Walk In My Shoes' campaign organised by St Patrick's Hospital Foundation to support mental health services for young adults.

May 5: The Johnny Fean Band play live at the *Festival Of The Fires 2012*, staged on the Hill of Uisneach in County Westmeath.

June 1: The band (with Eamon Carr) appear on a special 50th anniversary edition of 'The Late Late Show' alongside guests including Liam Neeson, Bono, Sinéad O'Connor, Imelda May, Sharon Corr and Daniel O'Donnell.

Lockhart: Inevitably, we played 'Dearg Doom', accompanied by the RTÉ Concert Orchestra, conducted by Brian Byrne. Dermot McEvoy, the pro-

gramme's music supervisor, organised for some well-known traditional players to join in at the end, including Sharon Shannon (accordion), Sharon Corr (fiddle), Mairéad Ní Mhaonaigh (fiddle), Gerry O'Connor (banjo), Eoin Dillon (uilleann pipes). The phenomenal line-up was mirrored by the 'who's who' of the Irish entertainment world at the after-show party.

June 3: Horslips headline the big top concert at the *Rory Gallagher International Tribute Festival* in Ballyshannon, County Donegal, with support from the Pat McManus Band and Moonchild. With Ray Fean absent due to his commitments with the *Celtic Woman* tour, long-time friend Sean Devitt (The Devlins) deputises on drums. The band pay homage to the Ballyshannon-born guitar hero by including his 1972 live classic, 'Bullfrog Blues'.

June 23: *Westport Festival of Music & Performing Arts*, Westport, County Mayo. Horslips share the first day's bill with Ray Davies, The Waterboys, Nick Lowe, The Dubliners, Beth Orton, Eric Bibb, The Undertones and many others. Ray Fean returns to the drum stool.

August 4: Horslips appear on 'Saturday Night With Miriam' on RTÉ 1, performing live.

August 25–26: Horslips play two 'Hot August Nights' at the National Concert Hall, Dublin (the location of Lockhart's first-ever public musical appearance, in the late 'sixties while at UCD), accompanied by the Orchestra of the National Concert Hall, with conductor David Brophy, using Brian Byrne's acclaimed arrangements from 2011.

September 28: McGrory's, Culdaff. *A Celebration Of Horslips Guitar Legend Johnny Fean* forms part of the *2012 Inishowen Guitar Festival*. Fean, along with Devlin, Lockhart, O'Connor (and his daughter Aphra) and Paddy Goodwin's Holy Ghosts, performs live to a packed audience.

October 27: INEC, Killarney.

October 28: The band and assorted guests play live at Ray Fean's belated 50th birthday party.

December 14–15: Christmas Party shows at the Olympia Theatre, Dublin (above and opposite) – supported by The Trouble Pilgrims, featuring Steve Rapid, Pete Holidai and Paddy Goodwin. Horslips begin their performance with an all-time first: an 'acoustic set' of extracts from their 1975 *Drive The Cold Winter Away* album, featuring the rare sight of Fean as banjo player.

After a romp through their greatest hits, the band close with a festive medley starring Aphra O'Connor as guest vocalist, reprising her earlier role with The Trouble Pilgrims.

February 16: Fean, Devlin and Lockhart guest with Paddy Goodwin & The Holy Ghosts and The Trouble Pilgrims at the *Men Against Cancer* charity event held at McKenna's Bar in Monaghan.

June 1: Paul Brady invites Devlin to join him on bass, at a gig in aid of North Tipperary Centre for Education for Autistic Children, at The Whiskey Still in Dromineer, County Tipperary.

June 21: At *A Night For Christy*, a fund-raising tribute for Aslan lead singer Christy Dignam at the Olympia Theatre, Dublin, Lockhart, Devlin and Fean perform Aslan's 'Different Man'.

LOOKING BACK TO THE FUTURE

Devlin: What we now have in front of us is a blank canvas. We're now a band that can gig, no question. There is a will for us to play more shows if the right offers come in, and that could be from anywhere at any time.

A full-length tour has been a possibility for a while, and we've not been short on options, but the reality is that modern touring is expensive and, although we're not in it just to make a ton of cash, there's no point in losing money either.

Lockhart: The period since we stepped out at the *History Of Horslips* exhibition seems to have flown by. Ten years ago, we had absolutely no idea that Horslips would rise from the dead in the way it has. Finding the ideal balance with the unpredictable demands of the day job can be tricky but thanks to my very supportive work colleagues I've been lucky to do more with Horslips than I expected.

O'Connor: Living in North Yorkshire and running an antiques business means that my world turns upside down every time I come over to Ireland for rehearsals, meetings and gigs.

I don't like the upheaval that much, but the reward of making a lot of people very happy with Horslips more than compensates for everything. I would love to tour with this band again, if we can make it work from a business perspective.

Fean: My situation is different, because I've never stopped being a professional musician and never will. It's who I am. I respect what the others do for a living, and they all have fascinating lives outside of music. But, of course, now that Horslips are back in the game, I would love to go all the way with tours and albums – I have no hesitation there. I get more of a thrill from playing Horslips songs now than I ever did.

Devlin: All of us are songwriters, and I think we're all capable of writing new material for this band if the right circumstances arose. Sometimes we get close; at other times it seems impossible. What that album might be, who knows?

Carr: How far forward this can go is anyone's guess, but the mood is lighter and there are all kinds of possibilities. I could easily revert back to being a drummer if we did some recording, and after *Roll Back*, that prospect still excites me. As *Arthur's Day* showed, playing live with the boys is also possible as long as there's minimum rehearsal and preparation, and it could happen out of the blue, depending on the timing.

O'Connor: We never had any great game plan as a band in the 'seventies, and that's still very much the case. We appreciate that many of our fans would like us to be more active, and that's no longer a heavy pressure. The good side is we can now cherry-pick what we want to do in a relaxed way.

Carr: There will almost certainly be further releases from the archives. Recordings exist that have never officially seen the light of day, and there are probably good reasons for letting them out of the bag in the future.

Devlin: This unexpected second life has shown us that not only are we remembered, we're also loved, and that's priceless. We are now more aware of the significance of what we created in that long ago, distant era – and of our mortality – than we ever were. There's no time in this life for 'what ifs' and 'maybes'.

We have had the most tremendous fun that five people could ever dare wish for, and we thank our families, friends and fans for being so supportive all the way.

CHAPTER 10

HORSLIPS
DISCOGRAPHY

ALBUMS

HAPPY TO MEET, SORRY TO PART
Original Release Date: 04-12-72, Oats MOO3 (Ireland) • RCA MOO3 (UK, 1973) • Atco SD 7030 (US, 1973) • Edsel/Demon CD EDCD661 06-06-00 • Strange Days POCE-1243 (Japan 2008) • Digipak CD MOOCCD003 24-02-12
Happy To Meet / Hall Of Mirrors / The Clergy's Lamentation / An Bratach Bán / The Shamrock Shore / Flower Amang Them All / Bím Istigh ag Ól / Furniture / Ace And Deuce / Dance To Yer Daddy / Scalloway Ripoff / The Musical Priest / Sorry To Part • *Digipak CD Reissue Bonus Tracks: Hall Of Mirrors / The High Reel / Rakish Paddy / Johnny's Wedding / Furniture / Bím Istigh Ag Ól [all live at Quartier Latin, Berlin, 1976]*

THE TÁIN
Original Release Date: 23-11-73, Oats MOO5 (Ireland) • RCA MOO5 (UK, 18-01-74) • Atco SD 7039 (US, 1974) • Edsel/Demon CD EDCD662 06-06-00 • Strange Days POCE-1244 (Japan 2008) • Digipak CD MOOCCD005 14-08-09
Setanta / Maeve's Court / Charolais / The March / You Can't Fool The Beast / Dearg Doom / Ferdia's Song / Gae Bolga / Cú Chulainn's Lament / Faster Than The Hound / The Silver Spear / More Than You Can Chew / The Morrigan's Dream / Time To Kill! • *Digipak CD Reissue Bonus Track: The Táin Live Extended Sequence [live at My Father's Place, New York, 1974]*

DANCEHALL SWEETHEARTS
Original Release Date: 27-09-74, Oats MOO7 (Ireland) • RCA APL 1-0709 (UK, 1974) • RCA CPL 1-0709 (US, 1974) • Edsel/Demon CD EDCD663 15-08-00 • Strange Days POCE-1245 (Japan 2008) • Digipak CD MOOCCD007 04-12-09
Nighttown Boy / The Blind Can't Lead The Blind / Stars / We Bring The Summer With Us / Sunburst / Mad Pat / Blindman / King Of The Fairies / Lonely Hearts / The Best Years Of My Life • *Digipak CD Reissue Bonus Tracks: Mad Pat / Blindman [live at Quartier Latin, Berlin, 1976] / King Of The Fairies [Sigma Sound, Philadelphia, 1978] / Lonely Hearts [live at My Father's Place, 1974]*

THE UNFORTUNATE CUP OF TEA!
Original Release Date: 11-04-75, Oats MOO8 (Ireland) • RCA SF 8432 (UK, 1975) • RCA CPL 1-1068 (US, 1975) • Edsel/Demon CD EDCD664 15-08-00 • Strange Days POCE-1246 (Japan 2008) • Digipak CD MOOCCD008 11-06-10
(If That's What You Want) That's What You Get / Ring-A-Rosey / Flirting In The Shadows / Self Defence / High Volume Love / The Unfortunate Cup Of Tea / Turn Your Face To The Wall / The Snakes' Farewell To The Emerald Isle / Everything Will Be Alright • *Digipak CD Reissue Bonus Tracks: High Volume Love [Live] / Locomotive Breath [Live]*

DRIVE THE COLD WINTER AWAY
Original Release Date: 06-11-75, Horslips Records MOO9 (Ireland) • Edsel/Demon CD EDCD665 12-12-00 • Strange Days POCE-1247 (Japan 2008) • Digipak CD MOOCCD009 11-03-11
Rug Muire Mac Do Dhia (Mary Bore A Son To God) / Sir Festus Burke – Carolan's Frolic / The Snow That Melts The Soonest / The Piper In The Meadow Straying / Drive The Cold Winter Away / Thompson's – Cottage In The Grove / Ny Kirree Fo Naghtey (The Sheep 'neath The Snow) / Crabs In The Skillet / Denis O'Connor / Do'n Oiche Ud I Mbeithil (That Night In Bethlehem) / Lullaby / The Snow And The Frost Are All Over – Paddy Fahey's / When A Man's In Love

HORSLIPS LIVE
Original Release Date: 23-04-76, Horslips Records MOO10 (Ireland) • Edsel/Demon CD EDCD666 12-12-00 • Strange Days POCE-1248 (Japan 2008) • Digipak CD MOOCCD010 11-06-10
Mad Pat / Blindman / Silver Spear / High Reel / Stars / Hall Of Mirrors / If That's What You Want / Self Defence / Everything Will Be Alright / Rakish Paddy / Rakish Paddy (cont.) / King Of The Fairies / Furniture / You Can't Fool The Beast / More Than You Can Chew / Dearg Doom / Comb Your Hair And Curl It / Johnny's Wedding

THE BOOK OF INVASIONS: A CELTIC SYMPHONY
Original Release Date: 12-11-76, Horslips Records MOO12 (Ireland) • DJM DJF 20498 (UK, 25-02-77) • DJM DJLPA-10 (US, 09-05-77) • Edsel/Demon CD EDCD667 26-09-00 • Strange Days POCE-1250 (Japan 2008) • Digipak CD MOOCCD012 14-08-09
Daybreak / March Into Trouble / Trouble (With A Capital T) / The Power And The Glory / The Rocks Remain / Dusk / Sword Of Light / Dark / Warm Sweet Breath Of Love / Fantasia (My Lagan Love) / King Of Morning, Queen Of Day / Sideways To The Sun / Drive The Cold Winter Away / Ride To Hell • *Digipak CD Reissue Bonus Tracks: Daybreak / Drive The Cold Winter Away / Ride To Hell / Sideways To The Sun / Sword Of Light / Dark [live at The Bottom Line, New York, 1978] / The Rights Of Man [live at Quartier Latin, Berlin, 1976] / Trouble (With A Capital T) [live at Park West, Chicago, 1979]*

TRACKS FROM THE VAULTS
Original Release Date: 07-05-77, Horslips Records MOO13 (Ireland) • Edsel/Demon CD EDCD669 13-02-01 • Strange Days POCE-1251 (Japan 2008) • Digipak CD MOOCCD013 11-03-11
Motorway Madness / Johnny's Wedding / Flower Amang Them All / Green Gravel / The Fairy King / Dearg Doom (Fritz Fryer Mix) / The High Reel / King Of The Fairies / Phil The Fluter's Rag / Come Back Beatles (Lipstick) / The Fab Four-Four (Lipstick) / Daybreak / Oisín's Tune • *Digipak CD Reissue Bonus Tracks: When Night Comes [Windmill Lane Studios, Dublin, 1979] / Motorway Madness [Live in Roosky, 1980] / Johnny's Wedding [live at My Father's Place, 1974] / Sword Of Light [live at Whitla Hall, Belfast, 1980]*

ALIENS
Original Release Date: 04-11-77, Horslips Records MOO14 (Ireland) • DJM DJF 20519 (UK, 1977) • DJM DJLPA-16 (US, 1977) • Edsel/Demon CD EDCD668 07-08-00 • Strange Days POCE-1252 (Japan 2008) • Digipak CD MOOCCD014 04-12-09
Before The Storm / The Wrath Of The Rain / Speed The Plough / Sure The Boy Was Green / Come Summer / Stowaway / New York Wakes / Exiles / Second Avenue / Ghosts / A Lifetime To Pay • *Digipak CD Reissue Bonus Tracks: New York Wakes [Sigma Sound, Philadelphia, 1978] / Speed The Plough [live in London, 1978] / Sure The Boy Was Green [live at The Bottom Line, New York, 1979]*

THE MAN WHO BUILT AMERICA
Original Release Date: 27-10-78, Horslips Records MOO17 (Ireland) • DJM DJF 20546 (UK, 19-01-79) • DJM DJLPA-20 (US, 1979) • Edsel/Demon CD EDCD670 13-03-01 • Strange Days POCE-1253 (Japan 2008) • Digipak CD MOOCCD017 14-08-09
Loneliness / Tonight (You're With Me) / I'll Be Waiting / If It Takes All Night / Green Star Liner / The Man Who Built America / Homesick / Long Weekend / Letters From Home / Long Time Ago • *Digipak CD Reissue Bonus Tracks: The Man Who Built America [live at Park West, Chicago, 1979] / Loneliness [Sigma Sound, Philadelphia, 1978] / Homesick [live at The Bottom Line, 1979] / Horslips Presents Horslips (An Advance Look Into The Man Who Built America)★ – ★digital version*

SHORT STORIES / TALL TALES
Original Release Date: 16-11-79, Horslips Records MOO19 (Ireland) • Mercury 9100-070 (UK, 30-11-79) • Mercury SRM-1-3809 (US, 1979) • Edsel/Demon CD EDCD671 13-03-01 • Strange Days POCE-1254 (Japan 2008) • Digipak CD MOOCCD019 11-03-11
Guests Of The Nation / Law On The Run / Unapproved Road / Ricochet Man / Back In My Arms / Summer's Most Wanted Girl / Amazing Offer / Rescue Me / The Life You Save / Soap Opera • *Digipak CD Reissue Bonus Tracks: Amazing Offer / Ricochet Man / Summer's Most Wanted Girl / Law On The Run / Unapproved Road / Soap Opera [all live in Roosky, 1980]*

THE BELFAST GIGS
Original Release Date: 18-07-80, Horslips Records MOO20 (Ireland) • Mercury SRM-1-3842 (US, 1980) • Edsel/Demon CD EDCD672 10-04-01 • Strange Days POCE-1255 (Japan 2008) • Digipak CD MOOCCD020 11-06-10
Trouble (With A Capital T) / The Man Who Built America / Warm Sweet Breath Of Love / The Power And The Glory / Blindman / Shakin' All Over / King Of The Fairies / Guests Of The Nation / Dearg Doom • *Digipak CD Reissue Bonus Track: Sword Of Light*

THE HORSLIPS COLLECTION
Original Release Date: 29-05-81, K-Tel Ireland KLP70 (vinyl only)
King Of The Fairies / Flower Amang Them All / Johnny's Wedding / Daybreak / Furniture / Loneliness / King Of Morning, Queen Of Day / Dearg Doom / Trouble (With A Capital T) / The Man Who Built America / I'll Be Waiting / The Power And The Glory / Speed The Plough / Long Weekend / Guests Of The Nation

THE BEST OF HORSLIPS
Original Release Date: 07-05-02, Edsel/Demon CD MEDCD700
Hall Of Mirrors / Furniture / Faster Than The Hound / Dearg Doom / More Than You Can Chew / Time To Kill! / Nighttown Boy / Mad Pat / Blindman / Blind Can't Lead The Blind / The Snakes' Farewell To The Emerald Isle / Flirting In The Shadows / Everything Will Be Alright / Trouble (With A Capital T) / Sideways To The Sun / Sword Of Light / Warm Sweet Breath Of Love / The Power And The Glory / Speed The Plough / Come Summer / Stowaway / Ghosts / Loneliness / I'll Be Waiting / The Man Who Built America / Long Weekend / Rescue Me / Summer's Most Wanted Girl / Guests Of The Nation

ROLL BACK
Original Release Date: 03-12-04, Horslips Records MOO23
Trouble (With A Capital T) / The Man Who Built America / Guests Of The Nation / Faster Than The Hound / Huish The Cat / Mad Pat / The Wrath Of The Rain / Flirting In The Shadows / Cú Chulainn's Lament / Ace And Deuce / Blindman / Furniture / The Power And The Glory / Long Weekend / My Love Is In America • *Roll Back Bonus Disc: Music From An Exhibition – Live at Orchard Gallery, Derry, March 20 2004 (Horslips Records MOO22) Flower Amang Them All / Furniture / The Musical Priest – The High Reel / Trouble (With A Capital T) / Video section: Flower Amang Them All / The Musical Priest / Trouble (With A Capital T)*

TREASURY – THE VERY BEST OF HORSLIPS
Original Release Date: 13-11-09, Horslips Records MOOCCD027
Furniture / Faster Than The Hound / Dearg Doom / Time To Kill! / Hall Of Mirrors / Flower Amang Them All / More Than You Can Chew / The Snakes' Farewell To The Emerald Isle / Nighttown Boy / Everything Will Be Alright / Trouble (With A Capital T) [Roll Back Version] / The Life You Save / Mad Pat / Blindman / The Blind Can't Lead The Blind / Flirting In The Shadows [Roll Back Version] / The Snow That Melts The Soonest / Warm Sweet Breath Of Love / Come Summer / Sword Of Light / Sideways To The Sun / The Power And The Glory / Trouble (With a Capital T) / Rescue Me / Loneliness / The Man Who Built America / Long Weekend / Speed The Plough / Ghosts / Guests Of The Nation / Stowaway / Ricochet Man / I'll Be Waiting / Dearg Doom [Acoustic Radio Version]

HORSLIPS – THE ESSENTIAL RECORDINGS
Original Release Date: 07-11-10
Issued free with *The Irish Mail On Sunday*
Trouble (With A Capital T) / Hall Of Mirrors / Charolais / Exiles / High Volume Love / Sunburst / The Power And The Glory / I'll Be Waiting / Amazing Offer / Dearg Doom

LIVE AT THE O2
Original Release Date: 19-11-10, Horslips Records MOOCCD028
King Of The Fairies / The Power And The Glory / Mad Pat / Blindman / The Wrath Of The Rain / Furniture / The High Reel / Faster Than The Hound / The Piper In The Meadow Straying / Long Weekend / Rescue Me / Maeve's Court / Charolais / Daybreak / Drive The Cold Winter Away / Ride To Hell / Sideways To The Sun / Sword Of Light / Flirting In The Shadows / Ghosts / Speed The Plough / Sure The Boy Was Green / I'll Be Waiting / The Man Who Built America / Trouble (With A Capital T) / Dearg Doom / Loneliness / Warm Sweet Breath Of Love / Shakin' All Over

LIVE WITH THE ULSTER ORCHESTRA
Original Release Date: 25-11-11, Horslips Records MOOCCD030
Daybreak / The Power And The Glory / Fantasia (My Lagan Love) / Drive The Cold Winter Away / Ride To Hell / Sideways To The Sun / Dusk / Sword Of Light / Setanta / Maeve's Court / Charolais / More Than You Can Chew / March Into Trouble / Trouble (With A Capital T) / Dearg Doom / Rescue Me / Ghosts / King Of The Fairies / I'll Be Waiting

SINGLES & EPs

Signing copies of 'Green Gravel' in 1972.

IRELAND

Johnny's Wedding/Flower Amang Them All
Oats MOO1 (pic sleeve) • 17-03-72

Green Gravel/The Fairy King
Oats MOO2 • 25-08-72

Dearg Doom/The High Reel
Oats MOO4 • 30-04-73

King Of The Fairies/Phil The Fluter's Rag
Oats MOO6 • 08-07-74

Daybreak/Oisín's Tune
Horslips Records MOO11 • 22-07-76

Exiles/Speed The Plough
Horslips Records MOO15 • 24-11-77

Tour-A-Loor-A-Loor-A-Loor-A (EP)
Sure The Boy Was Green/Red River Rock/
Trouble/Bridge From Heart To Heart
Horslips Records MOO16 • 28-07-78

Guests Of The Nation/When Night Comes
Horslips Records MOO18 • 16-10-79

Shakin' All Over/Sword Of Light
Horslips Records MOO21 • 20-07-80

UK

The High Reel/Furniture
RCA/Oats OAT 1 • 20-07-73

Dearg Doom/Shamrock Shore
RCA/Oats OAT 2 • 19-10-73

More Than You Can Chew/
Faster Than The Hound
RCA/Oats OAT 3 • 29-03-74

Nighttown Boy/
We Bring The Summer With Us
RCA Victor 2452 • 09-08-74

King Of The Fairies/Sunburst
RCA Victor 2505 • 24-01-75

(If That's What You Want) That's What You
Get/The Snakes' Farewell
RCA Victor 2564 • 13-07-75

Come Back Beatles/
The Fab Four Four (as Lipstick)
Polydor 2058 725 • 23-04-76

Warm Sweet Breath Of Love/
King Of Morning, Queen Of Day
DJM DJS 10754 • 25-02-77

The Power And The Glory/
Sir Festus Burke
DJM DJS 10792 • 25-07-77

Speed The Plough/
Bridge From Heart To Heart
Red River Rock (live)
DJM DJS 10859 • 23-06-78

The Man Who Built America/
Long Weekend
DJM DJS 10888 • 16-02-79

Loneliness/Homesick
DJM DJS 10916 • 02-06-79
DJM DJT 15001 (shamrock 12") • 09-06-79

Dearg Doom (Remixes) 4-Track EP
Dearg Doom (original)/Metisse vs.
Horslips/Ufeari vs. Horslips/Ear2Ear Mix
Edsel/Demon DEARG 1 / 112 • 07-05-02

OVERSEAS 45s

The High Reel/Furniture
ATCO 45-6935 • USA, 1973

The High Reel/Furniture
Atlantic ATL 10337 • Germany, 1973

SINGLES & EPs

The High Reel/Furniture
Atlantic/WEA 45-6935 • Australia, 1973

Dearg Doom/More Than You Can Chew
Atlantic ATL 19436 • Germany, 1974

Nighttown Boy (Edited) (stereo)/(mono)
RCA PB-10123 • USA, 1974

King Of The Fairies/Sunburst
RCA 2505 • Australia, 1975

Warm Sweet Breath Of Love/
Fantasia (My Lagan Love)
DJM 1238-1026 • Canada, 1977

Trouble (With A Capital T)/Daybreak
DJM 1238-1032 • Canada, 1977

The Power And The Glory/Sir Festus Burke
DJM 2043 103 • Germany, 1977

Sure The Boy Was Green/Exiles
DJM DJUS 1036 • USA, 1978

Sure The Boy Was Green/Exiles
DJM/Festival K7127 • Australia, 1978

Before The Storm/New York Wakes
DJM DJO-612 • Spain, 1978

The Man Who Built America/
Long Weekend
DJM/Festival K7427 • Australia, 1979

The Man Who Built America/
Tonight (You're With Me)
DJM DJO-620 • Spain, 1979

The Man Who Built America/
Long Weekend
DJM 2043 103 • Germany, 1979

Loneliness/Homesick
DJM DJMS-1105 (shamrock) • USA, 1979

Loneliness/Homesick
DJM/CBS-Sony 06SP319 • Japan, 1979

ASSORTED PROMOS

Warm Sweet Breath Of Love (stereo)/(mono)
DJM DJUS 1026 promo • USA, 1976

Warm Sweet Breath Of Love/
King Of Morning, Queen Of Day
DJM DJS 10754 promo • UK, 1977

Trouble (With A Capital T) (stereo)/(mono)
DJM DJUS 1032 promo • USA, 1977

The Power And The Glory (one-track)
DJM/Odeon P-50 • Spain, 1977

Horslips Present Horslips – An Advance
Look Into The Man Who Built America/
Warm Sweet Breath Of Love/
Sure The Boy Was Green
DJM MK-76 (12" promo) • USA, 1979

Rescue Me (stereo)/(mono)
Mercury 76030 promo • USA, 1979

Shakin' All Over (short)/(long)
Mercury 76072 promo • USA, 1980

Shakin' All Over/Shakin' All Over
Mercury MK 147 (12") • USA, 1980

Horslips: Radio Promo EP
Dearg Doom/Trouble (With A Capital T)/
Mad Pat/Ghosts/The Snakes' Farewell To
The Emerald Isle/Furniture
Horslips Records MOO22 • 06-06-00

Trouble (With A Capital T)
(one-track Roll Back promo)
Horslips Records MOO24 • 05-11-04

The Man Who Built America
(one-track Roll Back promo) • 05-11-04

POST-HORSLIPS

ZEN ALLIGATORS

SINGLES

Thrill Power/Having A Party/Just A Little Bit (as The Alligators)
AFG AFG 001 promo • 1980
Who Can That Someone Be?/Berlin Wall
Spider WEB 045 • 1981
Call Me Lucky/The Ticket
Auric AU 79005 • 1981
The Invisible Man/The Scorpio Function
Zodiac ZZA 82001 • 1982
You Make My Day (radio mix)/People Who Make People's Day
Zodiac ZZA 82002 • 1982
I Never Forget A Face/Caught In The Crossfire/
Diary Of A Forgotten War
Hotwire HSW-831 • 1983

BARRY DEVLIN

ALBUM

BREAKING STAR CODES
Starcode/RTÉ • BDLP1/RTE 79 • 1983
(Featuring Jim Lockhart on keyboards, flute,
string arrangements & DJ voice)
Twins (Gemini) / Who Can Tame The Lion? (Leo) / It's The
Cruelest Sign (Virgo) / Remember You're A Winner (Aries) /
When Two Stars Collide (Sagittarius) / Just Another Line (Pisces)
/ Let The Scales Decide (Libra) / December 21 (Capricorn) / The
Stars Said (Taurus) / Remember A Star (Cancer) / Aquarian Girls
(Aquarius) / Love With A Sting In Its Tail (Scorpio)

SINGLES

Who Can Tame The Lion? (Leo)/When Summer Comes Around
Starcode BAR 001 • 1983
When Two Stars Collide (Sagittarius)/
Love With A Sting In Its Tail (Scorpio)
Starcode BAR 002 • 1983
Remember You're A Winner (Aries)/December 21 (Capricorn)
Starcode BAR 003 • 1983

THE HOST

ALBUM

TRYAL
Changeling • CHRL 001 (Ireland) 1983 /
Aura • AUL 728 (UK) 1984 • Produced by Robbie McGrath

Witness Stand / First Kiss / Vows And Breezes / Safe World /
Declaring War / Walk On Love / Unearthly Shadows / Shadowy
Figures / I Wanted You / Strange Disease / Dark, Light And Air
(Break A Spell)

SINGLES

Walk On Love/The Long Walk
Changeling CRS 8301 • 1983
Witness Stand/Dark, Light And Air/
Excerpt from 'Love's Dark Light' (A Novel)★
(★Read by Joe Ambrose & Eamon Carr)
Changeling CRS 8401 • 1984
Walk On Love/Strange Disease
Aura AUS144 (UK) • 1985
The Hellhound Was My Name/The Trip, The King & The Creel
Hotwire HOST 10 • 1985

JIM LOCKHART

SINGLE

Theme From 'Glenroe'★/Thuas Ag Gort A Charnain
CBS 650301 7 • 1986 ★ Co-arranged with Barry Devlin

CHARLES O'CONNOR

ALBUMS

ANGEL ON THE MANTELPIECE
Koch Records CD 8008 • 21-02-95
Ocean Of Storms / Seachange / Comes A Calm / Bottom Buttons
/ In Your Own Time / Skinner's Treat / Circles Round The Moon
/ Angel On The Mantelpiece / Basket Of Bones / Chocolate Cats
/ The Grand Tour / When The Long Trick's Over / Fiddlehead /
Ocean Storms

BREAKING WAVES
[A Tribute to the HM Bark Endeavour & Crew]
Whitby Music WM 11002 • 2002
Breaking Waves / Lonorono / Transit Of Venus / The Hurricane /
Ice Blink

JOHNNY FEAN

PROMO / SINGLE

BLUES TRAX (promo) • Ramblin' On My Mind/I Wish You
Would/Hideaway • Recorded in Manchester • 28-02-91
I Am The One (single) • A1 Records A111 • 23-10-02

MISCELLANEOUS

THE COTTON MILL BOYS

Rainin' In My Heart/Orange Blossom Special (single)
Featuring Barry Devlin (bass) • Produced by Alan O'Duffy
Hawk HASP 396 • 1976

THE DEFENDERS

Happy Surfin' Santa/Xmas Up On Venus (single)
Featuring Charles O'Connor, Johnny Fean & Eamon Carr
Written by Carr/O'Connor • Guided Missiles ABM 1001 • 1979

U2

EARLY DEMOS (EP)
Street Missions/Shadows And Tall Trees/The Fool
Produced by Barry Devlin in 1978; included in the digital box set,
The Complete U2 • 23-11-04 • Island/Interscope 1978/2004

MAMA'S BOYS

PLUG IT IN (album) • Ultra! Noise ULTRA 1 • 1982
TURN IT UP (album) • Spartan • SPLP 001 • 1983
High Energy Weekend/Hitch-Hike★ (single)
Pussy PU006 • 1980
Silence Is Out Of Fashion/Rock & Roll Craze (single)
Pussy PU008 • 1981
Belfast City Blues/Reach For The Top (single)
Scoff DT015 • 1982
Needle In The Groove/Hard Headed Ways (single)
Ultra! Noise ION 1041 • 1982
Too Little Of You To Love★★/Freedom Fighters/Record Machine
Spartan 12 SP 6 (12") • 1983
Midnight Promises/Lonely Soul (single) • Spartan SP 11 • 1984
All produced by Barry Devlin except ★
★★ Featuring Jim Lockhart (keyboards)

THE CRACK

DAWN OF THE CRACK (album) • CBS Ireland 85680 • 1982
Co-produced by Barry Devlin
When The Time Comes★/Kickin' At The Kickham (single)
Cracked CRK006 • 1981
Go Away/Listen★ (single) • CBS 1710 • 1981
★ Produced by Barry Devlin

THE SHADE

Watching You★/Touch Sensitive (single) • EMI IEMI 5093 • 1982
★ Produced by Jim Lockhart

ALMA CARROLL

Only A Fool Would Stay★/One Night Stand (single)
CBS Ireland 2301 • 1982 • ★ Written & produced by Barry Devlin

NEURO

Nairobi/Loud Boys (single) • WEA IR19250 • 1982
Produced by Barry Devlin

ALBATROSS

Alberta/Too Late Now★ (single) • Stoic STS 004 • 1984
High School Queenie/Too Late Now (single) • STS 005 • 1984
Produced by Jim Lockhart except★

HIDDEN FEARS

Mirage/Robotic Man (single) • Shift RS 801 • 1986
Produced by Jim Lockhart

DERMOT MORGAN

Thank You Very Much Mr. Eastwood/
(Version Featuring Garret) (single)
Ritz 131/Stiff Records BUY 246 • 1985
No. 1 in Ireland for 3 weeks
Do You Know Bono?/Alsatian Once Again (single)
Dolphin DOS 190 • 1987
All produced by Barry Devlin
Country & Western Taoiseach/
Mama Mia What A Beautiful Team (single)
Lunar LOON62 • 1992 • Produced by Jim Lockhart

THE PEELERS

The Wind In The Willows/Sweet Memories (single)
Masquerade MASQ 1 • 1982 • Featuring Charles O'Connor

PROJECT AFRICA

Reach Out To Africa/Reach Out To Africa (Village Mix) (single)
ROTA RCA 001 • 1988 • Produced by Jim Lockhart

SHEELAGIG

Carnlough Bay/The Dancing Man (single) • LAR LS001
Produced by Jim Lockhart

WAXWORKS

So Lost/Train Of Thoughts (single)
WaxOnWax WOW100 • 1986 • Produced by Jim Lockhart

THE MIGHTY CLOUDS OF DUST

Flowers On The Wall/Champion The Wonder Horse/
Mister Custer (single) • Featuring Charles O'Connor as 'Hank Raven'.
Dead On DOR-001 7" • 1983 • Rogue 12 FMS 108 12" • 1989

THE SAINTS & SCHOLARS

A Hundred Thousand Welcomes For Boy George!/
The Land Of Your Father's (single) • Hotwire/Crashed BOY 1 • 1984
Produced by Eamon Carr • Written by Eamon Carr & Johnny Fean

AOIFE

19 Arches/Brian Boru's March/Jonathan's (single)
Yankee Doodle YD001 • 1984 • Produced by Jim Lockhart

THE GOLDEN HORDE

THE CHOCOLATE BISCUIT CONSPIRACY
(featuring Robert Anton Wilson) (album)
Hotwire HWLP 8502 • 1985
IN REALITY (album) • Media Burn MB6 • 1986
DIG THAT CRAZY GRAVE (EP)
Hotwire/Crashed WAY OUT 1 • 1984
Young And Happy/Little UFO/Fiona (single)
Hotwire HWS855 • 1984
All produced by Eamon Carr

THE LAST BANDITS IN THE WORLD

THE LAST BANDITS IN THE WORLD (album)
Hotwire HWLP 8504 • 1985
Produced by Eamon Carr • Featuring Johnny Fean
Three tracks co-written by Carr/Fean

LIGHT A BIG FIRE

GUNPOWDERS (album) • Hotwire HWLP 8501 • 1985
SURVEILLANCE (album) • Hotwire HWLP 8506 • 1986
Executive producer for both: Eamon Carr
Produced by Craig Leon

THE STARS OF HEAVEN

Clothes Of Pride/All About You (single)
Hotwire HWS 853 • 1986
Produced by Eamon Carr as 'Jah Teabag' (also on tambourine)

CHISEL

HONEST WORK (album) • Chisel Records CHIS 2 • 1985
Produced by Eamon Carr • Featuring Johnny Fean

THE CONCERNED

Show Some Concern/Show Some Concern (inst.) (single)
Featuring Johnny Fean & Eamon Carr
Revolving REV12 • 1985 – No.1 in Ireland for 3 weeks

BAD KARMA BECKONS

MUTATE AND SURVIVE (album) • Media Burn MB15 • 1986
Produced by Eamon Carr (brother Jude Carr on vocals)

THE STING-RAYS

CRYPTIC AND COFFEE TIME (album)
Kaleidoscope KSLP 001 • 1987
Behind The Beyond/Perverted Justice (single)
Kaleidoscope 7KS 102KS • 1986
June Rhyme/Militant Tendency/Wedding Ring (single)
BC S009T 12" • 1986
All produced by Eamon Carr

THE CHAPTERHOUSE

Scorch Avenue/Pressure (Right Now) (single)
Nouveau Wax NW179 • 1987 • Produced by Jim Lockhart

SHANTY DAM

THE REDUNDANCY CHEQUE /
THE SEVENTH LOCH (album) • 1987
Featuring Charles O'Connor • Produced by Robbie McGrath

DERVISH

THE BOYS OF SLIGO (album) • Sound SUNCD1 • 1989
Produced by Jim Lockhart

WATCH YOUR HOUSE (WITH PAUL McGRATH)

Ooh Aah Paul McGrath/
Ooh Aah Paul McGrath (The Deep Midfield Mix) (single)
Phonogram Ireland MCG1 • 1990 • Produced by Eamon Carr

REPUBLIC OF IRELAND FOOTBALL SQUAD

Put 'em Under Pressure★ (Mind Your House Mix)/
Put 'em Under Pressure★ (7" Mix)/Pacemaker/Heartbeat (single)
Son BUACD901 • 1990
★ Ireland's official Italia '90 FIFA World Cup single featuring the 'Dearg Doom' / 'O'Neill's Cavalry' guitar riff played by Anto Drennan • No.1 in Ireland for 13 weeks

MICK LALLY

The By-Road To Glenroe★/Theme From Glenroe★★ (single)
CBS Ireland • 1990 • No.1 in Ireland for 5 weeks
★Produced/written & ★★produced by Jim Lockhart

MURRAY HEAD

INNOCENCE (album) • Voiceprint • GAH 115CD 1993
Featuring Charles O'Connor on concertina, mandolin & fiddle
★ O'Connor also contributed sleeve design and art direction for many Murray Head releases, including albums Find The Crowd (Mercury, 1981), Shade (Virgin, 1982), Restless (Virgin, 1984), Sooner Or Later (Virgin, 1986), Some People (Virgin, 1986) & Wave (XIII BIS, 1992), and singles Maman (Mercury 7", 1982), Corporation Corridors (Virgin 7", 1983) and Picking Up The Pieces (Virgin 7", 1985)

COCA-COLA OFFICIAL IRISH TEAM

Watch Your House For Ireland/
Watch Your House For Ireland (version) (single)
RTÉ/BMG • 1994 • No.1 in Ireland for 1 week
Production, keyboards and programming by Jim Lockhart

THE STONE ROSES

CRIMSON TONIGHT (Live EP)
Geffen GEFDM-22081 • 1996 • Produced by Jim Lockhart

DEACON BLUE

I WAS RIGHT AND YOU WERE WRONG (EP)
Epic ESCA 5981 • 1996
★ 'Goin' Back (Live)' produced by Jim Lockhart

KERBDOG

Mexican Wave/Sally (Live)/ On The Turn (Live) (single)
Fontana KERCD 3 • 1997 • Produced by Jim Lockhart

LAL WATERSON & OLIVER KNIGHT

ONCE IN A BLUE MOON (album) • Topic TSCD478 • 1996
Featuring Charles O'Connor (fiddle) on 'At First She Starts'

A HOUSE

LIVE IN CONCERT (album)

In the signing tent at *Fairport's Cropredy Convention*, 2011.

Special thanks to Paul Callaghan, Stephen Ferris, Eamon Carr, Myles Lally, Stephen Matthews, Declan O'Connor and Tim Maher for their help in compiling this discography.

BBC/Strange Fruit SFRSCD077 • 1998
Tracks 1-7 produced by Jim Lockhart

THE DIVINE COMEDY

RE:REGENERATION (album) • Parlophone DCIND01 • 2001
'Love What You Do' & 'Generation Sex' produced by Jim Lockhart

JACOBITES

THE RAGGED SCHOOL (album)
Secretly Canadian SC56 • 2002
'Tell Me' produced by Eamon Carr • Slide guitar by Johnny Fean

BARRY McCABE

BEYOND THE TEARS (album)
McCabe 634479311413 • 09-08-06
Featuring Johnny Fean on 'Crazy Love', 'Trouble', 'Lonely Road'
and 'The Sunset Waltz'

VAN MORRISON

THE BEST OF VAN MORRISON: VOLUME 3 (album)
Manhattan/EMI • 19-06-07
'That's Life (Live)' produced by Jim Lockhart
That's Life (Live)★/Moondance/That's Life (single)
Exile/Verve • 1996 • ★ Produced by Jim Lockhart

SKULLY

WITHOUT A VOICE (album) • Blind Faith • 26-09-07
Features the artist's remix of Horslips' 'Trouble (With A Capital T)'.

HENRY McCULLOUGH

POOR MAN'S MOON (album) • There Wolf TW001 • 05-09-08
Seven tracks co-written with Eamon Carr

THE MIAMI SHOWBAND & FRIENDS

Joy To The World (single) • 2008 • Featuring Johnny Fean

THE TROUBLEMAKERS

Trouble (With A Capital T) (charity download) • 2009
Featuring Johnny Fean, Jim Lockhart & Barry Devlin

SHARON CORR

DREAM OF YOU (album) • Rhino 2564678839 • 13-09-10
Featuring Jim Lockhart (flute) on 'Jenny's Chickens'

THE RADIATORS FROM SPACE

SOUND CITY BEAT (album) • Chiswick CWK 3022 • 05-03-12
Features a cover of Horslips' 'The Lady Wrestler', and a spoken
word appearance by Eamon Carr on Phil Lynott's 'Dublin'

VARIOUS ARTIST COMPILATIONS

HIP CITY BOOGALOO (album) • Hotwire HWLP001 • 1984
Executive Producer: Eamon Carr
THE WEIRD WEIRD WORLD OF GURU WEIRDBRAIN
(album) • Hotwire HWLP8505 • 1985
'Project Architect': Eamon Carr
GAEL FORCE (live album) • RTE CD210 • 1997
Produced by Jim Lockhart

BIBLIOGRAPHY & ACKNOWLEDGEMENTS

References:

Seán Campbell & Gerry Smyth: 'Beautiful Day – Forty Years of Irish Rock' (Cork University Press, 2005).

Eamon Carr: 'The Origami Crow - Journey Into Japan, World Cup Summer 2002' (Seven Towers, 2008).

Ciaran Carson: 'Irish Traditional Music' (Appletree, 1986).

Tony Clayton-Lea, Richie Taylor: 'Irish Rock – Where It's Come From – Where It's At – Where It's Going' (Sidgwick and Jackson, 1992).

Mark Cunningham: 'The Shamrock Chronicles' (*Hot Press*, 1995); 'Good Vibrations: A History of Record Production' (Sanctuary Music Library, 1996/1999); 'An Audience With Steve Iredale' (*TPi Magazine,* 2005).

Polly Devlin: 'All Of Us There' (Blackstaff Press, 1994).

Martin Dillon: '25 Years of Terror' (Bantam Books, 1996).

Dave Fanning: 'The Thing Is...' (Collins, 2010).

Luke Gibbons: 'Transformations in Irish Culture' (Cork University Press/Field Day, 1996).

Christoph Grunenberg & Laurance Sillars: 'Peter Blake – A Retrospective' (Tate Publishing, 2007).

Colin Harper & Trevor Hodgett: 'Irish Folk, Trad and Blues: A Secret History' (Cherry Red, 2004).

John Kelly: 'Sophisticated Boom-Boom' (Vintage, 2003).

Thomas Kinsella (trans.): 'The Táin' (Oxford University Press, 1970).

Maurice Linnane: *The Return of the Dancehall Sweethearts* (Horslips Records/Long Grass Productions DVD, 2005).

Patrick McCabe: 'The Dead School' (Dial, 1995).

Terry McGregor: 'Crossing Borders of the Imagination – Religion, Politics and Cultural Identity in the Film-Making of Barry Devlin' (Dalarna University College, MA thesis, 2005).

David McKittrick & David McVea: 'Making Sense of The Troubles' (Blackstaff Press, 2001).

Paul Muldoon: 'The Horslips at the Whitla Hall, Belfast, Ireland, April 1980', from 'The Show I'll Never Forget' (ed. Seán Manning, Da Capo, 2007).

John L. Murphy: 'Horslips in Irish Musical and Literary Culture' (DeVryUniversity, 2008).

Tiffany Murray: 'Diamond Star Halo' (Portobello Books, 2011); 'The Time Freddie Mercury Came To Stay' (*The Guardian*, 2010).

Nuala O'Connor: 'Bringing It All Back Home: The Influence of Irish Music' (Merlin, 2001).

Rossa Ó Sioradáin: *The Road To The O2* (Horslips Records DVD, 2010).

Steven Rosenfield & Michael 'Eppy' Epstein: 'Fun & Dangerous – Untold Tales, Unseen Photos and Unearthed Music from My Father's Place, 1975-1980' (Ardent Artists, 2010).

Gerry Smyth: 'Noisy Island: A Short History of Irish Popular Music' (Cork University Press 2005).

Lora Lee Lorden Templeton: The ComeBackHorslips.com Archives (2005-present).

John Waters: 'Race Of Angels, Ireland and the Genesis of U2' (Fourth Estate, 1994).

Editions of *New Spotlight, Starlight, Hot Press, Melody Maker, Sounds, Disc, Record Mirror, New Musical Express, Music Week, Billboard* and *Cash Box* were cross-referenced, and information was also gleaned from back issues of the *Irish Independent, Evening Herald, Sunday Press, Sunday Post, Derry Journal, Irish Times, Belfast Telegraph, Meath Chronicle, Irish Post, Irish News, Skerries News, Daily Express, RTÉ Guide, Evening Standard* and isolated clippings from unidentifiable publications.

Research was also aided by scrapbooks owned by Jim Nelis, Jim Lockhart, Steve Iredale and Keith Johnston. Websites consulted include marmalade-skies.co.uk, irishrock.org, irishcharts.ie, irish-showbands.com and, of course, Horslips.ie and JohnnyFean.com.

The author would like to thank:

Barry Devlin, Jim Lockhart, Eamon Carr, Charles O'Connor and Johnny Fean for their time, patience, wisdom, humour, recollections, souvenirs ... and the incredible music. Maggie Fean and Numi Solomons for smoothing the path.

Shay Hennessy, Alan Hennessy, Ian Hennessy, Michael Deeny, Maurice Linnane, Steve and Sue 'Duchess' Iredale, and Myles Lally for guidance.

Everyone who agreed to be interviewed, including former band members, crew, fans and associates. Lora Lee Lorden Templeton for her tireless championing of this project, her eye for detail and her generous sharing of information.

Jim Nelis, Paul Callaghan, Stephen and Noel Ferris for their astonishing dedication to preserving the band's legacy, and for making their priceless collections available.

The loyal and feisty members of Horslips.ie's Fantasia Forum and Facebook group, who have encouraged me throughout this project and shared their memorabilia.

Michael, Ivan and Eoin O'Brien, Ruth Heneghan, Clare Kelly, Emma Byrne and everyone at The O'Brien Press Limited for their commitment and enthusiasm.

And Chrissy Brown for being Chrissy Brown.

Photography & Memorabilia:

Ian Finlay • Charles O'Connor • Jim Lockhart • Eamon Carr • Barry Devlin • Johnny Fean • Gail Fean • Steve Iredale • Paul Callaghan • Jim Nelis • Stephen Ferris • Daragh Owens • Guido DiVito • Myles Lally • Kieron Murphy • Shay Lattimore • Maurice Linnane • Stephen Matthews • Kathleen Murphy • Keith Johnston • Steve Katz • Pat Maguire • Christ & Marian Ceelen • Annie Lovejoy • Paul Gray • Mark Cunningham • Robert Aiken • Christopher Whalen • Andrew Basquille • Liz Bean • Molly Kavanagh • Daire Winston • David Creedon • Barney McGuinness • Fin Costello • Brendan Hearne • Daryl Feehely • Jim Corr • Marianne Ashcroft • Shay Hennessy • Sean Hennessy • Gearoid Lynch • Ted McCarthy • Fritz Fryer (RIP) • Sandy Harsch • George Doyle • Michael Stamp • Sean O'Connor • Tim Maher • Mark Wilson • Louise Edington • Sue Kurdziel • Iain Angus • Robin Dexter • John Ward • Mike Brown • Brian Tomany • Bob DeJessa • Matt Heineken • Ruth Medjber • Conor Horgan • Mike Mulcaire • Timmy Cupps • John Rea • Eamonn O'Dwyer • Robert Ellis • Liam O'Reilly • Patrick Brocklebank • David Dwane • Steven Rosenfield • Sarah Whelan • Michael Zagaris • Martin Nolan • Pat Maxwell • Rick Harbin • Declan O'Connor • Ian Tomey • Robert Mayne • Susan Byrne • Johnny Morris • Horslips.ie • JohnnyFean.com • Vicky Mitchell at BBC Television ('Old Grey Whistle Test') • RTÉ Stills Library • Gráinne Carroll (South Wind Blows) • Pat Gannon (Sligo County Libraries) • John Cooney (*RTÉ Guide*) • comebackhorslips.com • Gerry Gallagher (irish-showbands.com) • Eamonn Keane (irishrock.org)

All reasonable efforts have been made to contact the owners of photography to obtain permission. The author and publisher apologise to anyone whose name has been unintentionally omitted here. Please contact The O'Brien Press Ltd at books@obrien.ie and this will be rectified in future editions. Mark Cunningham can be contacted directly via his website, froog.net.

Official
Invitation

the history
HORSLIPS
an exhibition

THE Late La

TV Studio 4, RTÉ, Donnybrook, Dublin 4
Doors Open 8.00 pm • Doors Close 8.30 p

21st January, 2005

MCD PROMOTIONS PRES
HORSLIPS
PLUS SPECIAL GUESTS
ODYSSEY ARENA BELFAST
DOORS 6.30PM
THURSDAY 03-DEC-09
ENTER BY DOOR 7
ROW Q SEAT 27
SOUTH UPPER TIER

MCD PRESENTS
HORSLIPS
PLUS SPECIAL GUESTS
THE O2, DUBLIN
DOORS 6:30PM
SAT 05-DEC-09
ENTRANCE 2
ROW 26 SEAT 115

TOUR '03
HORSLIPS
AAA

TOUR 2010
AAA
TOUR CREW
HORSLIPS

MCD PRESENTS
HORSLIPS
THE O2, DUBLIN
DOORS 6:30PM TIMES MCD.
SAT 04-DEC-2010
ENTRANCE 2
ROW 7 SEAT 16

HORSLIPS
AAA

Old Fruitmarket
Candleriggs, Glasgow

Celtic Connections 2011
Presents
HORSLIPS
and Support

Tuesday
18-January-2011
Venue Opens 7:00 pm
Show Start 8:00 pm

Waterfront Auditorium
BBC NI & Belfast City Coun
HORSLIPS
with the Ulster Orche
Thursday 17-March-20
Performance Starts: 8:00 p
Doors Open: 7:15
Downst
A 405
£ 16.00

ENTE
UNRES

GUINNESS
IRISH
FESTIVAL
SION
4-5-6 AOUT 2011
TRI YANN
SULTANS OF SWING & THE MAHORES
CARLOS NUÑEZ
PUBSIDE DOWN & WOLFSTONE
HORSLIPS
ALAN KELLY & MARTIN O'CONNOR
PEATBOG FAIRIES
NO. 01763
PASSAGE DE TROIS JOURS
intransférable

BULMERS
LIVE LEOPARDSTOWN
RACING ROCKS!
at leopardstown
3
AAA

Fairport's
Cropredy
Convention 2011

13.08.11
12pm - Midnight
Before Jan 1st £58.94 Jan 1st - May 31st £60.00
June 1st - July 31st £65.00 After July 31st £70.00

BONDED

BONDED

RORY GALLAGHER FESTIVAL
SUNDAY NIGHT TICKET
BIG TOP - BALLYSHANNON
GATES OPEN 7PM
SUN 03-JUN-12
GEN ADMISSION
G1 1
000814396761

VIP

SATURDAY 23RD & SUNDAY 24TH JUNE 2012
— THE WEST IS CALLING —
westport
FESTIVAL OF MUSIC AND PERFORMING ARTS

VIP

INEC PRESENT
THE HORSLI
PLUS SPECIAL GU
INEC
DOORS 7.30PM, SHOW
FRI 03-AUG-20
STANDING
1 4

HORSLIPS
PAT MCMANUS BAND
MOONCHILD
30.00 (INC BKG FEE)

WARD/ MR. JOHN

BRUSH SHE
PAT MCMANUS OF
GL
29.90 (INC BKG FEE